LEE'S TIGERS

The Louisiana Infantry in the Army of Northern Virginia

TERRY L. JONES

Louisiana State University Press
Baton Rouge and London

Designer: Christopher Wilcox
Typeface: Baskerville
Typesetter: G & S Typesetters, Inc.
Printer: Thomson-Shore, Inc.
Binder: John Dekker & Sons, Inc.

10 9 8 7 6 5 4 3 2 1

Library of Congress Cataloging-in-Publication Data

Jones, Terry L., 1952–
  Lee's Tigers.
  Bibliography: p.
  Includes index.
  1. Louisiana—History—Civil War, 1861–1865—
Regimental histories. 2. United States—History—
Civil War, 1861–1865—Regimental histories.
3. Confederate States of America. Army of Northern
Virginia—History. 4. Virginia—History—Civil War,
1861–1865—Campaigns. 5. United States—History—
Civil War, 1861–1865—Campaigns. I. Title.
E565.4.J65 1987   973.7'455   86-27627
ISBN 0-8071-1314-X

To my wife, Carol

CONTENTS

ILLUSTRATIONS

PREFACE AND ACKNOWLEDGMENTS

As the sun slowly set, Generals Robert E. Lee and Jubal A. Early anxiously watched as Early's division advanced across a rugged, open plain toward the Union positions. The ragged gray line suffered occasional casualties as federal gunners found the range and pounded it with solid shot and canister. Steep hills and deep gullies further broke up the Confederate charge as the rebels closed in on the Union breastworks. Watching from his vantage point, Early became dismayed when it appeared that his division would be repulsed before even closing with the enemy. Suddenly, his spirits lifted as he watched General Harry T. Hays's Louisiana Brigade rush in and penetrate the enemy line. The blue defenders could be seen scampering back to a secondary position, only to be swept away again by the surging gray tide closing in behind them. As the victorious rebel yell rose over the field, Early momentarily forgot Lee beside him and jubilantly threw his hat on the ground, crying, "Those damned Louisiana fellows may steal as much as they please now!" [1]

General Early was only one of many Confederate officers who struggled with the paradox known as the Louisiana Tigers. He tended to agree with those who called the Tigers "wharf rats from New Orleans" and the "lowest scrapings of the Mississippi," who plundered and foraged on farms wherever they camped.[2] But the Tigers were reliable in combat, and the general readily forgave them their past transgressions as he watched the Louisianians

1. New Orleans *Times-Democrat,* in Reminiscences Division, n.d., Confederate Veteran Papers, DU.
2. Sidney J. Romero, "Louisiana Clergy and the Confederate Army," *Louisiana History,* II (1961), 280; Charles L. Dufour, *Gentle Tiger: The Gallant Life of Roberdeau Wheat* (Baton Rouge, 1957), 4.

swarm over two Union lines near Fredericksburg. Even though this charge of May 4, 1863, was finally contained and then repulsed by the federals, the Louisiana Tigers had once again proven themselves to be the premier shock troops of the Army of Northern Virginia.

The fierce reputation of the Tigers was well earned, for Louisiana probably had a higher percentage of criminals, drunkards, and deserters in its commands than any other Confederate state, probably because of the great number of poor foreigners who filled the state's ranks. The Irish and Germans made excellent fighters, but many were newcomers to America and had little enthusiasm for the war. Thus many deserted when a chance arose to escape the rigors and danger of campaigning. Other foreigners who enlisted off the rough New Orleans waterfront, where drinking, fighting, and thievery were a way of life, naturally brought their vices with them to the army. This is not to imply that all of Louisiana's foreign soliders fell into this category. The majority did not. Most of the Irish and Germans were dedicated soldiers who behaved as well as native-born Americans. Nevertheless, these foreign-dominated units were most often mentioned in connection with such deviant behavior.

No one Louisiana unit can be singled out as being responsible for creating the Tigers' infamous reputation. Major Roberdeau Wheat's 1st Special Battalion is most often cited by historians as being the unit first nicknamed the "Louisiana Tigers" and of spawning the image associated with that name.[3] One company in Wheat's Battalion, the Tiger Rifles, did lend its name to the entire Louisiana infantry, and no one can doubt that the battalion played a significant role in creating the reputation that surrounded the Tigers. But it was not Wheat's men who first spread the fear and apprehension that came to be associated with the Louisiana troops. Two other Louisiana commands, the 1st Battalion, Louisiana Zouaves (Coppens' Battalion), and the 14th Louisiana Volunteers, initiated this image by their wholesale rioting, looting, and robbery. These two

3. Douglas Southall Freeman, *Lee's Lieutenants: A Study in Command* (3 vols.; New York, 1942, 1944), I, 87; Henry E. Handerson, *Yankee in Gray: The Civil War Memoirs of Henry E. Handerson, with a Selection of His Wartime Letters* (Cleveland, 1962), 33; Leon Jastremski to Robert H. Hemphill, June 8, 1901, in Hemphill Family Papers, DU.

units did more to tarnish the image of Louisiana's soldiers during the first few months of the war than Wheat's Battalion did during its entire existence. In creating mayhem, even Wheat's desperadoes could not match the Irish, Germans, and Creoles of Coppens' Battalion and the 14th Louisiana Volunteers.

In an effort to glorify the Louisiana troops, some historians only lightly treat these negative aspects of the Tigers, or else make their deeds seem more like childish mischief than criminal behavior. Such apologies are unnecessary. Despite the Tigers' reputation, the Confederate commanders time and again called on them in the most desperate situations. From First Manassas to Appomattox they consistently played key roles in the most important campaigns. It was the Louisianians who held back the initial federal onslaught at First Manassas, made possible General T. J. "Stonewall" Jackson's famed Valley Campaign, contained the Union breakthrough at Spotsylvania's Bloody Angle, and led Lee's last offensive actions at Fort Stedman and Appomattox. For all their vices, weaknesses, and failings, Lee's Louisiana Tigers emerged from the Civil War with one of the most respected military records of any southern fighting unit.

Many works have dealt with the Louisiana Tigers, but no comprehensive study of them has ever before been undertaken. To portray accurately the role the Louisiana soldiers played in the Army of Northern Virginia it is necessary to go beyond the readily available sources and thoroughly research the numerous manuscript collections that have been neglected for so long. The letters, diaries, and muster rolls found in these collections contain a wealth of information that cannot be obtained elsewhere. To ferret out such material requires luck, patience, and the help of persons familiar with the documents. I was most fortunate, for the various library and archival personnel consulted during this project invariably proved to be most helpful and willing to make the extra effort often needed to turn up useful material. A special thanks is extended to the staff of the Inter-Library Loan Departments of Texas A & M University, College Station, Texas, and Northwestern State University, Natchitoches, Louisiana, for making available elusive printed sources. Thanks are also in order to the archival staffs of the following institutions for their indispensable aid in locating important manuscript collections: Louisiana State Archives and Louisiana State University, Baton Rouge, Louisiana; Virginia Historical Society and the Museum of the Confederacy, Richmond, Virginia; Duke University, Durham, North Carolina; the University of North Carolina, Chapel Hill, North Carolina; the National Archives and Library of Congress, Washington, D.C.; Centenary College and Louisiana State University at Shreveport, Shreveport, Louisiana; New York City Public Library, New York, New York; University of Michigan, Ann Arbor, Michigan; Northwestern State University, Natchitoches, Louisiana; East Carolina University, Greenville, North Carolina; University of Texas, Austin, Texas; Fredericksburg and Spotsylvania National Military Park, Fredericksburg, Virginia; the Huntington Library, San Marino, California; and the Mansfield State Commemorative Area, Mansfield, Louisiana. I would also like to recognize the Texas A & M University Graduate College's minigrant program, which helped fund a significant portion of my research at these institutions, and Donald Hunter, who prepared the maps included in this study.

Researching a historical topic is only half the task. One must then sift through thousands of pages of notes and present the narrative in a comprehensible form. This process requires advice, criticism, and editing. Robert Calvert, Don Hamilton, Larry Hill, and Betty Unterberger of Texas A & M University receive my sincere appreciation for their valuable input. I would especially like to thank Allan Ashcraft, without whom this study might never have been completed. Professor Ashcraft's kindly patience and constructive criticism helped immensely in guiding me through this project with a minimum of trauma.

ABBREVIATIONS

CC	Centenary College
DU	Duke University
ECU	East Carolina University
FSNMP	Fredericksburg and Spotsylvania National Military Park
HNLC	Historic New Orleans Collection
HL	Huntington Library
LC	Library of Congress
LHAC	Tulane University, Louisiana Historical Association Collection
LSA	Louisiana State Archives
LSU	Louisiana State University, Baton Rouge
LSUS	Louisiana State University, Shreveport
MSCA	Mansfield State Commemorative Area
NA	National Archives
NYPL	New York Public Library
NSU	Northwestern State University
SHC	University of North Carolina, Southern Historical Collection
TU	Tulane University
UM	University of Michigan
UT	University of Texas
VHS	Virginia Historical Society Library
VSL	Virginia State Library

LEE'S TIGERS

Chapter I

ON TO RICHMOND

Richmond! The threatened capital and symbol of the South was the goal of thousands of Louisiana recruits. By May, 1861, it was apparent that Virginia would be the focal point of the coming clash, and Louisiana's young men in gray were eager to be there. From Pensacola, Florida, a young soldier in the Shreveport Greys wrote that his comrades "had become tired of living like flounders and crabs in the deep sands of Pensacola, and the cry was 'on to Richmond.'" Andrew Newell of the Cheneyville Rifles exuberantly wrote his family on the eve of departure from Camp Moore, Louisiana, that the company was in good health and spirits and "eager to get into the fight." [1]

After the bombardment of Fort Sumter, Louisiana hastily organized scores of regiments and battalions to meet the threat of war, ultimately dispatching ten regiments and five battalions of infantry to Virginia. These were the 1st, 2d, 5th, 6th, 7th, 8th, 9th, 10th, and 14th Louisiana Volunteers; the 1st Special Battalion, Louisiana Infantry (Wheat's Battalion); 1st Battalion, Louisiana Volunteers (Dreux's Battalion); 1st Battalion, Louisiana Zouaves (Coppens' Battalion); 3d Battalion, Louisiana Infantry (Bradford's Battalion); and the Washington Infantry Battalion (St. Paul's Foot Rifles). The 4th Louisiana Battalion (Waddell's Battalion) was sent to Virginia in 1861 but is outside the scope of this study because it served there only briefly before being assigned to other areas.

Parades, parties, and pompous ceremonies were often held in

1. In this study, all direct quotes retain the soldiers' original grammar and spelling. Some punctuation, however, has been added for clarity. William E. Moore Diary, May 26, 1861, typescript copy, in William E. Moore Papers, UT; Andrew Newell to Robert A. Newell, June 20, 1861, in Box 1, Folder 2, Robert A. Newell Papers, LSU.

honor of the volunteer companies making up these commands. One function that garnered a great deal of attention was the presentation of flags to local volunteers. Such ceremonies were solemn rituals, as illustrated by the DeSoto Rifles' flag presentation. Handing the flag to the color guard, the spokeswoman for the seamstresses declared: "Receive then, from your mothers and sisters, from those whose affections greet you, these colors woven by our feeble but reliant hands; and when this bright flag shall float before you on the battlefield, let it not only inspire you with the brave and patriotic ambitions of a soldier aspiring to his own and his country's honor and glory, but also may it be a sign that cherished ones appeal to you to save them from a fanatical and heartless foe." The company's color-sergeant and corporals then stepped forward to receive the flag. The color-sergeant replied:

> Ladies, with high-beating hearts and pulses throbbing with emotions, we receive from your hands this beautiful flag, the proud emblem of our young republic. . . . To those who may return from the field of battle bearing this flag in triumph, though perhaps tattered and torn, this incident will always prove a cheering recollection and to him whose fate may be to die a soldier's death, this moment brought before his fading view will recall your kind and sympathetic words, he will . . . bless you as his spirit takes its aerial flight . . . May the God of battles look down upon us as we register a soldier's vow that no stain shall ever be found upon thy sacred folds, save the blood of those who attack thee or those who fall in thy defence. Comrades you have heard the pledge, may it ever guide and guard you on the tented field . . . or in the smoke, glare, and din of battle, amidst carnage and death, there let its bright folds inspire you with new strength, nerve your arms and steel your hearts to deeds of strength and valor.[2]

In their haste to enter the military, some prominent Louisianians bypassed state officials and appealed directly to Confederate authorities for permission to raise units for the Confederate army. Governor Thomas O. Moore bitterly complained of this practice to Secretary of War Leroy P. Walker because he wanted the regiments to be mustered into Louisiana service first so that the state could pick the field grade officers and have the prestige of naming the commands. Governor Moore was particularly incensed at George

2. Bell Irvin Wiley, *The Life of Johnny Reb: The Common Soldier of the Confederacy* (New York, 1962), 21–22.

Auguste Gaston Coppens, a graduate of the French Marine School. Coppens was highly regarded in New Orleans social circles and was described by one woman as "a fine example of grace and beauty." But Coppens earned the wrath of the governor because he received personal authorization from Jefferson Davis in early March to raise and equip a battalion of Zouaves for the Confederate army.[3]

Coppens, like many Louisianians, was impressed with the French Zouaves. In early 1861, a group of actors claiming to be veterans of the Crimean War toured the country as a drill team patterned after the Algerian Zouaves. The Zouaves' uniforms varied but usually consisted of a red fez, a dark blue, loose-fitting jacket trimmed and embroidered with gold cord, a dark blue vest with yellow trim, blue cummerbund, baggy red pantaloons, black leather leggings, and white gaiters. This Zouave drill team toured several cities in Louisiana and thrilled everyone with its close-order drill, colorful uniforms, and French drill commands. By March, 1861, the Zouaves were so popular in Louisiana that Coppens hoped to pattern his command after them.

Coppens quickly organized several companies, most of whose members were foreigners or Louisianians of French extraction. It was claimed that Coppens received permission from the mayor of New Orleans to set up recruiting stations within city jails to give criminals a choice between prison or military service. This is probably an exaggeration, but the battalion's subsequent record of lawlessness lends credence to the claim. In late March the battalion left New Orleans for Pensacola, Florida, where it was mustered into service as the 1st Battalion, Louisiana Zouaves.[4]

Competition for Louisiana's recruits became fierce as the war crisis deepened. By the end of April the state was offering ten dollars to anyone who joined a state regiment and an additional two dollars for each friend induced to sign up. Since some parishes also offered bounties, many potential recruits traveled from parish to parish looking for the best offer. Local planters and businessmen

3. Mrs. Roger A. Pryor, *Reminiscences of Peace and War* (New York, 1905), 172; *The War of the Rebellion: A Compilation of the Official Records of the Union and Confederate Armies* (130 vols.; Washington, D.C., 1880–1901), Ser. IV, Vol. I, 194–95 (hereinafter cited as *OR*). Unless otherwise indicated, all citations are to Series I.

4. Lee A. Wallace, Jr., "Coppens' Louisiana Zouaves," *Civil War History*, VIII (1962), 269–73.

even competed against one another by offering to supply weapons
and uniforms to volunteers, with the understanding that they would
be elected captain of the company or the company would be named
in their honor. This practice led to individualized uniforms and
weapons and caused regimental commanders much grief when trying to standardize their units' equipment.[5]

A. Keene Richards, a wealthy New Orleans citizen, outfitted the
famed Tiger Rifles. But unlike some businessmen, Richards apparently made no demands in return for his support. This company
adopted the popular Zouave dress and wore scarlet skullcaps with
long tassels, red shirts, blue jackets, baggy blue trousers with white
stripes, and white leggings. On each man's hatband were painted
such slogans as "Lincoln's Life or a Tiger's Death," "Tiger in Search
of a Black Republican," and "Tiger in Search of Abe." Recruited
from the back alleys, levees, and jails of New Orleans, the Tiger
Rifles became notorious for their thievery and brawling. The company was organized and led by Captain Alex White, a former mate
on a Mississippi River packet. Rumored to be the son of a prominent governor, the mysterious White supposedly had changed his
name and fled his native state after being convicted of killing a man
during a poker game.[6]

White's Tiger Rifles became part of Major Roberdeau Wheat's 1st
Special Battalion, Louisiana Volunteers. Born in Virginia to an
Episcopal minister, Wheat served as an officer in the Mexican War
and fought in Cuba, Mexico, and Nicaragua with various private
expeditions. The thirty-five-year-old lawyer and soldier of fortune
was serving with Garibaldi in Italy when South Carolina seceded.
He immediately returned to the United States and while in New
York was approached by his old commander, General Winfield
Scott, who urged him to join the Union forces. Wheat declined and
headed for Montgomery to try to obtain a commission in the Con-

5. Edwin Albert Leland, "Organization and Administration of the Louisiana
Army During the Civil War" (M.A. thesis, Louisiana State University, 1938), 19–
23, 31.
6. Dufour, *Gentle Tiger*, 121, 212; New Orleans *Daily Item*, August 25, 1896, in
David F. Boyd Scrapbook, David F. Boyd Papers, LSU; Thomas Cooper DeLeon,
*Four Years in Rebel Capitals: An Inside View of Life in the Southern Confederacy, from Birth
to Death* (Mobile, 1890), 66.

federate army. No commissions were available, however, so he continued on to his home in New Orleans to raise his own company—the Old Dominion Guards. Wheat was later elected major of the 1st Special Battalion and won a lasting place in history as commander of the famed Louisiana Tiger Battalion. A strapping six feet, four inches, in height and weighing 275 pounds, he proved to be the only man capable of handling the rowdy Tigers. "His men loved him—and they feared him," one soldier wrote, "the power or spell he had over his men was truly wonderful."[7]

Wheat's Battalion was a potpourri of men who ranged in status from lawyers and merchants to pickpockets and pimps. Richard Taylor wrote years later that "so villainous was the reputation of this battalion that every commander desired to be rid of it." One company, the Walker Guards, consisted of soldiers of fortune who had served under William Walker in Nicaragua. The Perret Guards, by contrast, were gamblers, and membership in the company was reserved for those able to "cut, shuffle, and deal on the point of a bayonet." Historians usually cite the Catahoula Guerrillas, a company of planters' sons, as being the tamest unit in Wheat's Tigers. Although they were not usually associated with the villainous acts committed by the rest of the battalion, they were referred to as "Free Booters and Robbers" by one officer when they left their hometown, which suggests that they may not have been as innocent as previously believed.[8]

Like many of Louisiana's commands, Wheat's Battalion contained a large number of foreigners, that is, men born in foreign countries, although some of them were naturalized citizens. In 1860, 11.44 percent of Louisiana's population was foreign-born—the most of any southern state. State officials recognized the importance of this segment of the population and made a special effort to incorporate it into the war effort. To promote foreign enlistments, newspaper advertisements frequently called for recruits for such

7. Dufour, *Gentle Tiger*, 7–120; *Southern Historical Society Papers*, XVII (1889), 47–54.

8. Richard Taylor, *Destruction and Reconstruction: Personal Experiences of the Late War* (1879; rpr. Waltham, Mass., 1968), 17; Dufour, *Gentle Tiger*, 120; J. W. Buhoup to St. John R. Liddell, April 26, 1861, in Box 14, Folder 91, Moses and St. John R. Liddell Family Papers, LSU.

companies as the Scotch Rifle Guards, British Guards, and Irish Brigade.[9]

The largest group of foreign-born in Louisiana was the Irish. State officials attempted to raise a brigade from among the thousands of Irishmen who were working as laborers on Louisiana's plantations, levees, and wharves. The attempt was a dismal failure, however, for only two companies were organized and later attached to Colonel Isaac G. Seymour's predominantly Irish 6th Louisiana Volunteers. Seymour was a fifty-seven-year-old Yale University graduate, a successful newspaper editor, and had been the first mayor of Macon, Georgia. Under Winfield Scott he led a company of volunteers against the Seminole Indians in 1836 and a regiment of volunteers in the Mexican War. In 1848, Seymour moved to New Orleans, where he became editor of the city's leading financial newspaper, the *Commercial Bulletin*. As commander of the 6th Louisiana, Seymour was described as being "a brave gentleman but [an] inefficient, slow officer." He often had difficulty controlling his Irishmen, for the 6th Louisiana was found to be "turbulent in camp and requiring a strong hand."[10]

In the spring of 1861, Major Gaspard Tochman, a native of Poland, arrived in New Orleans to promote foreign enlistments through the organization of a Polish brigade. Tochman first came to the United States after being exiled by Russia for his participation in the Polish Revolution of 1830. Once here, he became a popular lecturer on Poland and cultivated the friendship of prominent government officials. In May, 1861, Tochman received permission from his friend Jefferson Davis to raise two regiments of Poles. Since there were only 196 Polish men, women, and children residing in Louisiana in 1860, the real intent of the brigade was to induce other foreign groups to enlist. Tochman's plan was a success, for two "Polish regiments" were raised, although they mainly con-

9. Ella Lonn, *Foreigners in the Confederacy* (Chapel Hill, 1940), 30–31; New Orleans *Daily Delta*, May 2, 1861.

10. Campbell Brown, "Reminiscences of the Civil War," 2 vols., I, 33, in Campbell Brown Collection; Taylor, *Destruction and Reconstruction*, 39; Preface, Isaac G. Seymour Papers, in Schoff Civil War Collection, UM; New Orleans *Commercial Bulletin*, July 30, 1862, in New Orleans Civil War Scrapbook, 2 vols., TU; Leland, "Organization and Administration of the Louisiana Army," 45–46; Lonn, *Foreigners in the Confederacy*, 107–108.

sisted of other nationalities. These two regiments were separated instead of being consolidated into one brigade, with the 1st Polish Regiment designated as the 14th Louisiana Volunteers and the 2d Polish Regiment the 3d Battalion, Louisiana Infantry.[11]

Colonel Valery Sulakowski was made commander of the 14th Louisiana. Like Wheat, Sulakowski was a strict disciplinarian and perhaps the only officer capable of controlling the wild soldiers of his command. Born in Poland to a noble family, he received his military training during the 1848 Hungarian uprising against Austria. When the revolution failed, Sulakowski fled to the United States and settled in New Orleans as a civil engineer. Sulakowski eagerly supported Tochman's efforts to raise a Polish brigade and was rewarded with the command of the 1st Polish Regiment. His men's diverse nationalities and languages made them difficult to manage and forced Sulakowski to rule with an iron fist. He was described by one soldier as "a most exacting military commander, disciplinarian, and organizer" and as the "incarnation of military law—despotic, cruel and absolutely merciless." Sulakowski's men never became fond of him, although they did admire his talents. He was, one Louisianian claimed, "without doubt the best colonel in the service."[12]

Although thousands of foreigners joined Louisiana units, patriotism was not always the prime motivator. Shortages in state levee funds threw many Irishmen out of work before the war and forced them to enlist to survive. Other foreigners were literally shanghaied into the army. One English correspondent in New Orleans wrote, "British subjects have been seized, knocked down, carried off from their labor at the wharf and forced . . . to serve." Other foreign nationals were forced into barracks and hogtied until they agreed to enlist. The British consulate in New Orleans was so swamped by pathetic pleas from its subjects that it finally pressured

11. Sigmund H. Uminski, "Two Polish Confederates," *Polish American Studies*, XXIII (1966), 65–73; Lonn, *Foreigners in the Confederacy*, 101; Leland, "Organization and Administration of the Louisiana Army," 52–53.

12. *Confederate Veteran*, V (1897), 467; Napier Bartlett, *Military Record of Louisiana* (Baton Rouge, 1964), 43; Forrest P. Conner (ed.), "Letters of Lieutenant Robert H. Miller to His Family, 1861–1862," *Virginia Magazine of History and Biography*, LXX (1962), 71; Francis C. Kajencki, "The Louisiana Tiger," *Louisiana History*, XV (1974), 51–52.

Governor Moore to discharge all English citizens so impressed. One company of the 1st Louisiana Volunteers had eight members discharged for this reason.[13]

The forced enlistments of these unwilling soldiers caused severe problems for commands with large numbers of foreign members. These reluctant rebels quickly deserted, committed crimes, and generally failed to assimilate into army life. Invariably, the Louisiana commands most complained about for committing depredations were those with the greatest number of foreign-born members. This is not to say that the foreigners did not fight well, for the vast majority made excellent combat soldiers and brought much deserved praise upon their commands. Still, there were enough of the criminal and dissatisfied elements in the units to earn a bad reputation for all (the Appendix illustrates the high desertion rates in some companies).

Besides trying to fill its quota of men, Louisiana was also faced with the problem of providing a central training camp for its regiments. A site eighty miles north of New Orleans in the piney woods of St. Helena Parish was finally chosen. Named Camp Moore, it was a dry area with a good water supply and isolated from corrupting bars and taverns. Although several smaller camps were also used, the vast majority of the troops sent to Virginia received their initiation into army life at Camp Moore.

The first few days at Camp Moore were exciting for the new recruits as company officers wheeled and dealed to get their men assigned to a "fighting unit" destined for Virginia. Commissions in the newly formed regiments were also highly sought by company officers. Since regimental field offices were filled through elections, the atmosphere of Camp Moore was much like that of a political convention. Bribery and payoffs were common among the campaigning officers, and some commissions were bought and sold openly.[14]

The experience of Captain J. W. Buhoup's Catahoula Guerrillas

13. John D. Winters, *The Civil War in Louisiana* (Baton Rouge, 1963), 34; Bound #1, Record Roll, 1st Regiment Louisiana Volunteers, Army of Northern Virginia, in Association of the Army of Northern Virginia, LHAC; Sir William Howard Russell, *My Diary North and South*, ed. Fletcher Pratt (1863; rpr. New York, 1954), 137.

14. Leland, "Organization and Administration of the Louisiana Army," 33; Winters, *Civil War in Louisiana*, 24.

in these elections was representative. When the company was assigned to the 8th Louisiana Volunteers, Buhoup tried to get St.
John R. Liddell, a prominent Catahoula Parish planter, elected
colonel of the regiment. When this failed, Buhoup complained to
Liddell that the "Head Quarters Clique" tried to bring in field officers from outside the regiment—ignoring his own attempt to
do the same. After much bickering, Buhoup was nominated for
lieutenant-colonel, along with Captain Francis T. Nicholls of the
Phoenix Guards, but wrote, "They have only nominated me I think
to stop my mouth."

Buhoup claimed that all nominees for the regimental offices
agreed to support one another against outside influences. At the
last moment, however, three urban companies replaced three of
the regiment's rural companies and the tickets were redrawn, with
the rival Nicholls then nominated for colonel rather than lieutenant-
colonel. Nicholls supposedly approached Buhoup, stating that he
was not interested in the position, and asked Buhoup to support
retired army officer Captain Henry B. Kelly instead. Buhoup
agreed, but shortly before the election the camp was swamped with
circulars promoting Kelly for colonel and Nicholls for lieutenant-
colonel as originally nominated. When the election was held, Buhoup was beaten by Nicholls for the position of second in command.[15]

Buhoup claimed, "I publicly denounced Nichols . . . as a coward
and a puppy" for his deceitfulness and then followed the wishes
of the Catahoula Guerrillas to transfer to Wheat's Battalion. But
St. John R. Liddell, who was informed of the election, wrote his son
in the Guerrillas that Buhoup "sold the co. for a field office for
himself. . . . Buhoup has never succeeded in anything but diciving
those who were foolish enough to rely upon him—God help you if
you have such men for field officers." Liddell implied that Buhoup
transferred the company to Wheat's Battalion in an attempt to win
a field grade commission there—a commission he never received.[16]

Captain Nicholls explained the episode differently. As the election approached, some of his men accused him of intending to use
the company as a stepping stone to a higher command. Nicholls, a
twenty-seven-year-old West Point graduate, was certain to be tar-

15. Buhoup to Liddell, June 7, 1861, in Liddell Family Papers, LSU.
16. *Ibid.;* unsigned letter, but identified as St. John R. Liddell to son Moses, June
10, 1861, *ibid.*

geted for early promotion because he came from a military family and had served one year in the army before resigning to study law. But Nicholls promised his men he would stay with the Phoenix Guards for the duration of the war. Thus when he was nominated for colonel of the 8th Louisiana, he refused to campaign and threw his support to Kelly. At election time, however, the company released Nicholls from his promise and opened the way for his unsolicited election to lieutenant-colonel.[17]

Not all commands resorted to subterfuge and intrigue to elect their field grade officers. Some, like the 9th Louisiana, used logic in choosing a commanding officer who could best serve the regiment. The North Louisiana farmers of the 9th Louisiana asked Richard Taylor, son of President Zachary Taylor, to leave his position on General Braxton Bragg's staff in Pensacola and come serve as their colonel. Although Taylor had no prior military experience, the men of the 9th Louisiana knew this former state senator carried considerable political weight by being the son of a former president, brother-in-law of Jefferson Davis, and one of the most prominent planters in Louisiana. If anyone could get the regiment to the Virginia theater, it was Taylor.

Taylor proved a good choice, for the thirty-five-year-old scholar had attended Harvard, Yale, and the University of Edinburgh and possessed a brilliant mind and an aptitude for command. He had followed his father to numerous frontier outposts, served as his military secretary during the Mexican War, and was chairman of the Louisiana Military and Defense Committee during the secession convention. At Camp Moore, however, the 9th Louisiana almost regretted Taylor's efficiency. One soldier wrote, "Col. Taylor is a regular martinet in the line of discipline, and aspires to have the most orderly regiment in the service."[18]

17. Barnes F. Lathrop, ed., "Autobiography of Francis T. Nicholls, 1834–1881," *Louisiana Historical Quarterly*, XVII (1934), 249, 250; Ezra J. Warner, *Generals in Gray: Lives of the Confederate Commanders* (Baton Rouge, 1959), 224–25; C. Howard Nichols, "Some Notes on the Military Career of Francis T. Nicholls," *Louisiana History*, III (1962), 297–304.

18. Handerson, *Yankee in Gray*, 91; for background information on Taylor, see Taylor, *Destruction and Reconstruction*, 4–8; New Orleans *Times-Democrat*, January 31, 1897, in Scrapbook, Boyd Papers, LSU; Warner, *Generals in Gray*, 299–300; Kenneth Trist Urquhart, "General Richard Taylor and the War in Virginia, 1861–1862" (M.A. thesis, Tulane University, 1958), 1–17.

To enlisted men like Henry E. Handerson, Camp Moore was not a political arena but a place where "we were fairly initiated into the mysteries and miseries of a soldier's life." Handerson was an Ohio native who came to Louisiana to tutor planters' families around Alexandria and then joined the Stafford Guards with his friends when war came. At Camp Moore he found the army much less glamorous than expected. The Stafford Guards found it difficult to adjust to hauling garbage, digging ditches, and clearing brush, but Richard Taylor, in whose regiment the company belonged, said his men were determined to become soldiers despite the menial labor. It was, he claimed, "'niddering' in gentlemen to assume voluntarily the discharge of duties and then shirk." This determination was characteristic of most soldiers, but W. G. Ogden of the 7th Louisiana wrote his father that he felt like "the Rich Man in the Bible and biseach the officers to let me warn my brothers against the folly which has brought me here. . . . I do implore you to think well before telling any more of the family [to] enter [the] ranks." [19]

The constant drill and drudgery of Camp Moore quickly erased the initial excitement of army life and encouraged men to find ways to make the monotony bearable. Drinking became a favorite pastime, but acquiring liquor posed a problem because all camp alcohol was channeled through regimental sutlers and no taverns existed close to camp. Officers could buy liquor directly from the sutlers, but enlisted men had to secure the written permission of a company officer before purchasing any. For a brief time this regulation kept liquor a privileged item. Andrew Newell wrote home that "Tom Furlong is in good health; quit drinking per necessity can't get it." The Louisiana privates, however, quickly learned to circumvent such rules. One wrote, "The enlisted men secured the signature of captains when they could do so, but to save time and chances of being met by a refusal, most frequently forged the name of their officers." [20]

The rigors and boredom of camp life, plus the availability of liquor, corrupted many innocent boys. One of Francis T. Nicholls' men wrote, "I was told today that men even to Captains & Lieuten-

19. Handerson, *Yankee in Gray*, 9; Taylor, *Destruction and Reconstruction*, 40; W. G. Ogden to father, n.d., in Ogden Family Papers, TU.

20. Newell to Newell, June 20, 1861, in Newell Papers, LSU; Dufour, *Gentle Tiger*, 124.

ants had been drunk and had played cards that were never known to have touched them before coming to this place."[21] This taste for the spirits had a devastating effect on the reputation and behavior of the Louisiana troops in the next few months. Most of the incidents of lawlessness attributed to them were directly related to too much liquor.

Some Louisiana troops were sent to Pensacola, instead of Camp Moore, to strengthen General Bragg's forces there. Among these was the 1st Battalion, Louisiana Volunteers, under the dashing twenty-nine-year-old New Orleans socialite, Lieutenant-Colonel Charles D. Dreux. Dreux was educated in France, at Amherst College, and at two military institutes in Kentucky. After college he studied law and became one of Kentucky's Whig delegates at the 1851 national convention, where he delivered an inspiring speech promoting Winfield Scott for president. Returning to New Orleans, he was later elected district attorney and state legislator and organized the Orleans Cadets when war loomed closer. This company consisted of New Orleans' most prominent young bachelors and claimed to have thirty-four men under eighteen years of age, with Dreux being the only married member. With four other companies, Dreux's men were dispatched to Pensacola and mustered into Confederate service as the 1st Battalion, Louisiana Volunteers—the first Louisiana unit to be accepted into the Confederate army. Dreux was elected lieutenant-colonel of the battalion and won the admiration of his men by mixing strict military discipline while on duty with friendly familiarity while off.[22]

Coppens' Zouaves joined Dreux's Battalion to help protect Pensacola from the Union forces still occupying Fort Pickens on Santa Rosa Island. With their colorful uniforms and French aura, the Zouaves were the center of attention at Pensacola. One foreign correspondent who dined with them noted that many of Coppens' officers were veterans of European wars and that they were the only unit at Pensacola "with a military exactness." Mornings on the sandy

21. R. S. Jackson to David F. Boyd, June 7, 1861, in Box 1, Folder 1, David F. Boyd Civil War Papers, LSU.

22. A. Meynier, Jr., *The Life and Military Services of Col. Charles D. Dreux* (New Orleans, 1883), 11–14, in Civil War Manuscript Series, TU; *Confederate Veteran*, XV (1907), 307.

beach were uniquely French, this Englishman wrote, as "the well
known *reveille* of the Zouaves, and then French clangors, rolls, ruf-
fles and calls ran along the line."[23]

As at Camp Moore, the Louisianians quickly became bored with
their duty station at Pensacola; the monotony of camp life was relieved only by persistent rumors of an impending attack by the
Union fleet. But after weeks in the broiling sun, even this threat of
combat failed to arouse the men. As one put it, "I dread the mos-
quitoes and sand flies more than the black republicans." This same
soldier reported that the insects and heat combined to make conditions miserable and tempers flare. In a fit of anger, a Shreveport
Grey once used a musket to crack the head of a New Orleans soldier who called him a liar, and a nearby saloon was placed off limits
when the Louisiana soldiers engaged in a barroom brawl there with
civilians. Some of the men found this punishment unbearable—
"kill me," they cried, "but don't take my whiskey."[24]

By late spring most of the commands destined for Virginia were
organized and ready to ship out. In addition to the twelve thousand
men who made up these units, a sizable number of camp followers
went along as well. One New Orleans correspondent wrote that
Coppens' Zouaves "had the good taste" to bring women with them
to Pensacola to wash, cook, and clean their quarters, and four fe-
male companions of Wheat's Battalion had to be hauled from the
front lines in a wagon just before the First Battle of Manassas. They
were described by one observer as being "disgusting looking creatures," who were "all dressed up as men." Rose Rooney, however,
was one woman who earned the respect of all the Louisiana soldiers. After enlisting as a regular member of the Crescent Blues to
serve as the men's cook and nurse, she tore down a rail fence while
under heavy fire during the First Battle of Manassas to allow a battery of artillery to enter the fight. She served with her company for

23. Sir William Howard Russell, *Pictures of Southern Life, Social, Political and Military* (New York, 1861), 45–48.
24. Moore Diary, May 1–8, 1861, in Moore Papers; for details on the Louisianians' preparation for battle in Pensacola, see New Orleans *Daily Delta,* May 24,
1861; Moore Diary, April 20, 1861, in Moore Papers, UT; J. W. Minnich article on
Coppens' Zouaves, in Reminiscences, Executive and Army of Northern Virginia,
LHAC; Taylor, *Destruction and Reconstruction,* 7–8.

four years and was still on the rolls as a regular company member when Lee surrendered at Appomattox.[25]

At least twenty-four nationalities were represented among the 12,000 Tigers who left Louisiana in 1861. Original muster rolls give the birthplaces of approximately 7,000 of these men. Of these, only 2,303 were native Louisianians, with the largest group of recruits (2,485) being from other states—mostly poor white farmers who migrated to the piney woods of North Louisiana from other southern states. There were almost as many foreign-born soldiers as native Louisianians. The muster rolls show 2,268 men born outside the United States, most of them serving in New Orleans companies. The breakdown of these men according to place of birth is as follows:[26]

Ireland	1,463	Belgium	5
German states	412	Denmark	4
England	160	Norway	4
France	74	Italy	4
Canada	50	Cuba	3
Scotland	31	Brazil	3
Switzerland	13	Russia	2
West Indies	12	Hungary	1
Sweden	7	Holland	1
Mexico	6	Spain	1
Poland	6	Martinique	1
Nassau	5		

On June 1, 1861, Coppens' Battalion departed from Pensacola for Richmond on what became one of the stormiest train rides in military history. The Zouaves' officers precipitated trouble when they chose to leave their men unattended and rode in a special car at the end of the train. At the first stop the officers left their car to

25. New Orleans *Daily Delta*, May 6, 1861; Susan Leigh Blackford (comp.), Charles M. Blackford and C. M. Blackford (eds.), *Letters from Lee's Army or Memoirs of Life in and out of the Army of Virginia During the War Between the States* (New York, 1947), 23.

26. The statistics on places of birth were obtained from Bound Volumes 1–10 and 12, in Association of the Army of Northern Virginia, LHAC, which include the Record Rolls of the 1st, 2d, 5th, 6th, 7th, 8th, 9th, and 15th Louisiana Volunteers. See also the Appendix for a breakdown by regiments of places of birth.

enjoy a quiet breakfast at the station, but they were quickly inter-
rupted by a shrill whistle and the low rumble of moving cars. Rushing to the windows, the startled officers saw their special car sitting
beside the station while their men and train slowly disappeared
down the tracks. The Zouaves had quietly uncoupled the officers'
car and hijacked the train. Cursing in their respective languages,
the officers quickly wired for another locomotive and were soon in
hot pursuit of their runaway men.

The Zouaves arrived in Montgomery, Alabama, long before their
enraged leaders. The tension and frustration built up at Pensacola
were unleashed as the Zouaves embarked upon a drunken spree of
looting, robbery, and harassment. After an hour of rampant destruction, city officials called out the 1st Georgia Volunteers to
restore order. With loaded muskets and fixed bayonets, the Georgians were forcing the Zouaves out of the stores when the abandoned officers finally pulled into town.

With drawn revolvers, the fuming officers sprang from the moving train and ran toward the drunken mob. "The charge of the
Light Brigade," one witness recalled, "was surpassed by these irate
Creoles." Into the midst of the mob they ran, cursing some, pistol
whipping others. One young lieutenant noticed a huge sergeant
emerging from a store with an armload of shoes. The startled soldier only hesitated when the young officer yelled for him to drop
his loot, so the lieutenant ran up, grabbed him by the throat, and
cracked his head with the pistol barrel. The sergeant collapsed as if
pole-axed, but the officer simply roared, "Roll that carrion into the
streets!" as he stalked off to seek more of his men.[27]

After a half hour of cursings and beatings, the Zouaves finally
dropped their plunder, fell into line, and reluctantly reboarded the
train to continue their trip toward Richmond. Bloodied and sullen
from the experience, Coppens' men were hardly in a cooperative
spirit. Along the way one Zouave was shot and killed by a company
officer and another was accidentally killed under unknown circumstances. The train crew was horrified when others began riding
on top of the train and on the couplings between the cars. When

27. DeLeon, *Four Years in Rebel Capitals*, 72–80; Wallace, "Coppens' Louisiana
Zouaves," 274–75. The material in the following two paragraphs is from the same
source.

warned of the danger, the Zouaves only cursed the crew, laughed hysterically, and clung tighter. One was killed when the train passed under a low bridge, and three others on the couplings were crushed to death when the train lurched suddenly.

At Columbia, South Carolina, the Zouaves again ran amuck. "Sich a shooting of cattle and poultry, sich a yelling and singing of their darned french stuff—sich a rolling of drums and a damning of officers, I arn't hear yit," declared one railroad agent. Reflecting on the trip so far, he added, "and I'm jest a-thinkin' . . . ef this yere reegement don't stop a-fightin' together, being shot by the Georgians and beat by their officers—not to mention a jammin' up on railroads—they're gwine to do darned leetle sarvice a-fightin' of Yanks!"

Despite their riotous reputation, Coppens' Zouaves impressed civilians with their Gallic uniforms and military bearing. After watching them pass through Petersburg, Virginia, one onlooker wrote a friend:

> The greatest sight I have yet seen in the way of military was a body of about 600 Louisiana Zouaves, uniformed and drilled it was said in the true French Zouaves style. Most of them were of foreign extraction— the French predominant—but there were Irish, Italians, Swiss, etc., etc. Their uniforms consisted of loose red flannel pants tied above the ankles, blue flannel jackets, and for headgear a kind of red flannel bag large enough at one end to fit the head and tapering to a point at the other where it was generally decorated with a piece of ribbon. This end fell behind. In this cap which, you see, did not protect their faces from the sun in the least, they had been wasting for a month or two in the burning sun of Pensacola, and of course were as brown as they could well get—browner than I ever saw a white man. Add to their costume and complexion that they were hard specimens before they left the "crescent city" as their manner indicated and you may perhaps imagine what sort of men they were. In fact they were the most savage-looking crowd I ever saw.[28]

When the Zouaves stormed Richmond a few days later, a local newspaper reported that the city was "thrown into a paroxysm of excitement" by their arrival. One man who witnessed their entry wrote home that the battalion was "composed of 'Wharf Rats' of

28. H. B. Cowles, Jr., to unknown, June 20, [1861], in John Buxton Williams Papers, ECU.

New Orleans. . . . & look wilder, & are usually drunker than any indians. They are the lions of the town now & cut out all the other uniforms."[29]

The citizens of Richmond had heard of the Louisianians' wild train ride and were curious about the much publicized Zouaves. Their curiosity was soon satisfied: "From the time of their appearance in Richmond," remembered one resident, "robberies became frequent. Whenever a Zouave was seen something was sure to be missed." Housed at first on the second floor of a warehouse, the Zouaves eluded guards posted at doorways by using their sashes as ropes and exiting out the windows. They then "roamed about the city like a pack of untamed wildcats." Stalking into saloons, they ordered "what they wished to eat and drink, and then direct[ed] the dismayed proprietor to charge their bill to the government." "Thieving, burglary, and garroting in the streets at night" were common as long as the Zouaves were in town. Understandably, "the whole community, both military and civil, drew a long breath of relief" when they were dispatched to Yorktown on June 10.[30]

The 14th Louisiana Volunteers rivaled Coppens' Battalion for being the most feared Louisiana command. While making the trek to Virginia the regiment turned a routine stop at Grand Junction, Tennessee, into a bloody fratricidal battle. During the layover, Colonel Sulakowski ordered the closure of all liquor stores and posted guards to prevent the men from entering them. Many of the soldiers were inebriated before Sulakowski issued his orders, however, for they had smuggled aboard the train two barrels of whiskey and were even issued rations of liquor during the ride to Tennessee. Infuriated by the colonel's orders, these intoxicated men proceeded to defy Sulakowski openly by slipping into the stores through back windows. An underlying tension of personal jealousies and petty grievances over the election of certain officers combined with this drunkenness to set off a vicious riot.

Sulakowski's guards tried to prevent the men from entering the stores, but they were quickly overpowered by the drunkards. When

29. Wallace, "Coppens' Louisiana Zouaves," 275; Edward Porter Alexander to wife, June 8, 1861, in Edward Porter Alexander Collection, SHC.

30. Sallie A. Putnam, *Richmond During the War: Four Years of Personal Observation* (New York, 1867), 36–37; Alfred Hoyt Bill, *The Beleaguered City: Richmond, 1861– 1865* (New York, 1946), 50–51.

some officers and guards tried to subdue the men at one saloon, a
bloody brawl erupted after a guard bayoneted one soldier. The
drunken mob quickly disarmed the guards and began pouring into
the town's streets. Luckily, the regiment had not been fully equipped
and the weapons seized by the rioters were empty; only the officers'
revolvers were loaded.

As the mob became uncontrollable, a pistol shot rang out from a
young lieutenant's revolver, followed in quick succession by others.
Several rioters fell, but the surviving horde of screaming, cursing
men chased the officers into a nearby hotel and set fire to the building even though several hundred civilians were also inside. Loyal
soldiers and civilians were able to extinguish the fire, but the rioters
succeeded in breaking into the hotel. They "rushed in like a mob of
infuriated devils," wrote one newspaper. "Drawers were torn open,
the contents were destroyed, the furniture was broken and pitched
out, the dining room table was thrown over and all the table furniture broken, the chairs smashed to pieces, and such a general
wreck you have never witnessed in a civilized community."[31]

Into the midst of this wreckage swaggered Colonel Sulakowski.
Eyes flashing and lips blue with rage, he screamed to the mutineers, "Go to your quarters!" One man hesitated and was dropped
by a pistol ball from the colonel's drawn revolvers. Another was shot
in the face by Sulakowski but jumped back to his feet, spit out a
tooth, and continued on his way. A sergeant trying to help officers
control the men failed to move quickly enough for Sulakowski and
was mistaken for a rioter. The sergeant was killed by the quick-
shooting colonel in front of his wife, who had traveled to Grand
Junction to visit him.

The pistol-wielding Sulakowski soon cleared the hotel of rioters
with the help of other officers who followed his example. The
battle then continued in the streets for another hour, but finally,
after seven men lay dead and nineteen wounded, the mutineers
were subdued. Surveying the carnage, one newspaper reported,
"The hotel looks like a hospital after a hard fought battle. The
dead and wounded are strewn all over the second floor." Sulakowski was enraged over the incident and bitterly denounced sev-

31. Memphis *Appeal,* n.d., in Browning Scrapbook, Amos G. Browning Papers,
64, DU.

eral of his officers for allowing the situation to get out of hand. He later had the Franco Rifle Guards disbanded for being the major instigators of the riot. The company's officers were forced to resign by the secretary of war, and the enlisted men were distributed among the regiment's other companies.[32]

The violent nature of the foreign-dominated 14th Louisiana Volunteers and Coppens' Battalion convinced many people that all Louisiana soldiers were cut from the same mold. As word of their exploits spread, and as they continued their depredations in Virginia, fear and dread of Louisiana soldiers began to permeate civilian and military life in the Old Dominion. Of course, the belief that all Louisianians were thieves, drunkards, and brawlers was wrong, for other Louisiana commands made the trip to Virginia without incident. Drinking was just as prevalent among these men, but it did not cause the trouble it did with Coppens' and Sulakowski's troops. Lieutenant-Colonel Charles de Choiseul of the 7th Louisiana wrote that his regiment "rattled quietly along, for a couple of days, nothing more exciting happening than the contest between the officers, & a portion of the men. The latter seemingly bent on trying the experiment of how much whiskey they could consume, while the former were endeavoring to make them members of the total abstinence society."[33]

For most Louisianians the journey to Virginia was a gay outing, with civilians jubilantly welcoming them to their towns and hailing the Tigers as liberating heroes. B. C. Cushman of the 1st Louisiana wrote, "At every little town and village [in Tennessee], the inhabitants (especially the ladies) greeted us with cheers and welcomed us to their soil, opened their doors to us all and treated us to the best fare they had without charging any one a single cent." After crossing into Virginia, the 1st Louisiana was treated "more in the manner of the Prince of Wales than as common soldiers." Sometimes the officers wired ahead to the next station to alert the citizens of their impending arrival. By the time the regiment arrived, "we would find [the town] thronged with ladies moving their hand-

---

32. *Ibid.;* Bartlett, *Military Record of Louisiana,* 44–46; Compiled Service Records of Confederate Soldiers Who Served in Organizations from the State of Louisiana, War Record Group 109, Microcopy 320, Roll 253, NA.

33. Charles de Choiseul to Emma Louisa Walton, June 30, 1861, in Folder 5, Walton-Glenny Family Papers, HNLC.

kerchiefs, tossing us flowers, and bidding us to be of good cheer, and fight like brave fellows." [34]

Similar receptions greeted other Louisiana commands. The spring of 1861 was an exciting time; war was still glorious—and bloodless. Within a few months, it was believed, the Yankees would be vanquished and the gray-clad warriors of the Pelican State would be returning to Louisiana in victory. The only concern for most Tigers was to reach the contested field before peace broke out.

34. B. C. Cushman to Boyd, May 16, 1861, in Box 1, Folder 1, Boyd Civil War Papers, LSU.

Chapter II

THE LOUISIANA TIGERS

As the Louisiana Tigers streamed into Virginia, they were quickly dispatched to the two critical military theaters—to the north around Manassas and Centreville to help block any Union advance from Washington and to the southeast on the peninsula formed by the James and York rivers to check the enemy at Fortress Monroe. By summer's end the 6th, 7th, 8th, and 9th Louisiana Volunteers and Wheat's Battalion were assigned to the Potomac District and stationed eighty miles north of Richmond at Centreville. These five commands were first assigned to several different brigades, but in August they were consolidated into the 8th Brigade under General W. H. T. Walker of Georgia. In late summer St. Paul's Foot Rifles also left Richmond to join these forces around Manassas. This command was placed with the Washington Artillery but by May, 1862, was back on the Peninsula in Colonel Micah Jenkins' Brigade.

The 2d, 5th, 10th, and 14th Louisiana Volunteers and Coppens' and Dreux's battalions were ordered to the Peninsula to serve in General J. Bankhead Magruder's Department of the Peninsula. These Louisianians were separated into several small brigades and were often shifted from point to point and reassigned to various commanders. The 1st Louisiana Volunteers were stationed at Norfolk under General Benjamin Huger. Their colonel, Albert Gallatin Blanchard, was promoted to brigadier-general, but he left Virginia within a year for the Trans-Mississippi Department.[1]

The Tigers came to Virginia expecting quickly to engage the enemy, rout them in a great battle, and return home to a victory parade and a heroes' welcome. Since no forethought was given to the

1. *OR,* V, 815, 961, 1030; *ibid.,* Vol. XI, Pt. I, 569; *ibid.,* Vol. LI, Pt. II, 316; *ibid.,* IV, 668–69; *ibid.,* IX, 472; Taylor, *Destruction and Reconstruction,* 14–15.

more mundane aspects of army life, the monotony of soldiering came as a complete shock. "Dull, dull, dull," is the way William E. Moore of Dreux's Battalion described the realities of campaigning.[2] Leon Jastremski, an eighteen-year-old member of the 10th Louisiana, complained to a friend of his daily routine:

> Reveille at 5 o'clock a.m. Roll call. Then we cook our breakfast which of course we are supposed to eat. Half past eight, guard mounting, which is equal to a small parade as it each day consists of 40 men, 1 Lieut., 1 sergt. & 3 corporals. At 9 o'clock company drill until 10 o'clock, after which we are free until 12 o'clock when we have dinner call, after which comes what is called fatigue duty which means Spades and [illegible] and when there is no digging to be done, we have to clean up Quarters. After which we are again free until 6 o'clock. Then dress parade & dismiss [to] cook our supper, eat, loaf & spin yarns until 9 o'clock when tattoo beats & are all sent to bed like a parcel of schoolboys. . . . This occuring every day makes it very tiresome.[3]

Although the men complained about the seemingly constant drilling and lack of free time, for some the worst part of military life was preparing for each day's routine. The 9th Louisiana's Sergeant Edmond Stephens described a typical morning to a friend:

> About one hour before the brake of day you are interrupted by a loud beating of a base drum which they call revile. You then at once rise & on double quick time drag on your old dust wallowed coat, & as for your pants it [is] contrary to the rules of camp to take them off during the hours of rest. You then lay an old wool hat on your head which [you] have picked up in the road while traveling up on some wild march & it having been refused to be owned by some layboring Negro. You then lay your feet into a pair of Shoe soles without any uper leather being attached to them. You start with said clothing around you with the speed of some wild flying fowl for the parade ground to answer your name at Roll call. You then proceed to kindle you a fire with a few sticks of wood which was hauld [to] you [a] number of miles, & that [is] nearly imposible with me because there [is] not

---

2. Moore Diary, September 24, 1861, in Moore Papers, UT.

3. Leon Jastremski to Charlie, September 2, 1861, in Folder 2, Leon Jastremski and Family Papers, LSU.

the first splinter of lightwood here. . . . By chance you get you a little smothered fire to burning, then aply your cooking utensils which are near nothing, iron mashed to geather. . . . You take from the pan some burnt biscuit without either salt, flour or water in them & from said kettle you take a little beefs neck boil[ed] without any water. You then seat your self with four or five of your filthy handed, snot nosed, frisele headed mess mates which would seem to white men not only to be wild but naturally breathed filth & after this is finished about one third are detailed to guard the others & keep them all to wollern in one hole as if they were a parcel of hogs.[4]

Although army life had obviously lost its appeal for Stephens, he and many other Louisianians were proud of some of their newly found talents. Before coming to Virginia, most of the soldiers had little experience in cooking and housekeeping—two tasks that were now required daily of them. Stephens proudly boasted, "I can just stack the world a cooking. I can bake a plate of bisquit without any water, fire or flour." Apparently, the Tigers did not worry about the usual drudgery of washing up after meals, for one of Stephens' messmates remarked that "the general rule in camp is not to wash the dishes as long as you can recollect what was in them last."[5]

Cooking was a duty the Louisianians accepted for it was an accomplishment in which they could take pride. More demanding, and more insulting, was the constant digging of earthworks. Charles I. Batchelor, an eighteen-year-old Atchafalaya Guard, declared, "The sound of spade and axe handled by individuals who never before dreamed of becoming experienced in an art so extremely fatiguing and unprofitable would remind a visitor of the Sable Sons of Africa felling timbers for their masters. . . . Among those becoming experienced in the use of the spade you might find your humble sevt." Henry C. Monier of the 10th Louisiana wrote in his diary that "spades and pickaxes [were] so disgustingly plentiful that the mere sight of them was enough to send men to the hospital." This exhausing work caused some of the more prominent soldiers to reflect upon times past. Lieutenant Alfred Flournoy, a weary member of the 2d Louisiana, promised his wife, "If I ever

4. Edmond Stephens to William W. Upshaw, November 22, 1861, in Judge Paul Stephens Collection, NSU.

5. Stephens and J. Monroe Thomas to Mrs. Pickens, November 21, 1861, *ibid.*

get home I will give the negroes a heap more Saturday evenings than I ever did before. Bless the name of Saturday."[6]

The worst problem in the Virginia camps was not the drilling or digging but the threat of disease. During their first year of military service, many more Tigers were struck down by disease than by Yankee bullets. Exposure and crowded, unsanitary living conditions were the major causes of sickness among the Louisianians. When performing picket duty, men were often required to live for weeks at a time without any shelter; and even in permanent camps, they had only flimsy tents, which offered little protection against the elements. Once near Manassas the men of the 7th Louisiana were drenched and battered when their tents were destroyed by a violent wind storm. The soldiers were on the parade ground when the storm hit and rushed back to camp in a futile attempt to save their tents. When the storm subsided, many of the tents lay collapsed, and clothes, equipment, and other personal items were strewn in every direction. Despite their predicament, W. G. Ogden recalled that it was amusing to see "officers' heads every now and then popping up from admist the ruin."[7]

More substantial housing was finally constructed as the harsh Virginia winter began. The Louisianians, unused to cold weather, proved particularly adept at building winter quarters of logs and mud. Ogden told his father, "The extreme cold here brought out all the house building knowledge our Regiment possessed. With astonishing rapidity the La. Regiments have felled almost all the trees for miles around." The region around Bull Run, he reported, soon had "the appearance . . . of one immense plantation." These log houses were comfortable but crowded—a sixteen-by-twelve-foot structure often lodged as many as eight men. Although protecting the Tigers from the elements, these quarters also helped spread disease because the men were often confined in their small huts for days at a time during bad weather. The stale air and cramped living space made the soldiers particularly susceptible to such contagious

6. Charles I. Batchelor to Albert Batchelor, October 10, 1861, in Box 1, Folder 4, Albert A. Batchelor Papers, LSU; "spades and pickaxes" quote in Bartlett, *Military Record of Louisiana*, 26; Alfred F. Flournoy, Jr., to wife, typescript, September 22, 1861, in Alfred Flournoy Papers, LSU.

7. W. G. Ogden to father, June 26, 1861, in Ogden Papers, TU.

illnesses as mumps and measles, and the unsanitary practices of waste disposal spawned outbreaks of typhoid and dysentery. The soldiers' latrines, or "sinks," were dug two hundred yards from the camps but consisted of an open ditch with a fresh layer of dirt thrown over the contents each morning. At best, such accommodations were a health hazard, and many of the undisciplined men refused to use even these rudimentary facilities.[8]

Typhoid, pneumonia, and measles were the primary killers of Louisiana's soldiers, but nearly every ailment can be found on the hospital rolls. The 7th Louisiana's hospital ledger shows that 645 men out of a total regimental strength of 920 were taken ill during the month of August, 1861. By month's end most of the sick were able to return to duty, but 62 men were forwarded to a general hospital, 15 were discharged from the service, and 3 died. Acute diarrhea was the most common ailment listed, but medical discharges were given for hernias, epilepsy, lead poisoning, syphilis, opium addiction, old age (sixty-two years old), under age (sixteen years old), and idiocy.[9]

All of the Louisiana commands suffered heavily from disease that summer of 1861. During August, 239 of 421 men in Wheat's Battalion and approximately one-half of Dreux's Battalion were taken ill. Of the 600 men in Coppens' Battalion, fewer than 100 were fit for duty that September. No other unit, however, matched the farm boys of Taylor's 9th Louisiana in falling victim to epidemics. Their Centreville campground was the first place most had ever been exposed to such diseases as measles, mumps, and typhoid. By August nearly 100 men had died or been medically discharged, and so many others were sick that the regiment could barely muster 300 men for duty. Everyone hoped cooler weather would slow the raging epidemics, but winter brought severe cases of pneumonia. That winter 6 of the Bienville Blues contracted the dreaded illness and died within a three-week period. Death became so commonplace, wrote Richard Colbert, that "the death of one of our poor soldiers is hardly noticed. One of the Bossier boys died

8. *Ibid.*, January 16, 24, 1862; Urquhart, "General Richard Taylor," 25.
9. Record Book of the Hospital of the 7th Regiment of Louisiana Volunteers, 1861, War Record Group 109, Chap. VI, Vol. 486, 1–4, NA.

day before yesterday and one of ours yesterday and it seemed to me that it was not noticed no more than if a dog had died."[10]

Regimental doctors desperately tried to alleviate the suffering, but their primitive cures did little good and crowded, unsanitary hospitals often only made patients worse. Suffering from typhoid fever, Sergeant Stephens complained from his hospital bed that "we get nothing to eat but bread and coffee, [and] in addition to that it is very filthy and nasty." The 5th Louisiana's Theodore Mandeville echoed Stephens' sentiments when he wrote of his liver ailment: "I believe these damn quacks we have got for Drs. in this regt. are doing me more harm than good. They know nothing but Calomet & Quinine. . . . Yesterday they dosed me with Elixor of Vitriol and to day, intend giving me Iodine of Potash & paint me in the region of the liver with Iodine which burns like the devil."[11]

Since the hospitals were filled to capacity, many Louisianians were sent to civilian homes that were opened to care for the sick soldiers. Because of the improved sanitary conditions in the private homes, those men fortunate enough to be taken in had a much better chance for survival than in the army hospitals. A welcomed result of this civilian care was the many friendships and romances that blossomed between the sick Louisiana soldiers and the Virginia girls who nursed them. Correspondence throughout the war contains numerous mention of girl friends and affairs, many of which originated during times of illness. Sergeant Stephens wrote in early 1864: "There is hardly a young man in our company but what has a Virginia sweetheart—at any rate a friend correspondent in Va." He added poignantly, "We get a great many articles of clothing in that way." Apparently clothing was not all the Tigers received from their girl friends, however. In the back of his diary,

10. Richard Colbert to sister, August 11, 1861, in Folder 58, North Louisiana Historical Association Collection Archives, CC; Dufour, *Gentle Tiger*, 153; Moore Diary, August 2, 1861, Moore Papers, UT; Cornelius M. Buckley (trans. and ed.), *A Frenchman, a Chaplain, a Rebel: The War Letters of Pere Louis-Hippolyte Gache, S.J.* (Chicago, 1981), 47; Ogden to father, January 24, 1862, in Ogden Papers, TU; J. B. Walton to Emma Walton, August 19, 1861, in Folder 7, Walton-Glenny Papers, HNLC; Stephens to unknown, January 9, 1862, in Stephens Collection, NSU; Taylor, *Destruction and Reconstruction*, 15.

11. Stephens to parents, September 14, 1861, in Stephens Collection, NSU; Theodore Mandeville to Jose, August 24, 1861, in Box 2, Folder 12, Henry D. Mandeville Family Papers, LSU.

Captain Boling Williams listed three prescriptions for gonorrhea—one paste and two injections.[12]

Some Tigers were not completely honorable in their relationships. The Richmond *Daily Dispatch* warned its readers in 1863 that soldiers with wives back home were marrying unsuspecting Virginia women. As an example it cited an anonymous Louisiana officer who wrote two long, affectionate letters to his wives in Louisiana and Virginia—and then put them into the wrong envelopes.[13]

Disease, monotony, and for some men the shock and horror of combat at Manassas caused the soldiers to lose their youthful enthusiasm for war and long to return home. On the Peninsula, Benjamin Smith told of changing attitudes in the 5th Louisiana:

> We all take things rather easy now. . . . Not so much gas about exterminating unfortunate yankees, and a great deal more solicitude about our bodies wants and comforts. Once we waked up in the dead of night to repel an expected attack. We were assigned to a certain post and instead of waiting with breathless expectations for the ruthless invader, as the newspapers would express it, all the men just rolled themselves in their blankets and went to sleep with many an expression of pity for the poor devils, who should have to be tramping toward us that time of night . . . I loaded my musket once or twice with the expectation of hurting somebody, but was disappointed. . . . As for my bayonet it had only been stained by the blood of a unfortunate pig, who was foolish enough to tempt a hungry soldier. I devoutly hope, that, he was a Yankee pig.[14]

The Tigers' mental and physical comforts dictated how well they adjusted to military life in Virginia. When affairs at home were going badly or when supplies of food and clothing ran short, they naturally ached to return to Louisiana. The spring of 1862 proved to be a season of depressing homesickness when news of New Or-

12. Stephens to Mr. and Mrs. Paxton, January 14, 1864, in Stephens Collection, NSU; Boling Williams Diary, p. 150, in MSCA; see also Flournoy to wife, typescript copy, May 22, 1861, in Flournoy Papers, LSU; Batchelor to father, October 18, 1861, in Folder 6, Batchelor Papers, LSU; James H. Beard to wife, August 21, 1861, in James H. Beard Papers, LSUS.

13. Wiley, *Johnny Reb,* 281; see also Sallie Garland Young to Louis Marcel Rambin, September 23, 1864, in Young-Spicer Family Papers, ECU.

14. Benjamin Smith to R. H. Carnae, August 25, 1861, in Benjamin Smith Letter, LSU; Andrew B. Booth (comp.); *Records of Louisiana Confederate Soldiers and Louisiana Confederate Commands* (3 vols.; New Orleans, 1920), III, Book III, 602.

leans' capture reached the soldiers. Robert H. Miller spoke for many Louisianians when he wrote that his physical suffering "is nothing to the mental anxiety I have undergone since the whole state of Louisiana has been abandoned to the enemy." General La-fayette McLaws noted that his Tigers showed their feelings of grief openly and that several officers begged him for permission to go home, "as the enemy were in New Orleans and their 'wives and chil-dren would be homeless wandering on the face of the earth.'" The soldiers vented their anger more on General Mansfield Lovell, who lost the city, than on Union General Benjamin Butler, who ruth-lessly ruled over it. Edward Randolph wrote a friend that "it does seem to me that there was a screw loose somewhere" in the city's defense, and another Louisianian declared that "curses 'not loud but deep,' are freely bestowed upon Genl' Lovell." Some men, like Colonel Isaac Seymour, even believed traitorous activity might have caused the city's loss. In camp, he wrote, "there is no mincing of words in giving expression to those opinions and feelings." [15]

During their first year in Virginia, the Tigers could attribute little homesickness to shortages in food and clothing. Unlike later times, when the Confederate soldier was usually ill-clothed and poorly fed, the Louisianians enjoyed a fairly comfortable rookie year. In July, 1861, the four companies from Caddo Parish received $1,500 each to buy supplies, and that autumn the 9th Louisiana re-ceived several large shipments of goods. One such delivery con-tained 12 cases of blankets, 872 pairs of drawers, 400 flannel shirts, 400 jackets, 400 pairs of pants, and 22 dozen pairs of socks. Along with these regimental supplies were numerous bundles addressed to individual soldiers. Typical of these was the one received by R. L. Tanner containing three towels, two blankets, one pillow, a pair of pants, a pocketknife, a necktie, a cake of soap, a comb, and a bottle of medicine. [16]

15. Conner, "Letters of Lieutenant Robert H. Miller," 83–84; Lafayette McLaws to wife, May 1, 1862, in Folder 5, Lafayette McLaws Collection, SHC; Edward G. Randolph to Boyd, June 1, 1862, in Boyd Civil War Papers, LSU; Ben Hubert to Letitia, May 2, 1862, in Ben Hubert Papers, DU; Isaac G. Seymour to William J. Seymour, May 2, 1862, in Seymour Papers, UM.

16. J. H. Mackensie to Boyd, October 21, 1861, in Box 1, Folder 2, Boyd Civil War Papers, LSU; 9th Louisiana Quartermaster Document, *ibid.;* W. Ezra Denson to John F. Stephens, November 16, 1861, in John F. Stephens Correspondence, LSU; J. M. Batchelor to Albert Batchelor, December 20, 1861, in Folder 4, Batchelor Papers, LSU; Richmond *Enquirer,* July 11, 1861; *OR,* VI, 748.

Food was usually plentiful that first year, and few complaints were registered about its quality or quantity. The 2d Louisiana's B. C. Cushman wrote from Norfolk, "We fare finely here, get more vegetables, and strawberries and cream than we know what to do with. I think this is the greatest vegetable market in the world. And besides we get any quantity of fish of every description. I am living and growing fat on oysters and soft shell crabs." Despite the plentifulness of food and clothing, the Louisianians did have to suffer through a few lean times. During a June retreat on the Peninsula, all the extra clothing in Coppens' Battalion was destroyed. When the remaining clothes wore out, the familiar Zouave uniforms were lost forever. Two months later, other Louisianians on the Peninsula endured a temporary food shortage and for a short time subsisted on "five ears of green corn & a piece of fat pork." Even during these rare times of want, however, the Tigers were usually able to purchase needed goods from camp sutlers and local merchants.[17]

Because of this abundance of food, large, elaborate dinners were often held by enlisted men and officers alike. Major Roberdeau Wheat became famous for his gourmet meals at Manassas, where he and Colonel Frederick A. Skinner of the 1st Virginia Volunteers engaged in a friendly contest to see who was better at creating excellent cuisine. Skinner found it difficult to top Wheat's "cabeza de buey al ranchero"—an ox head, with skin and horns intact, covered in a pit of coals and baked like a potato. To prepare the meal, Wheat decapitated an ox, sewed loose skin over the neck cut, and buried the head in the coals at tattoo. At next morning's reveille, Skinner returned to watch the unearthing: "The head, when dug up and brought into the tent covered with ashes and dirt, was, I think, about as repulsive an object as my eyes ever beheld, but giving out a most appetizing odor. The dirt and ashes were brushed off and the skin and horns speedily and skillfully removed, and lo! a metamorphosis occurred. . . . We had before us a dish as grateful to the eye as it was to the nostrils." After stuffing themselves,

17. B. C. Cushman to Boyd, May 16, 1861, in Box 1, Folder 1, Boyd Civil War Papers, LSU; see also Charles I. Batchelor to Albert Batchelor, August 25, 1861, in Folder 4, Batchelor Papers, LSU; Stephens to L. W. Stephens, January 4, 19, 1862, in Stephens Collection, NSU; Wallace, "Coppens' Louisiana Zouaves," 275–76; Mandeville to Rebecca Mandeville, August 27, 1861, in Box 2, Folder 12, Mandeville Papers, LSU; Fannie A. Beers, *Memories: A Record of Personal Experience and Adventure During Four Years of War* (Philadelphia, 1889), 229–30.

Wheat's guests declared that the unusual breakfast was a "gas-tronomic triumph" and proclaimed the major a culinary genius. Wheat's hospitality did not end here. In the autumn of 1861 he entertained Generals Joseph E. Johnston, Jubal Early, Gustavus Smith, and Earl Van Dorn with a "Tiger Dinner." While the gener-als wined and dined inside the party tent, Wheat's Tigers became roaring drunk outside and spent the night racing around the tent on the generals' horses.[18]

Because of their unique use of the French language, several Loui-siana commands became the objects of bemused curiosity upon their arrival in Virginia. After witnessing one Louisiana officer put his men through battalion drill, a Georgian declared, "That-thur furriner *he* calls out er lot er gibberish, an them-thur Dagoes jes maneuver-up like Hell-beatin' tanbark! Jes' like he was talkin' sense!" The 15th Alabama once camped beside Sulakowski's regiment and took delight in sitting around the parade ground each day after completing its own drill sessions to watch "Colonel Sooli Koski" take out his men. One Alabama officer recalled, "The foreign ac-cent of Sooli Koski and the alacrity and precision with which his men obeyed his commands, not a word of which we could under-stand, presented a good entertainment for the edification of our officers and men." To integrate the Louisianians more fully into the command structure, Confederate authorities eventually ordered the Tigers to abandon the use of French and to adopt English commands.[19]

General McLaws, under whom the 10th Louisiana was eventually placed, found it difficult even to communicate with that regiment's officers. The 10th was led by Colonel Mandeville Marigny, son-in-law of Louisiana's first governor, William C. C. Claiborne, and a former French cavalry officer who had been invited by the French to study at the Saumur Military College. Marigny organized his regiments along the lines of a French army unit. Consisting of sol-

18. Quoted in Dufour, *Gentle Tiger,* 157; New Orleans *Daily Item,* August 25, 1896, in Scrapbook, 96, Boyd Papers, LSU.
19. James Cooper Nisbet, *Four Years on the Firing Line,* ed. Bell Irvin Wiley (1914; rpr. Jackson, Tenn., 1963), 19; William C. Oates, *The War Between the Union and Con-federacy and Its Lost Opportunities with a History of the 15th Alabama Regiment and the Forty-eight Battles in Which It Was Engaged* (New York, 1905), 75–76 (hereinafter cited as *15th Alabama*); Wiley, *Johnny Reb,* 322–23.

diers from a dozen different nations, the 10th Louisiana seemed to be an army from Babel with the strange, bewildering jabbering of its members. When Marigny and his adjutant first reported to McLaws, the resultant interview was difficult because of this language barrier. The general wrote his wife, "Indeed, the Colonel & Adjutant who have just left my tent speak English but indifferently well. The Adjutant did not say much. I think but two words & I do not believe he can talk English."[20]

The off-duty activities of the Tigers were not as amusing as their speech, for all the Louisiana commands on the Peninsula openly killed livestock and created havoc in any town unlucky enough to be located near one of their camps. Dreux's Battalion and the 5th Louisiana publicly bayoneted hogs, and McLaws once claimed that in the twelve hours the 10th Louisiana was camped on Jamestown Island its members "eat up every living thing on the Island but two horses and their own species." The Richmond provost marshal's record of arrests for this time also shows numerous Tigers being arrested for robbery, desertion, forgery, and drawing double pay through fraudulent means.[21]

While en route to North Carolina for a brief tour of duty, Sulakowski's 14th Louisiana reenacted its famous Grand Junction riot. As on their earlier train ride, some men prepared for the journey by freely indulging in whiskey and began brawling among themselves aboard the train. Upon reaching Petersburg, Virginia, the feuding soldiers had to disembark and march into town because tracks were not yet laid through the city. It was not long before the soldiers took their squabble into the streets, using "paving stones, clubs, bowie knives, and every available weapon that was at hand." As at Grand Junction, the regiment's officers tried to quell the

20. McLaws to wife, August 18, 1861, in Folder 4, McLaws Collection, SHC; Bartlett, *Military Record of Louisiana*, 26; New Orleans *Daily Picayune*, April 29, 1861; Buckley, *A Frenchman, a Chaplain, a Rebel*, 53.

21. McLaws to wife, August 18, 1861, in Folder 4, McLaws Collection, SHC; Register of Arrests, 1862–64, War Record Group 109, Chap. IX, Vol. 244, NA; Moore Diary, September, 1861–February, 1862, in Moore Papers, UT; Fred Ober, "The Campaign of the Peninsula," in Reminiscences, Executive and Army of Northern Virginia, LHAC; James Stubbs to father, June 25, 1861, in Folder 1, Jefferson W. Stubbs Family Papers, LSU; List of charges against an anonymous private, 1st Louisiana Volunteers, October 1, 1861, in Box 1, Folder 1, James Calvert Wise Papers, LSU.

rioters but were attacked immediately. One lieutenant was seriously injured with three stab wounds, and a store owner's wife was chased by knife-wielding Tigers when she protested the looting of her business. Order was finally restored by the officers and loyal soldiers, but not before the Tigers' reputation for violent behavior was further enhanced.[22]

Coppens' Battalion had the most lawless reputation of all the Louisiana commands on the Peninsula. One Virginian camped near the Zouaves conceded that they were excellent soldiers but wrote, "The pirates are from the dregs of all nations and the ten days they were here, they killed some eighteen or twenty head of cattle." Another soldier, hearing that his company was to be transferred to Coppens' Battalion, exclaimed, "The men swear they will be shot first." So blatantly did Coppens' men raid neighboring farms and pastures that General Magruder was forced to denounce them publicly one hot, sultry day in June during an inspection of his six thousand troops. After a short speech thanking certain regiments for their bravery during a skirmish at Big Bethel, Magruder cautiously approached Coppens' Battalion. Standing rigidly at attention in their fezzes and blue flannel jackets, the Zouaves sweated profusely while their commanding officer berated them for the rash of cattle killings. One witness wrote that Magruder "informed the Zouaves that he had heard of their depredations and that they must be stopped, or every man who was guilty of [such] conduct . . . should be shot immediately." One Tar Heel claimed that the reputation of the Zouaves was so fierce that officers felt they might mutiny if pressed too hard on the issue, and many soldiers believed Magruder chose this particular time to deliver his harangue because he had six thousand men behind him.[23]

The tension that developed between the Tigers and their generals gradually diminished as McLaws and Magruder learned to enjoy the lighter side of their feisty soldiers. In October, McLaws wrote his wife that the 10th Louisiana had "warmly invited" him several times to Williamsburg, where the soldiers were "giving par-

22. New Orleans *Daily Picayune*, September 20, 1861.

23. Charles W. Turner (ed.), "Major Charles A. Davidson: Letters of a Virginia Soldier," *Civil War History*, XXII (1976), 20; anonymous letter, June 17, 1861, in Carrington Family Papers, VHS; Manly Wade Wellman, *Rebel Boast: First at Bethel—Last at Appomattox* (New York, 1956), 62–63.

ties and picnics, singing and serenading." He also told her some Tiger anecdotes that were circulating around camp. One Frenchman, who was lying prostrate in high grass hiding from officers and waiting for a nearby pig to wander within reach, was beaten to his prey by a North Carolina soldier, who suddenly appeared and boldly shot the hog. Rising up on his hands, the Tiger surprised the Tar Heel by shouting, "A, Ha! De Zouave is not the only one who stole de pig, some body else is the damned rascal besides." When two other Louisianians were caught redhanded pulling boards off a house, the owner demanded to know their units. With a straight face, one Tiger replied in a heavy French accent, "Ve belongs to the first Georgiy." Nonsense, the civilian shot back: Georgians did not have that accent. "Vera well," shrugged the soldier, "Bon jour," and off the two went, clutching the boards.[24]

In his attempt to win the Tigers' confidence, General Magruder sometimes overplayed his hand. He once issued a general order for the Louisianians immediately to engage any enemy encountered— even if faced with fifty-to-one odds. The Tigers were pleased that Magruder held such confidence in them, but one of Dreux's men later recalled, "Crazy as we were at that period regarding our ability to eat up such and such a number of live Yankees before breakfast, it began to dawn upon the intellects of most of us that fifty to one was slightly in excess of what we had calculated upon."[25]

In early 1862 Dreux's men found an opportunity to impress Magruder in a way other than fighting Yankees. A "burlesque circus" was organized to entertain residents of the surrounding area, and during the festival season a Mardi Gras parade was held. This event involved about two hundred battalion members, who wanted to show the people of Williamsburg a real Mardi Gras celebration. Materials for costumes were gathered from all over town, and on Mardi Gras day a long, wild procession wound through the streets, halting at Magruder's headquarters. As a practical joke, Billy Campbell, one of Dreux's men, dressed as a girl and strode gracefully into Magruder's office on the arm of Ned Phelps, another member of the battalion. Phelps very properly introduced his escort to the un-

24. McLaws to wife, August 18, 1861, in Folder 4, McLaws Collection, SHC.

25. *Confederate Veteran*, VIII (1900), 105; also see Flournoy to wife, typescript copy, July 8, 1861, in Flournoy Papers, LSU.

suspecting general and claimed the baby-faced Campbell was a sister of one of the battalion's soldiers. The gallant Magruder quickly took the "lady's" hand and began entertaining Campbell with food, drink, and lively conversation. During this interlude, other battalion members entered the room above Magruder, ripped apart a feather mattress and shoveled the feathers through cracks in the floor. Magruder was covered with feathers, but the Tigers simply laughed and yelled that it was a "Louisiana snowstorm!" While the confused Magruder tried to make sense of all this, Campbell and Phelps quietly slipped away, leaving the puzzled general standing alone amid his Louisiana "snow." [26]

Ned Phelps, the ringleader of the Mardi Gras caper, had another encounter with Magruder on the Peninsula. During a night march, Phelps slipped away from the battalion to forage and at daybreak came upon a farmhouse where he discovered Magruder and his staff about to sit down to breakfast. Seeing a vacant chair, the private plopped down as well and hungrily eyed the meal. Amazed at the man's gall, Magruder leaned back in his chair and asked, "Young man, are you aware whom you are breakfasting with?" "Well," mused Phelps, "before I came soldiering I used to be particular whom I ate with, but now I don't care a damn—so [long as] the victuals are clean." Magruder snickered helplessly at this honest retort and declared, "Young man, stay where you are and have what you want." Despite his begrudging admiration of Phelps's style, Magruder must have had his fill of the impetuous soldier for in June, 1862, the general personally granted a transfer for Phelps to the Washington Artillery.[27]

The tumultous activity of Coppens', Sulakowski's, and Marigny's Louisianians created a tarnished image of the Pelican soldiers that never faded. From the Peninsula, the 10th Louisiana's Father Louis-Hippolyte Gache wrote, "The Louisiana soldiers have gained a reputation for pilfering and general loutishness that as soon as any-

26. *Confederate Veteran*, V (1897), 55–56; Beard to wife, April 4, 1862, Beard Papers, LSUS.

27. Booth, *Records of Louisiana Confederate Soldiers*, Vol. III, Book III, 130; unidentified newspaper clipping in Civil War Scrapbook, 1862–64, TU; *Confederate Veteran*, V (1897), 55; *ibid.*, VIII (1900), 108; J. H. Cosgrove, "Reminiscences and Recollections," *Cosgrove's Weekly*, June 24, 1911, in Melrose Scrapbook #230, NSU.

one sees them coming they bolt the doors and windows. Usually any affiliation at all with the Louisiana boys is enough to assure one a cold welcome no matter where he shows his face." [28]

Although the Peninsula was where the Tigers' reputation was largely born, it was near Manassas and Centreville that the term "Louisiana Tiger" came into being. Wheat's Battalion earned its *nom de guerre* because of its fierce fighting at First Manassas and subsequent career of unbridled lawlessness. The title was most probably taken from the Zouave company, Tiger Rifles, because its members were the most conspicuous and proved to be the wildest of Wheat's men. The term was widely used by the autumn of 1861, and because the deeds of the Peninsula Louisianians received so much publicity, it was soon applied to all of the state's soldiers in Virginia.

Wheat's Battalion quickly became a command that was feared by civilians and soldiers alike. In recalling his first view of these original Louisiana Tigers, one Alabaman wrote that they were dressed in "half-savage uniforms" and were "adventurers, wharf-rats, cut-throats, and bad characters generally." Another soldier remembered years later, "I was actually afraid of them, afraid I would meet them somewhere and that they would do me like they did Tom Lane of my company; knock me down and stamp me half to death." Even other Louisianians were leery of Wheat's men. Henry Handerson and the Stafford Guards found "considerably to our horror" that their company had to stand in line next to the Tiger Battalion during brigade drill. [29]

These soldiers had good reason to be fearful, for Wheat's men proved to be a reckless lot. Shortly after their baptism of fire at First Manassas, Captain Alex White challenged one of General Richard S. Ewell's aides to a duel after the officer spoke disparagingly of White's men. Choosing rifles, the two officers proceeded with the duel, which ended tragically when White's opponent was "bored through just above the hips, and died in great agony." Soon after this incident, the men whose honor White defended engaged

28. Buckley, *A Frenchman, a Chaplain, a Rebel,* 43.
29. Oates, *15th Alabama,* 30–31; "I was actually afraid" quote in Lonn, *Foreigners in the Confederacy,* 105; Handerson, *Yankee in Gray,* 34.

in a bloody, drunken brawl in the streets of Lynchburg. These Tiger Rifles so threatened the town's safety that its citizens were finally compelled to organize an armed guard and forcibly jail the drunken mob before the town was wrecked.[30]

Wheat's men were involved in two other melees within a few months. Somehow, Wheat's Battalion and the 1st Kentucky Volunteers developed bad blood and had to be separated in camp to keep the peace. At one new camp near Centreville, however, this routine procedure was overlooked and the two commands were bivouacked adjacent to each other. That night while out on the town, two gangs of drunken Tigers and Kentuckians met in the streets and engaged in a violent street battle, each band attacking the other with paving stones. The noisy rocks bouncing off the frame houses awakened the town and created such a ruckus that a company of infantry had to be sent from camp to separate the men.[31]

Later that winter a dozen Tigers took on an entire company of the 21st Georgia Volunteers when the Georgians absconded with the Louisianians' whiskey after the Tigers offered them a drink from their bottle. The Georgians' captain emerged from his tent to investigate the row and found several Tigers crumpled in the snow. The battered soldiers were gathered up and taken into the captain's tent, where they were treated to a drink and an apology by the Georgian when he learned of the circumstances. As they were leaving, however, the captain warned them that they could have been killed if he had not intervened. The Tigers were reluctant to leave an unfinished fight and called defiantly over their shoulders, "We are much obliged, sor, but Wheat's Battalion kin clean up the whole damn Twenty-first Georgia any time."[32]

Whiskey proved to be the common denominator in the incidents of misbehavior among the Louisianians at Centreville and on the Peninsula. Although enlisted men were officially forbidden to have whiskey in the camps, the "Louisiana Brigade," wrote one soldier, "being mostly city or river men, knew the ropes; and could get it from Richmond." One member of the 8th Louisiana paid a heavy

30. New Orleans *Daily Item*, August 25, 1896, in Scrapbook, Boyd Papers, LSU; Leland, "Organization and Administration of the Louisiana Army," 37–38.

31. W. G. Bean, *The Liberty Hall Volunteers: Stonewall's College Boys* (Charlottesville, 1964), 65.

32. Nisbet, *Four Years on the Firing Line*, 26.

price for his drinking when he froze to death in November, 1861, after getting drunk and passing out in the snow.[33]

Officers seemed to be the greatest abusers of liquor because they were free to purchase it from camp sutlers. The 7th Louisiana sutler's ledger shows that one captain bought eight and a half gallons and one canteen of whiskey in less than two weeks, and Colonel Harry T. Hays purchased five bottles of brandy, one canteen of whiskey, and one bottle of wine in nine days. The account of Captain J. Moore Wilson, however, put all others to shame. It reads as follows:

August	20—one pint of brandy
	21—two quarts of brandy
September	12—one canteen of brandy
	19—one bottle of brandy
	20—three bottles of brandy
	22—one bottle of brandy
	23—one bottle of brandy and one canteen of whiskey
	24—three gallons of whiskey
	25—one canteen of whiskey
	26—one flask of brandy
	28—two gallons of whiskey and four bottles of brandy
	29—two gallons of whiskey[34]

Although it can be assumed that a good proportion of such purchases were made for other men, the Louisiana officers like Captain Wilson were famous for their heavy consumption of spirits. Colonel Isaac G. Seymour complained bitterly about his officers' drinking habits and reported to his son that "some dozen or so of them are low vulgar fellows . . . [who] habituat whiskey tubs." Drinking so affected the performance of the 6th Louisiana that Seymour once pointed out the offenders by name and publicly rebuked them in front of their men during dress parade. The officers of the 2d Louisiana were nearly as bad. During a patrol in December, 1861, they allowed their men to stand outside in freezing weather while they adjourned to a nearby house to get drunk.[35]

33. *Ibid.;* John Devine to mother, November 27, 1861, in John Devine Letters, MSCA.

34. Washburne and Hesler Ledger, LSU.

35. Isaac G. Seymour to William J. Seymour, May 2, 1862, in Seymour Papers, UM; Williams Diary, notation for December, 1861, in MSCA.

Because of the Tigers' recklessness and abuse of alcohol, court-martials became a familiar occurrence in the Louisiana camps. Fighting, often alcohol-induced, was one of the most common reasons for such trials. From August 3 to September 3, 1861, there were four reported fights within the 2d Louisiana, two of which resulted in stabbings. Sentences were the same at Centreville as on the Peninsula and appear to have been cruel and unusual punishment by today's standards. When convicted of killing a hog, some members of the 9th Louisiana were sentenced to carry a rail on their shoulders for alternating periods of two hours for eight days. Drunkenness was often punished by days of hard labor in the trenches, and insubordination usually carried sentences of wearing a ball and chain. One Louisianian found guilty of this latter offense drew twenty days at hard labor with a ball and chain, and one of Coppens' Zouaves had to wear the dreaded device for the duration of his three-year enlistment. Other common penalties for minor offenses were public reprimands, forfeiture of pay, confinement in the guardhouse, standing on the head of a barrel, and wearing a "barrel shirt" with a placard attached declaring the offense. On rare occasions men were cashiered from the service for certain offenses. When this occurred they were normally marched out of camp to the tune of the "Rogue's March." At the suggestion of Colonel Harry Hays, however, the Army of Northern Virginia eventually substituted "Yankee Doodle," because, as Hays put it, more rogues marched to its tune on any given day than to the "Rogue's March." [36]

Not all discipline was handed out by official courts. The sergeant-major of the unruly Tiger Rifles was a former New Orleans prize fighter, who at six feet, six inches, in height, had no need for such formalities. About once a month he simply lined up his men,

36. Williams Diary, August 3–September 3, 1861; unidentified newspaper clipping, in William H. Wharton Scrapbook, MSCA; Orders for October 10 and December 27, 1862, in Louisiana Troops, 7th Regiment Orderly Book, 1862–64, NYPL; Court-martial sentences signed by Lieutenant Colonel W. G. Vincent, September 12, 1861, in Army of Northern Virginia Papers, Part I, LHAC; General Order #123, "Headquarters Army of Northern Virginia," October 28, 1862, *ibid.;* Mandeville to Ellwyn Mandeville, August 31, 1861, in Box 2, Folder 12, Mandeville Papers, LSU; General and Special Orders, 1861, 2d Louisiana Infantry, in Box 48, Folder 2a, Jean Ursin LaVillebeuvre Family Papers, LSU; Thomas Benton Reed, *A Private in Gray* (Camden, Ark., 1905), 52.

stripped off his coat, and menacingly growled, "Now men, yez have
seen me lay down me sthripes. If any of yez has anything agin
me let him step out like a man and settle it with me." There were
few takers.[37]

Lieutenant-Colonel Charles de Choiseul found the Sulakowski
method of discipline more appealing. After Major Wheat was badly
wounded at First Manassas, de Choiseul was ordered temporarily
to take command of Wheat's Battalion. "I am," he wrote a friend,
"the victim of circumstances, not of my own will. . . . Whether the
Tigers will devour me, or whether I will succeed in taming them,
remains to be seen." His moment of truth came when "the whole
set got royally drunk." During the day one drunken soldier twice
snapped his loaded musket at de Choiseul's orderly when the orderly tried to arrest him outside the colonel's tent. Luckily the musket failed to discharge and the orderly was able to subdue him.
Later in the day, de Choiseul reported, other unknown Tigers succeeded in "knocking down & badly beating & robbing . . . a washer-
woman of the battalion in a thicket not a hundred yards from the
guard house." The camp gradually settled down after that and de
Choiseul retired for the night, only to be awakened at 10:30 P.M.,
by a free-for-all at the guard tent. Grabbing his revolver, he rushed
out and found his guards battling seven or eight Tigers who were
apparently trying to free some of their comrades. De Choiseul
slugged one man who approached him threateningly and finally
restored order "with seven or eight beauties bucked & gagged in
the guard tent."[38]

The next day de Choiseul noticed two Tigers casually walking
out of camp toward Centreville. No privates were to leave camp
without a signed pass, so the colonel rode over to investigate and
was told that the orderly sergeant had given them permission to
leave. Suspicious, de Choiseul then went to question the sergeant
but wound up arresting him when the sergeant gave "an impudent
answer" to his inquiry. Ordered to his quarters by de Choiseul, the
soldier swaggered off uttering oaths under his breath, while another Tiger came up to the colonel and began taking the side of the
departing sergeant. When de Choiseul ordered this man to the

37. Handerson, *Yankee in Gray*, 34.
38. Charles de Choiseul to Emma Louise Walton, September 5, 1861, in Folder 8,
Walton-Glenny Papers, HNLC.

guardhouse, the soldier refused. Furious at such insubordination, the mounted colonel picked the man up by the collar and threw him heavily to the ground. After picking himself up, the soldier still refused to leave, so de Choiseul knocked him to the ground a second time. By then several other Tigers had encircled de Choiseul and were pressing closer menacingly. Realizing the danger, the colonel fingered his revolver and sternly warned that he would shoot the first man who "raised a finger." The words were no sooner uttered than a "big double fisted ugly looking fellow came at me & said 'God damn you, shoot me.'" Not one to bluff, de Choiseul immediately drew his pistol and fired. "He turned as I fired & [I] hit him in the cheek, knocking out one upper jaw tooth & two lower ones on the other side & cutting his tongue." The other Tigers quickly broke their encirclement and recoiled from the obviously dangerous colonel. "That quelled the riot," de Choiseul nonchalantly recalled.[39]

It was possibly this two-day episode that led to two of Wheat's Tigers becoming the first soldiers executed in the Virginia army. Michael O'Brien and Dennis Corcoran (or Corkeran) were convicted of being the ringleaders of a gang that beat up an officer and tried to free some of their friends from the guardhouse. Whether this was the same incident de Choiseul described is uncertain, but it likely was because de Choiseul's brawl occurred approximately one month before the executions took place. When O'Brien and Corcoran were sentenced to death, Wheat made an impassioned plea for leniency since one of them had risked his life by carrying the wounded Wheat from the Manassas battlefield. Brigade commander Richard Taylor, however, rejected Wheat's request because he felt strict discipline had to be established.

At 11:30 A.M., on December 9, the entire division formed a three-sided square around a slight depression used as a natural amphitheater for the executions. Twelve men chosen by Taylor from the condemned men's own Tiger Rifles were drawn up to serve as executioners. While a band played the "Death March" the silent division watched as a covered wagon escorted by two companies with fixed bayonets slowly drove to the open side of the square. One witness described what happened:

39. *Ibid.*, January 1, 1862, Folder 1; also see letter of November 6, 1861.

Then six men get out of the wagon—two "Tigers," a catholic priest in long black cassock and three-cornered cap, and three officers. These step forward a little when the Colonel rides up to them and, speaking to the "Tigers," reads to them the charges of which they have been found guilty and the sentence of the court condemning them to death. The two "Tigers" have their hands tied behind them with rope. They are then led backward a short distance and made to kneel with their backs resting against two strong posts driven into the ground. Their hands are also tied tightly behind them to the posts. The priest is seen going constantly from one to the other of the two criminals, comforting them in preparing them for the awful death. . . . He holds to their lips a crucifix, which they passionately kiss and over which they pray. In a few minutes the signal is given, the priest leaves them alone with an officer, who put a bandage over their eyes and retires.[40]

Despite their crime, sympathy for the two Tigers was expressed among the onlooking soldiers. In a last pathetic gesture, the two men had published their final thoughts in a local newspaper. They pleaded for others not to fall victim to the vice of liquor and forgave those who were involved in their execution. Many soldiers recalled this statement as they watched the twelve executioners advance to within twenty yards of the condemned men. The firing squad was not aware of it, but one company of Colonel Henry B. Kelly's 8th Louisiana was standing behind them with loaded muskets. Fearing the Tigers might refuse to fire when ordered, Colonel Kelly was prepared to execute the executioners if the need arose. His concern was unwarranted, however, for Captain White ordered, "Ready! Aim! Fire!" and a dozen muskets split the crisp December air with a thunderous volley. The two men were dead by the time the echoes faded into the hills. In the hushed silence that followed, a lone Tiger broke ranks, ran up to one body, and gently held and caressed it. "It was heart-rendering," a correspondent wrote, "to see the poor brother's agony." Wheat, the only man in the division excused from attending the execution, broke down and cried in his tent at hearing the discharge of muskets. After the burial, many soldiers ghoulishly combed the death site for pieces of posts and

40. Quoted in Michael R. Thomas, "Confederate Firing Squad at Centreville," *Northern Virginia Heritage,* June, 1980, p. 6; unidentified newspaper clipping in Confederate States of America Archives, Army Units, Louisiana Volunteers, DU.

other relics until the distraught Tiger Rifles angrily dispersed them with fixed bayonets.[41]

These two Tigers paid with their lives for attacking one of their officers at the guardhouse. Although this case was extreme, enlisted men often did not hesitate to assault their officers verbally and physically, just as line officers sometimes took drastic measures to oust unpopular field grade officers. Nearly every Louisiana command on the Peninsula was racked by such personal rivalries and internal turmoil. In June, 1861, the company officers of Coppens' Battalion met en masse with General Magruder and threatened to resign and serve as privates if Coppens continued in command. They conceded that he was "a brave and good man" but said he was "entirely without energy or the faculty to command." Magruder tried to defuse the situation by adding two Virginia companies to the battalion, raising it to regimental strength, and bringing in a new colonel, but this plan was rejected by Richmond and Coppens remained in command.[42]

Lieutenant-Colonel Charles M. Bradford of the 3d Louisiana Battalion had similar problems. His officers complained to President Davis that he was unfit, immoral, and a drunkard, but since Bradford had been personally appointed by Davis, he remained until his resignation in June, 1862. Captain Henry Gillum of the Quitman Rangers led the fight against Bradford. He was finally able to get his company transferred to the 14th Louisiana, but he and one of his lieutenants were ambushed and seriously wounded the night before their scheduled departure. Gillum believed Bradford was responsible for the attack, but there is no evidence for this claim. Bradford resigned after being court-martialed on charges of being disrespectful to a superior officer and for conduct prejudicial to good order and discipline.[43]

    41. Michael R. Thomas, "Unearthing Two Tigers' Graves," *Northern Virginia Heritage,* June, 1980, pp. 7–8; Dufour, *Gentle Tiger,* 160–63; Taylor, *Destruction and Reconstruction,* 17; New Orleans *Daily Item,* August 25, 1896, in Scrapbook, Boyd Papers, LSU; John Devine to mother, December 27, 1861, in Mansfield Museum MSS., NSU; Richard Colbert to sister, December 26, 1861, in Folder 60, North Louisiana Historical Association Archives, CC.

    42. Wallace, "Coppens' Louisiana Zouaves," 276.

    43. Henry Gillum to B. F. Post, December 11, 1892, in Reminiscences, Executive and Army of Northern Virginia, LHAC; Buckley, *A Frenchman, a Chaplain, a Rebel,* 31.

The 2d, 10th, and 14th Louisiana Volunteers lost their respective colonels through resignations. Colonel Louis G. DeRussy of the 2d Louisiana reportedly resigned from fear of having to fight an older brother stationed with the federal force at Fortress Monroe, and Colonel Mandeville Marigny resigned in disgust at Richmond's favoritism of others over him. Sulakowski's resignation came as a shock, for he was considered by many to be the best officer on the Peninsula. He was also thoroughly trusted as an engineer by Magruder, who had him construct some of the most formidable Confederate works of the war. But the Polish soldier was impatient and ambitious, and when Howell Cobb was promoted over him to brigadier-general, Sulakowski offered his resignation. After a bitter farewell to his men, the colonel left Virginia to continue his career in the Trans-Mississippi Department.[44]

The men of the 14th Louisiana handled this crisis in typical style—they rioted. Sulakowski's departure left Lieutenant-Colonel Richard W. Jones in command of the regiment. Described by one soldier as "a whining methodist class leader," Jones was very unpopular with his men. As Sulakowski took his leave, "the Regiment became *wild* and *uncontrollable*," tore down the sutler's shop, and physically threatened Colonel Jones. The colonel reportedly took shelter in the surgeon's quarters while the soldiers ran rampant. Wisely, the sutler poured all his whiskey out on the floor, and the officers were finally able to control "the same demoniac spirit that broke out at Grand Junction." Nearly half the regiment's officers were said to have tried to resign because of Jones's appointment as colonel but were refused by army headquarters.[45]

Stationed near Centreville, the Louisiana Brigade seemed to be more stable in its political and personal affairs. The only controversy that occurred there was in October, 1861, when a new commander was appointed to replace W. H. T. Walker, who was departing to take over a Georgia brigade. Walker was a former officer in the old army, a veteran of the Seminole and Mexican wars, and well liked by the Louisianians. His replacement was to be Colonel

44. Bartlett, *Military Record of Louisiana,* 27; Eugene Janin to father, November 21, 1861, in Folder 1, Eugene Janin Collection, SHC; Flournoy to wife, July 8, 21, 1861, in Flournoy Papers, LSU; Smith to Carnae, August 25, 1861, in Smith Letter, LSU; Kajencki, "Louisiana Tiger," 52–53.
45. Conner (ed.), "Letters of Lieutenant Robert H. Miller," 69–75.

Richard Taylor of the 9th Louisiana. Taylor's appointment was not welcomed by the other Louisiana officers, however, because he was the junior officer of the four brigade colonels and, unlike two of the other colonels, had no previous military experience. Adding insult to this perceived injury, Taylor was the brother-in-law of Jefferson Davis. His appointment smacked of nepotism, the officers thought. The Louisiana colonels had been through this before when it was rumored that Taylor, not Walker, originally was to command the Louisiana Brigade. At that time Colonel Isaac G. Seymour wrote a friend, "The powers in Richmond would have given the place to Taylor but they did not dare to do it." Apparently, the brigade's colonels had enough political clout then to overturn the decision—but now the situation was different.

Taylor was embarrassed by the decision to promote him. Acutely aware of his delicate position, he met personally with Davis to ask that the appointment be canceled. Davis promised to consider the request, but instead wrote the other three Louisiana colonels and explained that he alone had made the appointment for the good of the service. This personal note helped soothe their ruffled feelings and persuaded the colonels to support Taylor. Taylor then accepted the promotion and soon became one of the outstanding brigade commanders in the army.[46]

For the vast majority of Louisianians the first year in Virginia proved to be a bore. Inactivity bred restlessness and petty grievances, which often erupted into violent outbursts of lawlessness and mayhem. The thefts, drunken brawls, and unmilitary behavior engaged in by some forever pegged all Louisianians as misfits and unruly "Tigers." Most of the Louisianians desperately wanted to prove themselves in combat to offset this black image. They were eager to meet the enemy and receive their baptism by fire.

46. Taylor, *Destruction and Reconstruction*, 14–16; Urquhart, "General Richard Taylor," 27–32; Isaac G. Seymour to unknown, September 2, 1861, in Seymour Papers, UM.

Chapter   III

BAPTISM BY FIRE

very Louisiana soldier was obsessed with the same goal in
1861—to meet the Yankee invaders in combat and end the
war swiftly in one glorious, textbook battle. Regiments fiercely
competed with one another for the honor of drawing first blood,
and the embarrassment was almost unbearable for those commands still untried in combat by year's end. Wheat's Tigers were en-
vied by the other Louisianians when they became the state's first
veterans after engaging the enemy in a brief skirmish on June 28
while on picket duty along the Potomac River. Such encounters
usually made headlines in Louisiana newspapers, but this action
largely went unnoticed because it was overshadowed a week later by
a lesser but more tragic clash on the Peninsula.[1]

Soon after arriving on the Peninsula, Lieutenant-Colonel Charles
Dreux was placed in command of Young's Mill, an important link in
General Magruder's defensive line, which ran from Yorktown to the
Warwick River. Although Magruder intended for Dreux to stay on
the defensive, the fiery young Creole was determined to win fame
for his battalion and anxiously watched for an opportunity to strike
the enemy. A Fourth of July celebration sponsored by Dreux seemed
to intensify his impatience. In 1861 Independence Day was a holi-
day celebrated by the South as well as the North because the Confederates saw a great similarity between their struggle and the
cause George Washington and other southerners fought for in
1776. To honor the occasion, Dreux invited General McLaws to the
battalion's camp, where a barbeque was being held, complete with
eloquent patriotic speeches and free whiskey. Caught up in the
day's martial excitement after his men honored him with a special
jug of whiskey, Dreux made what McLaws described as "a most ex-

1. Dufour, *Gentle Tiger*, 126; *OR*, Vol. LI, Pt. I, 32.

citing, stirring speech." Standing before his battalion, the young officer closed his oratory by touching his sword hilt and solemnly promising the men that "this is our day, and we will have it."[2] The tipsy crowd responded with enthusiastic cheers, unaware that Dreux fully intended to back up his pledge with action.

The colonel was in a fighting mood by day's end and hastily made plans to cap off the festivities with a bold move against the enemy. His intended victim was a squadron of federal cavalry that regularly passed through a crossroads just outside Young's Mill. Dreux handpicked twenty men from each of his five companies and, with a small detachment of cavalry and one gun from the Richmond Artillery, silently led them out of camp during the predawn hours of July 5. By daylight he had prepared an ambush at the chosen crossroads. His men were huddled quietly along the brushy roadside, and the lone howitzer was posted at the far end of his line. The eastern sky was rapidly growing lighter when Dreux dispatched two scouts down the road the Yankees were expected to use. Within minutes they hurriedly reappeared and told the colonel in hushed but excited whispers that a large cavalry column was coming their way. To ensure that the Yankees would ride into the ambush and get within range of the howitzer, word was quickly passed down the line not to fire until Dreux gave the signal.

Hammers clicked noisily in the brush as the men prepared for action, but no Yankees appeared. Suddenly a single musket shot boomed on the Confederate left in the direction of the approaching enemy. Realizing something was dreadfully wrong, Dreux and some of his officers stepped out of the bushes into the dark road to investigate. With sword in hand, Dreux was straining to see through the dim light when several Union scouts suddenly materialized in the shadowy road. The Confederate officers silently melted back into the underbrush but not before being spotted by one Yankee, who raised his musket and fired. The soldier's aim was true, and his minié ball killed Dreux almost instantly when it lodged deep in the colonel's abdomen after cutting through his swordbelt and shattering his pocketwatch. This lone musket shot touched off several more thunderous rounds from the hiding Confederates and startled

2. Lafayette McLaws to wife, July 8, 1861, in Folder 4, McLaws Collection, SHC; *Confederate Veteran*, V (1897), 55.

Yankees, who jerked their triggers in fright. If it had not been so tragic, the scene would have been comical as bullets whistled through the air, rattled officers yelled confusing commands, and men ran frantically in every direction. The artillery officer ordered his gun rolled out on the road to fire into the Union cavalry, but the horses spooked in the confusion and broke loose. The team began galloping pell-mell in the opposite direction with the cursing artillerymen chasing their runaway howitzer.

The "battle" was soon over, the clever ambush spoiled by an anonymous soldier who fired prematurely and alerted the enemy to the danger that lay ahead. Colonel Dreux and Private Steve Hacket, of the Shreveport Greys, were dead—victims of a botched ambush that netted no offsetting Yankee casualties. In the following days, volleys of accusations flew as wildly as the Tiger's bullets. Some men claimed the untimely shot was fired by one of Dreux's scouts who killed a snake at that crucial moment. Others accused certain officers of hiding behind trees when the shooting began, or worse, of shamelessly running away through the forest. Everyone agreed that the entire affair was badly mishandled, but few held the beloved Dreux responsible. Eugene Janin, however, probably best summed up the incident when he wrote that "a 4th of July barbeque & a jug of whiskey presented to Dreux by [Captain S. M.] Todd had more to do with it than we like to have known out of the battalion."[3]

Most contemporary accounts claimed that Dreux was the first Confederate soldier to die during the war, but this is untrue. At least one Confederate was killed in an earlier cavalry skirmish. But Dreux's death was mourned throughout the South, for not only was he the first Louisianian killed in the war, he was also the first Confederate field grade officer to fall. A large portion of the Peninsula army paid its last respects to the slain soldiers before their bodies were placed aboard a black-draped train for New Orleans. Accompanied by six honor guards, the train was met in the Crescent City by a huge crowd that silently watched as Dreux's coffin was un-

3. Janin to Germain Vincent, August 2, 1861, in Janin Collection, SHC; *OR*, II, 188–89, 964–65, 990–92, 1003–1005; Meynier, *Life of Col. Charles D. Dreux*, 11–17; *Confederate Veteran*, III (1895), 146; *ibid.*, V (1897), 54–55; *ibid.*, XV (1907), 307; Alfred Flournoy, Jr., to wife, typescript copy, July 8, 1861, in Alfred Flournoy, Jr., Papers, LSUS.

loaded and escorted to City Hall by a company of militia. There the colonel's body lay in state for several days and was viewed by thousands of mourners. On July 13, following a funeral service that involved forty Catholic priests, the casket was placed on a velvet-covered artillery carriage drawn by six coal-black horses and was escorted by a squadron of cavalry to St. Louis Cemetery. Buildings along the funeral route were draped in mourning, flags flew at half-mast, and scores of church bells solemnly tolled every minute during the ninety-minute procession. Two hundred carriages carrying such dignitaries as Governor Moore and Mayor John Monroe followed the casket, while another ten thousand mourners walked along behind. The funeral procession was viewed by an estimated sixty thousand people and was the largest ever held in New Orleans. It was an event, one correspondent claimed, "which will never be forgotten . . . whilst one of the rising generation lives."[4]

Dreux's sudden and shocking death was only a harbinger of things to come. A week after the funeral other Tigers first learned of war's ghastly horror along the sluggish Virginia stream known as Bull Run. In July, 1861, the war's first major campaign began when federal troops left Washington heading south toward Richmond. General P. G. T. Beauregard's Army of the Potomac was stationed along Bull Run near Manassas to guard its fords against any Union crossing. The long-awaited federal attack began on July 18, when Union General Daniel Tyler cautiously advanced his division to feel out the Confederate positions at Blackburn's Ford. When a brisk fight erupted there between Tyler and General James Longstreet's brigade, Longstreet was forced to call for support from Jubal Early's brigade camped a mile or so away. Early's brigade consisted of the 7th and 24th Virginia Volunteers and Colonel Harry T. Hays's 7th Louisiana. The three regiments were eager and ready for action, Hays's men having already pocketed forty rounds of ammunition and pinned strips of red flannel to their shirts to identify themselves as Confederates. The Louisianians could clearly hear the battle for some time, but without orders there was nothing to do but patiently sit, listen to its roar, and watch the plumes of bluish-white smoke rise lazily above the tree-lined creek. After

4. Unidentified newspaper clipping in Civil War Scrapbook, 1861–62, TU; Meynier, *Life of Col. Charles D. Dreux,* 11–17.

what seemed an eternity, Early finally received urgent orders to move his men and two guns of the Washington Artillery to the ford and shore up Longstreet's faltering line. Commands were quickly shouted around camp, and in an instant the brigade was up and shuffling down the hot, dusty road toward the sound of the firing.

While marching to the battle, the brigade passed a small farmyard where Beauregard sat on his horse watching the men file past. Dressed in a sparkling new uniform, the general took care to speak to each of the Louisiana companies as Hays's regiment trotted by. Bursting with pride, the men were anxious to enter the fray under the watchful eye of their commanding general. These thoughts were soon dispelled, however, when the brigade crested a hill and walked headlong into a stream of bloodied soldiers stumbling up the slope toward the rear. Some clutched shattered limbs and gaping wounds, but all urged the brigade on, nonetheless, for the federals were forcing a crossing at that very moment. Suddenly the idea of entering the boiling contest below lost its appeal, but Early quickly deployed the Louisianians out front and sent them careening down the hill with the Virginians following in support. The noise of battle and visions of the wounded so unnerved some of the Virginians that they fired volleys of musketry dangerously close over the Tigers' heads before reaching the ford. Luckily, no casualties resulted from the nervous volley and Hays's men arrived at the stream "just in time to save the day."[5]

Hays took up a position astride the ford while the Virginians filed in on his right. The brigade remained in this position for several hours, unable to advance and subjected to a terrific, plunging fire from the blue-clad soldiers atop the much higher opposite bank. When it was evident that neither side could advance, the Yankees accepted the stalemate and withdrew, allowing Early to send pickets across the stream to sound the alarm if they reappeared.

The Louisianians were pleased with their conduct during the Battle of Bull Run, as they called it, but the fight had not been the spectacular battle they expected. Hemmed in by brush and trees and having to hug the muddy creek bank for protection from the enemy's fire was hardly a heroic way to fight. Spirits were further

5. A. J. Dully to unknown, July 19, 1861, in Army of Northern Virginia Papers, Part I, LHAC.

dampened by the sight of the nine dead and fifteen wounded Tigers who lay strewn grotesquely along the stream's edge. As the exhausted men glumly reflected on this first fight, a cold, steady rain set in for the night. Daylight was slow in coming through the overcast sky, and the creek was still shrouded in darkness when Hays's pickets trudged back to the ford from their all-night vigil across Bull Run. Mistaken for a Union advance by their jittery comrades, the surprised pickets were greeted by a shower of minié balls that added one more Tiger to the fatality list.[6]

The skirmish at Blackburn's Ford convinced Union General Irwin McDowell that the ford was too heavily defended to force a crossing, and he decided to cross Bull Run above the Confederate left. By doing so he could destroy the rebel army by smashing its left flank and steamrolling down the length of Beauregard's line.[7]

Guarding the Confederate left at the Stone Bridge were Wheat's Battalion and the 4th South Carolina Volunteers of Colonel N. G. Evans' brigade. Before daybreak on Sunday, July 21, Evans' pickets heard the low rumble of a massive troop movement beyond the bridge. Evans quickly sent one company of Wheat's Battalion and some of his Carolinians across the creek as skirmishers while the rest of the brigade took up positions on nearby hills overlooking the bridge. A single federal gun opened the contest at daylight by sporadically shelling Evans' position. This diversion did not deceive Evans and Wheat, however, for a huge dust cloud could be seen boiling up across Bull Run, slowly snaking beyond the Confederate left. In a hurried strategy session, the two Confederate officers surmised McDowell's flanking maneuver and agreed that their only option was to split the brigade. The Carolinians would remain to hold the bridge while Wheat's Tigers sidestepped almost a mile upstream to try to hold back the enemy long enough for Generals Beauregard and Joe Johnston to send help.[8]

6. *OR*, II, 310–12, 440–50, 463–65; Jno. to Charley, July 28, 1861, in Army of Northern Virginia Papers, Part I, LHAC.

7. *OR*, II, 318.

8. Dufour, *Gentle Tiger,* 134–36; P. G. T. Beauregard, "The First Battle of Bull Run," in R. V. Johnson and C. C. Buel (eds.), *Battles and Leaders of the Civil War* (4 vols.; New York, 1884–88), I, 207; Jesse Walton Reid, *History of the Fourth S.C. Volunteers, from the Commencement of the War Until Lee's Surrender* (1892; rpr. Dayton, Ohio, 1975), 23–25.

After getting into position, Wheat aligned his men perpendicular to the stream in a rolling field interspersed with patches of trees. The Catahoula Guerrillas had just been deployed as skirmishers at 9:45 A.M., when General Ambrose Burnside's Rhode Island brigade slipped through the forest with bayonets brightly reflecting the early morning sunlight. A sporadic fire broke out along the line as Burnside's 2d Rhode Island unexpectedly flushed out the Cata-houla boys, who were hiding in the brush and weeds at the edge of the woods. These individual shots soon merged into long, roaring volleys as the rest of Burnside's line and six of his artillery joined in the fight. "The balls came as thick as hail," wrote one Guerrilla, "[and] grape, bomb and canister would sweep our ranks every minute." Outnumbered six to one, Wheat's men desperately hugged the ground or took cover behind scattered trees and answered the fire as best they could.[9]

For crucial minutes the Louisianians and Rhode Island brigade fought alone, their battle lines surging back and forth across the rolling hills. But Wheat soon received help when the 4th South Carolina and two pieces of artillery finally arrived from the Stone Bridge. Evans placed the Carolinians in a patch of woods on Wheat's left, but in the smoke and confusion they mistook Wheat's men for federals and fired a volley into their flanks. The mistake was quickly corrected, but not before the Tigers turned and peppered the South Carolina line in return.[10]

The din of battle became deafening as Evans' men were slowly forced back by the increasing federal numbers. Wheat and some of his Tigers drifted to the left in the confusing retreat and tried to make a stand around a field of haystacks. Dismounting, Wheat held his reins in one hand and with the other drew his sword and waved it overhead, calling on his men to rally around. Handfuls of Tigers were beginning to respond to his call when there was the sickening thud of lead hitting flesh. The major collapsed, drilled through the body by a ball that entered under his upstretched left arm and tore through one lung before passing out on the other side. Captain

9. Debra Nance Laurence, "Letters from a North Louisiana Tiger," *North Louisiana Historical Association's Journal*, X (Fall, 1979), 132; see also Augustus Woodbury, *The Second Rhode Island Regiment: A Narrative of Military Operations from the Beginning to the End of the War for the Union* (Providence, 1875), 97–98.

10. *OR*, II, 558–62.

Buhoup rushed to Wheat's side and called on his Catahoula Guerrillas to roll the major onto a blanket and use it as a litter to carry
him to the rear. Grabbing the blanket's corners, the Tigers began
their journey, when a couple of the bearers were shot down. Wheat
tumbled hard to the ground and gasped, "Lay me down, boys, you
must save yourselves." The Tigers adamantly refused to abandon
him and called on others to lend a hand with the makeshift litter.
Several more men rushed up, placed the Old Dominion Guards'
flag over the stricken Wheat, and hustled him safely to the rear.[11]

Although Wheat's and Evans' eleven companies had been steadily pushed back, they had maintained order and were effectively
slowing the advance of thirteen thousand Yankees. The wounding
of Wheat seriously threatened this resistance, however, for the
sight of their apparently mortally wounded leader being carried
from the field destroyed the Tigers' morale. Without effective
leadership, the battalion quickly disintegrated, and the men drifted
away in small groups to continue the fight alone or attached to
other commands.

The federals saw the growing confusion in the Confederates'
ranks and pressed their attack with increased vigor. One Tiger, his
thigh shattered by a musket ball, struggled up on one elbow as his
comrades began falling back past him. "Tigers, go in once more,"
he cried. "Go in my sons, I'll be great gloriously God damn if the
sons of bitches can ever whip the Tigers!" A number of Tigers then
rallied, turned, and met this new Union charge with the aid of two
newly arrived Confederate brigades under General Barnard Bee
and Colonel F. S. Bartow. One survivor of the carnage that followed
wrote, "I have been in battles several times before, but such fighting
never was done, I do not believe as was done for the next half-hour,
it did not seem as though men were fighting, it was devils mingling
in the conflict, cursing, yelling, cutting, shrieking." It was during
this phase of the battle that the Tigers earned their reputation as
fierce fighters. Newspapers later claimed that the Tiger Rifles and
Catahoula Guerrillas threw down their slow-firing Mississippi Rifles
in disgust and charged the federals armed only with drawn knives.
Some Louisianians, no doubt, did resort to their trusted blades in

11. Dufour, *Gentle Tiger*, 136–42; unidentified newspaper clipping, in M. J. Solo-
mons Scrapbook, 312, DU; Frank to "Darling," July 26, 1861, in Folder 11, John T.
Wheat Collection, SHC.

the bloody fight, but it is unlikely that two entire companies did so en masse—especially since the battalion's companies were so disorganized. Nevertheless, the story of the knife-wielding Tigers received national attention, and a legend was born.[12]

Some order was restored to the confused Confederate ranks by noon, when other brigades arrived to establish a new line around the famous Henry House. After a series of charges and countercharges, the federals finally massed a determined assault in mid-afternoon that began crumbling the rebel resistance. If not for the timely arrival of Early's brigade at this crucial moment, the entire Confederate army might have given way.

Since early morning, Early's men had been marching constantly from ford to ford trying to block other threatened federal crossings. At no place did they encounter much resistance, although the dust they kicked up along the march did attract a number of enemy shells, one of which killed and wounded a handful of men in the 7th Louisiana. Early was several miles away at Blackburn's Ford when the battle began building to its climax around noon. Although his men were exhausted from having marched miles back and forth between the fords in the hot July sun, Early was ordered to move immediately to the left toward the fighting. With the 7th Virginia, 13th Mississippi, and the 7th Louisiana, Early headed for the sound of battle, which by now had increased to a sustained thunder as the federals began their final push. At approximately 3:00 P.M., Early found General Johnston and was told to find the federal right flank and attack it to relieve some of the pressure on the Confederate front. Unable to obtain guides, Early had to judge where the Union flank was by the sound of firing. Hays's Louisianians "were much blown" from their earlier marching, but the column quickly moved away and soon found the Union flank positioned along a sharp ridge. Early placed the 7th Virginia in front, with Hays and the 13th Mississippi slightly behind to its left. Then "whooping and yelling, like so many devils," wrote one Tiger, the men rushed up and over the slope.[13]

Johnston was startled by the sudden commotion on his left. Leading the screaming horde was a large blue Louisiana state flag

12. Quoted in Dufour, *Gentle Tiger,* 140–41; Richmond *Enquirer,* July 26, 1861.
13. Unidentified newspaper clipping in Civil War Scrapbook, 1861–62, TU.

with a pelican emblazoned across it much like a United States eagle. Thinking this was a Union flag, Johnston was about to order a general retreat when he saw Early's men pounce on the federal flank. McDowell's line disintegrated before Early's determined attack. The Union army was then put to headlong flight as Beauregard and Johnston sent the rest of the Confederate line charging in as well. Muskets, knapsacks, and other equipment littered the ground as the Yankees threw away their gear in their haste to escape. Hays's men scooped up discarded letters during the chase and amused themselves by reading aloud the Yankees' plans to hang Jefferson Davis and end the war in six weeks. Colonel Hays even stumbled upon and kept a complete set of elegant china, which his men believed was abandoned by one of the northern picknickers who came to witness the downfall of the Confederacy.[14]

When darkness and confusion in the Confederates' ranks finally ended the chase, the exhausted but ecstatic rebels halted and huddled around sputtering campfires to recount their day's experiences. Both sides had about eighteen thousand men engaged in the bloody day's work, with the South losing approximately two thousand men, the North three thousand. Wheat's Battalion and Hays's 7th Louisiana could be proud of their performance in this first great southern victory. Wheat's Tigers had helped hold back the Union onslaught until Beauregard and Johnston could organize a defense, and Hays had led the way in breaking the federal flank at the most critical moment of the battle. Losses among the Louisiana commands were surprisingly light considering the heavy fire they were subjected to. Wheat had eight men killed, thirty-eight wounded, and two missing, while Hays lost only three killed and twenty-three wounded.[15]

The Louisianians, and in particular Major Wheat, were treated as bona fide heroes because of their actions. In the days following the fight, dignitaries frequently visited the wounded Wheat, and the camp grapevine predicted his promotion to brigadier-general.

14. *Ibid.;* OR, II, 488, 499, 555–58; Lieutenant-Colonel Charles de Choiseul to Emma Louisa Walton, November 6, 1861, in Folder 8, Walton-Glenny Papers, HNLC; William B. Ratliff to P. G. T. Beauregard, July 4, 1884, in Pierre Gustave Toutant Beauregard Papers, DU; Jubal A. Early, *War Memoirs: Autobiographical Sketch and Narrative of the War Between the States,* ed. Frank Vandiver (1912; rpr. Bloomington, 1960), 16–27.
15. *OR,* II, 327, 570.

Wheat was fortunate to be alive to hear such accolades, for the surgeon who first examined him believed his wound was fatal. During the night, when Wheat asked the doctor about his chances of surviving, the surgeon slowly shook his head and said, "Major, I will answer you candidly that you can't live 'til day." Wheat defiantly answered, "I don't feel like dying yet." "But," the surgeon replied, "there is no instance on record of recovery from such a wound." Thinking this over, the major resolutely declared, "Well, then, I will put my case on record," and he astounded the surgeon by making a full recovery.[16]

The Louisiana commands that missed the fight were envious of their veteran comrades. Richard Taylor's 9th Louisiana heard of the impending battle while still in Richmond and managed to procure a train to try to reach Manassas in time to participate in the fight. Leaving the night of July 20, his men were shocked to find the locomotive so worn out that they had to get off and help push it over the steeper grades. All through the morning of July 21 the raging battle could be heard over the puffing engine. The men's worst fear was realized—they arrived at Manassas soon after the battle was won.

Several of Hays's companies and all of the 6th and 8th Louisiana Volunteers were particularly outraged because they were detailed to guard supplies and act as reserves during the historic battle. Although it took many Tigers a long time to recover from this jealousy, a few of the 6th Louisiana counted themselves lucky after visiting the battlefield. These men were horrified at the human wreckage that lay scattered across the field and in nearby hospitals and quickly decided that combat was not the glorious excitement they previously thought.[17]

Soon after the epic Battle of Manassas the Louisianians around Bull Run were formed into the 8th Brigade under General W. H. T.

16. *Southern Historical Society Papers,* XVII (1889), 55; Section V in Henry T. Owen Papers, Accession 28154, Personal Papers Collection, Archives Branch, VSL; Richmond *Enquirer,* July 26, 1861; unidentified newspaper clipping in Civil War Scrapbook, 1861–62, TU; Dufour, *Gentle Tiger,* 143–46.

17. Early, *War Memoirs,* 15; William F. Ogden to father, July 23, August 1, 1861, in Ogden Papers, TU; Nicholas Herron to Anne McCarthy, August 8, 1861, in Herron Family Correspondence, TU; unidentified newspaper clipping in Civil War Scrapbook, 1861–62, TU; Brown, "Reminiscences," I, 7–12, in Brown Collection, SHC; Taylor, *Destruction and Reconstruction,* 8–10.

Walker of Georgia. The only active campaigning conducted during
the remainder of the year was in late September, when Walker took
the brigade to the Potomac River on a reconnaissance mission. For
many Tigers this excursion was their first real experience in soldiering, and they found the outing pleasant. On several occasions
the brigade slipped to the river's edge opposite Union encampments and banged away at surprised bathers before waving the pelican flag in triumph and melting back into the woods. Such tactics
were fun and relatively harmless, for the only casualties suffered
during the sortie were blisters on the feet of soldiers from the long
forced marches.[18]

The Louisianians on the Peninsula joined in celebrating the victory at Manassas. But as the excitement faded, they were left unnoticed in their muddy Tidewater trenches while Wheat's and
Hays's soldiers basked in glory. Throughout the remainder of 1861
these men stoically performed the vital but dreary task of guarding
Richmond against the enemy garrison at Fortress Monroe. Much of
this important work was overseen by Colonel Sulakowski, who was
placed in command of Magruder's entire left flank in January,
1862. Perhaps Sulakowski's most lasting contribution to Richmond's
defense was the building of a series of trenches and earthworks
that were described by one Union engineer as the "most extensive
known to modern times." But even mundane tasks like sprucing up
the hamlet of Ship's Point also came under the colonel's watchful
eye. One Louisianian wrote that Sulakowski turned the town "from
the muddiest, and most miserable looking place, [into] a neat little
village with every convenience of civilized life . . . including an
opera-house" run by the band members of Sulakowski's regiment.
Sulakowski's guiding hand was lost in February, however, when he
resigned in a huff over real or perceived incidents of governmental
favoritism.[19]

18. History of the 6th Louisiana Volunteers in Army of Northern Virginia Papers, Part II, LHAC; Bound Volume 8 in Association of the Army of Northern Virginia, LHAC; Compiled Service Records, War Record Group 109, Microcopy 320,
Rolls 163 and 175, NA; Frank E. Vandiver (ed.), "A Collection of Louisiana Confederate Letters," *Louisiana Historical Quarterly*, XXVI (1943), 942; *Confederate Veteran*, X
(1902), 389; *ibid.*, XVII (1909), 557.

19. Conner (ed.), "Letters of Lieutenant Robert H. Miller," 71–72; Special Order #580, January 6, 1862, in Association of the Army of Northern Virginia, Part I,
LHAC; Moore Diary, July 22, 1861, in Moore Papers, UT; McLaws to children, July
21, 1861, in Folder 4, McLaws Collection, SHC; Kajencki, "Louisiana Tiger," 52.

In late March, 1862, Union General George B. McClellan's Army of the Potomac began arriving at Fortress Monroe in preparation for a strike up the Peninsula toward Richmond. To meet this threat, Johnston sent a large segment of his Army of Northern Virginia to the Peninsula and arrived there himself on April 12 to take command. By the end of April, Johnston had sixty thousand men available to face McClellan's one-hundred-thousand-man army. The long-awaited campaign began on April 5, when McClellan's huge army lumbered up the Peninsula and probed both of Magruder's flanks. Although these advances were easily repulsed by Magruder's men, the skirmishes kept the Confederates on edge awaiting the inevitable main assault. The tense waiting caused nerves to fray and sometimes led to tragic encounters. In separate incidents a sergeant in Dreux's Battalion and Lieutenant Alfred Scanlon of the 10th Louisiana were killed by their own jittery men when they were mistaken for Yankees while inspecting their picket lines at night.

Daily shelling by huge Union siege guns further broke down Confederate morale. At Young's Mill, Eugene Janin reported the federal gunners were "quite accurate" in lobbing shells into the works held by Dreux's Battalion. The men of the 14th Louisiana endured daily shelling for three weeks, during which time they never left their trenches and had only raw pickled pork and biscuits to eat. In one twenty-four-hour period some three hundred shells were fired into the 14th Louisiana's position, but surprisingly only three men were wounded. Robert H. Miller found the shells' characteristics strangely intriguing. "The first thing we knew of them," he wrote, "is a shrill whistle unlike any thing you or I ever heard before, then the sharp bell-like crack of the bomb—the whistle of the little balls like bumble-bees—then the report of the Guns."[20]

For many Louisianians the weather made life more miserable than the Union artillery. Rain—steady, soaking, bone-chilling rain—set in and continued for days, filling up at night trenches freshly dug that morning. The early spring air was also exceedingly cold, and the men were not allowed to light fires lest they give away their positions to the enemy. Some commands, like the 14th Louisiana,

20. Conner (ed.), "Letters of Lieutenant Robert H. Miller," 80; Janin to father, April 11, 1862, in Folder 1, Janin Collection, SHC; *OR*, IX, 405–406; *ibid.*, Vol. XI, Pt. I, 403–404; Bartlett, *Military Record of Louisiana*, 27–28.

were forced to spend days at a time huddled in cold, thigh-deep water awaiting the Union advance.[21]

Occasionally the Confederate artillery became as great a nuisance to McClellan as his was to Magruder. One such gun was a lone six-pounder stationed at Dam Number One on the Warwick River. Dam Number One was one in a series of dams Magruder designed to impede the Union advance by creating small lakes across McClellan's front. The dam was held by Colonel William Levy's 2d Louisiana, with General Howell Cobb's 15th North Carolina, Cobb's Legion, and the 11th and 16th Georgia strung out in trenches to Levy's right. On the morning of April 16, General W. T. H. Brooks's Vermont brigade was ordered to slip across the shallow, thirty-yard-wide pond and seize this annoying cannon and the trenches surrounding it.

At 8:00 A.M., several Union guns opened fire on Levy's position from a range of eleven hundred yards. With the Louisianian's lone six-pounder barking back with only limited effect, this exchange continued until 3:00 P.M., when eighteen federal pieces began blasting the Confederate works. At the same time three companies of the 3d Vermont eased into the waist-deep water, holding their muskets and cartridge boxes high, and began weaving their way through the flooded forest toward the opposite shore. The dead brush and timber clogging the pond concealed the approaching Yankees, but it also tripped many and sent them tumbling headlong into the stagnant water. Under the covering artillery barrage, the Yankees managed to reach the hostile shore undetected and quickly captured the trenches and the six-pounder when they surprised the 15th North Carolina on Levy's right. The Tar Heels and 16th Georgia attempted a bold counterattack, but the death of the former's colonel and the arrival of two more Vermont companies sent the Confederates reeling back a second time. Quickly reforming, General Cobb hurled the 7th and 8th Georgia, part of the 16th Georgia, and two companies of the 2d Louisiana under Major J. T. Norwood back toward the trenches. This charge pushed the outnumbered Yankees back into the pond, where they were further cut up by devastating volleys from two other Louisiana companies

21. *OR*, Vol. XI, Pt. I, 408–409; Robert Stiles, *Four Years Under Marse Robert* (4th ed.; New York, 1910), 75, 83; Conner (ed.), "Letters of Lieutenant Robert H. Miller," 79–80.

occupying the dam. The plucky federals regrouped on the opposite bank and attempted a second crossing. After losing eighty men and having their flag riddled by eleven balls, however, they finally gave up the mission.

This bloody skirmish has received little attention from historians, but it was the first assault made on an entrenched position by the Army of the Potomac. The sortie carried a high price—63 of the Vermont men were dead and 127 wounded, along with 60 to 75 Confederates killed or wounded. For two days the federal dead lay sprawled along the muddy banks and bobbing in the putrid water before Colonel Levy crossed the dam under a flag of truce to arrange for their burial. In the ensuing discussions, Levy inquired what regiment had made the initial assault that drove the Tar Heels from their trenches. When told it was only a "detachment" of the 3d Vermont, the Louisianian sighed and declared, "It was lucky for us that you did not send over many such detachments." [22]

Probes such as this heightened tensions in the southern camps. Johnston was heavily outnumbered along the Yorktown-Warwick line, and everyone knew little could be done if McClellan launched an all-out assault. To make matters worse, Johnston stood to lose a sizable portion of his army when the twelve-month enlistments for thousands of his men ran out that April. Luckily, on the same day the Vermont brigade stormed across the Warwick River, the Confederate Congress passed the Conscription Act. This bill drafted all eligible males from eighteen to thirty-five years of age and required those volunteer companies still on active duty on April 16 to reelect officers and reorganize for the duration of the war.

This law had a sobering effect on the Louisianians, for many were tired of military life and eagerly looked forward to returning home. Complaints and oaths were loud and numerous in such commands as the 1st Louisiana, seven of the ten companies of which were due to disband less than two weeks after the law went into effect. A unique situation arose in Dreux's Battalion, however. That unit was to disband on April 11, but Magruder personally ap-

22. G. G. Benedict, *Vermont in the Civil War: A History of the Part Taken by the Vermont Soldiers and Sailors in the War for the Union, 1861–5* (2 vols.; Burlington, 1886), I, 265; *OR*, Vol. XI, Pt. I, 363–67, 406–408, 415–21; *Confederate Veteran*, VIII (1900), 197; Compiled Service Records, War Record Group 109, Microcopy 320, Roll 102, NA.

pealed to its members to stay on the firing line until the immediate
Union threat passed. In a special order, Magruder thanked the battalion for its faithful service and sympathized with the soldiers' disappointment over their lack of a chance to fight. But he hoped
"that it may be never said that a La. Batl. . . . moved to the rear
at the sound of the enemy's cannon." In closing, the general authorized the battalion's disbandment but stated that "he is satisfied
that no co. will avail itself of it—at least until reinforcements have
arrived."[23]

The Louisianians accepted this challenge and agreed to remain
in the trenches an additional month without pay. On May 1, however, Colonel N. H. Rightor was told of Johnston's plan to evacuate
the Yorktown-Warwick line and took his retreat as a release from
the battalion's agreement. Calling the men together, Rightor gave a
fiery speech before ordering the drummer boys to beat taps and
the battalion to disband. Only one company, the Shreveport Greys,
was still officially on duty when the Conscription Act became law, so
it was transferred to the 1st Louisiana Volunteers. Most of the remaining battalion members returned to Louisiana and reorganized
as Fenner's Louisiana Battery. The other Louisianians in Virginia
reluctantly went through reorganization and reelected officers in
elections that were reportedly marred by "whiskey, promises and
bribes of various sorts."[24]

After weeks of planning and maneuvering, McClellan was ready
to move against Yorktown on May 5. Upon advancing, however, he
found that Johnston had abandoned the Yorktown-Warwick line on
May 3 and had withdrawn closer to Williamsburg. Dawn of May 5
was slow in coming through a sky heavy with fog and misty rain.
Sporadic skirmish fire broke out as the Union forces began prob-
ing this new rebel line. On the Confederate right Union General
Joseph Hooker charged through a rain-soaked forest and put so

23. General John B. Magruder's Special Order 701, March 27, 1862, in MC-3/
MSS. 3, Museum of the Confederacy, Richmond, Va.
24. *Confederate Veteran*, III (1895), 146; *ibid.*, V (1897), 54–55; Paul E. Daugherty,
"W. E. Moore in the Civil War," in Moore Papers, UT; *OR*, Vol. XI, Pt. III, 435; un-
known to Colonel W. G. Vincent, April 2, 1862, in Box 1, Folder 1, Wise Papers,
LSU; William E. Huger to O. L. Putnam, July 20, 1899, in Flags, LHAC; Bound Vol-
umes 1 and 2, in Association of the Army of Northern Virginia, LHAC; Thomas
Taylor to Miles Taylor, April 12, 1862, in Box 1, Folder 3, Miles Taylor Family Papers,
LSU; Williams Diary, 119–21, 144, in MSCA.

much pressure on the brigades of Cadmus Wilcox and George Pickett that Colonel Richard Jones's 14th Louisiana and three Alabama companies had to be rushed in as reinforcements. Placed on the far right of the Confederate line, Jones sent two of his companies out as skirmishers and ordered the rest of the men to slip off their knapsacks and prepare to advance. When the order to charge was given, the Louisianians clambered over a rail fence and gingerly picked their way through a tangled abatis of downed trees. After a great deal of slipping and falling on the slick logs, Jones's skirmishers finally made contact with Hooker's men. But they were blasted back onto the main line just as it was struggling through the jungle of wet, twisted foliage. The confusion was great in the dark, misty woods, and Jones could not be found. Other officers had to take control of the situation and were able to deploy the regiment to resist the oncoming enemy. When a counterattack was attempted by the Confederate line, the rebels "were staggered and embarrassed for a moment" by the accurate Yankee fire. But the Louisianians quickly rallied and charged again, this time forcing Hooker's men back a mile. The rebels captured a sizable number of prisoners, three pieces of artillery, and "a small mountain of knapsacks," which the famished Tigers put to good use.

The Confederates finally halted the advance from fear of overextending themselves and being cut off in the rear. While the Louisianians laid down on the wet leaves for rest and protection, other Confederate units drifted in and were quickly put into line next to Jones's men. Within minutes, the Yankees came crashing back through the dripping underbrush "with extreme fury." They sent volleys of musket fire tearing through the Louisiana line, dreadfully wounding several of Jones's men in the head, neck, and shoulders as they lay prone on the ground. When this final assault was beaten back, the Confederate regiments pulled themselves together and withdrew to their original line.[25]

The Louisianians played a crucial role in holding back McClellan's army during the Battle of Williamsburg, but they were badly shot up in the process. In the brutal fire fight on the Confederate right, the 14th Louisiana lost 194 men, with Lieutenant-Colonel Zebulon York and Major David Zable among the wounded.

25. Henry Gillum to B. F. Post, December 11, 1892, in Reminiscences, Executive and Army of Northern Virginia, LHAC.

In the center of Johnston's line, the St. Paul's Foot Rifles garrisoned
an earthwork dubbed Fort Magruder during the day and lost
twenty-nine men while under a heavy fire from the Yankee artillery
and sharpshooters.[26]

The good conduct displayed by Jones's and Henry St. Paul de
Lechard's men during the Battle of Williamsburg should have improved the reputation of Louisiana's soldiers on the Peninsula. But
the actions of one man during the campaign negated their contribution and almost irreparably blackened the name of the Tigers.
Sometime during the retreat a number of captured wounded federals were carefully laid out on the ground near Fort Magruder.
Soon a large group of curious Confederates crowded around the
prisoners to catch a glimpse of a real live Yankee. One pitiful Union
soldier was shot through the abdomen and rolled in agony on the
ground, pleading with the Confederate guards to kill him and end
his misery. At that moment, Coppens' Battalion marched by. Seeing
the crowd of onlookers, several Zouaves dropped out of rank,
walked over, and peeped through the encircling crowd. They were,
remembered one Virginia soldier, "the most rakish and devilish
looking beings I ever saw." After hearing the poor Yankee's agonizing pleas, one Zouave elbowed his way through the crowd, stood
over the wounded man, and asked, "Put you out of your misery?
Certainly, sir!" He then swiftly brought down his musket butt and
crushed the man's skull. The crowd gasped and moved back from
"this demon" in horror, but the Zouave simply looked around at
the other wounded men and asked matter-of-factly, "Any other
gentlemen here'd like to be accommodated?" When no one answered, he disappeared through the crowd before anyone could
react. Apparently the perpetrator of this gruesome deed was never
brought to justice. Coppens' Battalion disappeared down the road
toward Richmond, and a new atrocity was registered under the
name of the Louisiana Tigers.[27]

26. *OR*, Vol. XI, Pt. I, 275, 441–43, 450–60, 467, 475, 487–91, 564–71, 581–
89; Leon Jastremski, "Yorktown and Williamsburg," in Reminiscences, Executive
and Army of Northern Virginia, LHAC; Fred Ober, "The Campaign of the Peninsula," *ibid.;* McLaws to Adjutant General Right Wing, May 16, 1862, in Folder 5,
McLaws Collection, SHC; John Y. Foster, *New Jersey and the Rebellion: A History of
the Services of the Troops and People of New Jersey in Aid of the Union Cause* (Newark,
1868), 133.

27. Stiles, *Four Years Under Marse Robert*, 80–81.

Chapter IV

SOMETHING TO BOAST OF

J ohnston's Army of Northern Virginia was reorganized after the
victory at Manassas. Taylor's Louisiana Brigade was placed in
Richard S. Ewell's division along with the brigades of Generals
George H. Steuart, Arnold Elzey, and Isaac Trimble. The Louisianians found their new divisional commander rather odd—even by
the Tigers' own strange standards. Colonel Isaac Seymour wrote,
"We are all exceedingly dissatisfied with Gen. Ewell, who is very eccentric and seems half the time not to know what he is doing." An
1840 graduate of West Point, Ewell had experienced army life
mostly on cavalry duty on the frontier—he once claimed he knew
all there was to know about handling a squadron of cavalry but
little else. This lack was illustrated while his division was camped
along the Rappahannock River in the early spring of 1862. Disap-
pointed that his men were reaping few supplies from such a rich
area, Ewell went foraging for his destitute men himself and returned to camp with a fine bull. When Ewell proudly showed his
prize to Taylor, the Louisianian admired the catch but pointed out
that it would hardly feed the division's eight thousand men. Ewell's
face went blank, then he sighed, "Ah! I was thinking of my fifty
dragoons."[1] Such idiosyncrasies elevated Ewell in the eyes of the
Tigers. His very appearance drew sympathy. Taylor wrote of Ewell,
"Bright, prominent eyes, a bomb-shaped bald head, and a nose like
that of Francis of Valois, gave him a striking resemblence to a wood-
cock, and this was increased by a bird-like habit of putting his head
on one side to utter his quaint speeches." Ewell was also extremely
nervous and had the peculiar habit of sleeping "curled around a
camp-stool, in positions to dislocate an ordinary person's joints."[2]

1. Isaac G. Seymour to William J. Seymour, May 2, 1862, Seymour Papers, UM;
Taylor, *Destruction and Reconstruction,* 29–31.
2. Taylor, *Destruction and Reconstruction,* 29–31.

Perhaps one reason the Tigers grew so fond of Ewell was because they were used to strange behavior. Taylor had as many personality quirks as his commander. He, too, was a nervous man, often afflicted with "nervous headaches," rheumatism, and strokes of paralysis that left his right side so weak and useless that he sometimes had to be helped onto his horse. Such seizures made him ill-tempered. As one of Taylor's officers remembered, "Taylor well was charming company [but] Taylor sick was not a pattern of patience and amiability."[3]

Taylor's short temper often exploded and stirred up the Louisiana camp. When the regiments were reorganized under the Conscription Act, Taylor wanted his artillery to reelect its captain. But the artillerymen bolted and chose a new leader instead. This disobedience "caused much swearing" by Taylor, and he declared the whole battery worthless. Every artilleryman was relieved of duty, sent to Richmond, and replaced by some of Taylor's infantry, who were put under the former artillery captain. The irate artillerymen persuaded Confederate officials to countermand Taylor's order and eventually rejoined their guns under the newly elected captain but not before missing the glorious Valley Campaign.[4]

Taylor's famous temper at times even caused friction between himself and the usually placid Ewell. On one occasion Taylor was sitting in Ewell's quarters when a courier arrived with a report. When the courier remarked, "I passed Taylor's Brigade," the proud Louisianian shouted out, "How dare you speak in that manner! I am *General* Taylor, sir." Ewell glowered at Taylor for this outburst and silenced him with a curt reply. "This is *my* courier, sir," he said coldly, and then directed the embarrassed soldier to continue.[5]

In reinforcing Magruder on the Peninsula, General Johnston was forced to evacuate Manassas and Centreville. On March 8, 1862, the Army of Northern Virginia pulled back to Orange Courthouse. There it would be in position to head off any Union thrusts up the Peninsula or out of Washington. Rumors of such a withdrawal circulated through the rebel camps for days before it actu-

---

3. New Orleans *Times-Democrat*, Confederate Veteran Papers, Reminiscences Division, n.d.

4. Brown, "Reminiscences of the Civil War," I, 27–28, Brown Collection, SHC.

5. Frank M. Myers, *The Comanches: A History of White's Battalion, Virginia Cavalry, Laurel Brig., Hampton Div., A.N.V., C.S.A.* (1871; rpr. Marietta, Ga., 1956), 39.

ally occurred, causing Taylor's brigade hastily to assemble all the possessions it had accumulated over the last few months. By the day of the evacuation, small mounds of items lay scattered around the men's quarters as each soldier attempted to stuff his knapsack and blanket roll with the numerous little conveniences he felt he could not live without.[6]

Early on March 9, the Tigers torched their cherished winter huts and served as rear guard when the army headed south in a cold, drizzling rain. Thus began a long, arduous night march over roads turned into quagmires by the late winter rains. "We had," summed up W. G. Ogden, "a wet, miserable time of it." The Irishmen of Seymour's 6th Louisiana brought up the army's rear and soon noticed pots, pans, clothing, boots, and various equipment littering the darkened roadside as the exhausted Confederates discarded their precious cargo. By daylight most men carried only the clothes on their backs—their tents, blankets, and cooking utensils had been burned at Manassas or thrown away during the night.[7]

Many of Taylor's men collapsed from exhaustion on the muddy roadside. Taylor stopped the brigade several times to let these stragglers catch up and finally rode in the rear to give them some respite by carrying their muskets—a gesture soon followed by several other officers. Taylor further garnered respect from his Tigers by giving friendly advice throughout the miserable, rainy night on how to bathe blistered feet and readjust ill-fitting shoes during the short halts. The men appreciated these helpful hints and took pride in their improved marching ability. In the months to come, Taylor's brigade often set the pace for Stonewall Jackson's "foot cavalry," and the Tigers "soon held it a disgrace to fall out of ranks." Despite Taylor's efforts, however, a number of the slower Tigers were captured by the enemy during the withdrawal.[8]

After safely crossing the Rappahannock River, Johnston's army bivouacked and the Louisianians picketed the river crossings. The

6. Handerson, *Yankee in Gray*, 39; Taylor, *Destruction and Reconstruction*, 27–28.

7. W. G. Ogden to father, March 24, 1862, in Box 1, Folder 8, Ogden Papers, TU; Thomas Taylor to Ann Steel, March 21, 1862, in Box 1, Folder 3, Taylor Papers, LSU; Edmond Stephens to parents, April 13, 1862, in Stephens Collection, NSU; Bartlett, *Military Record of Louisiana*, 32.

8. Taylor, *Destruction and Reconstruction*, 28–32; J. E. B. Stuart to Joseph Johnston, March 12, 1862, in James Ewell Brown Stuart Papers, DU; Ogden to father, n.d., in Ogden Papers, TU.

Tigers saw little action along the river because heavy spring rains put a halt to most maneuvering. But in April they were forced to blow up one bridge after Union cavalry threatened to cross it. The torrential rains continued to fall, and many of the men frequently wandered out of camp to seek more substantial shelter than their scanty pup tents offered. During one particularly bad storm a number of Tigers went into a nearby church to keep dry. The cozy chapel was soon crowded with soldiers, who began joking and singing as they dried out. One man sang a vulgar little tune that brought peals of laughter from his comrades. When another soldier was about to follow suit, however, Tom Jennings, Major Wheat's huge sergeant-major, slowly rose in the pulpit, where he had been smoking quietly. "See here boys!" he said sternly. "I am just as bad as any of you, I know. But this is a church and I'll be damned if it's right to sing any of your smutty songs in here, and it's got to be stopped!" A hush fell over the crowd, and the men went back to their subdued chatter. Three months later, Sergeant-Major Jennings was taken from the Gaines' Mill battlefield mortally wounded through the abdomen.[9]

After several weeks of picket duty, the Louisiana Brigade moved to a new campground at Gordonsville. Johnston's Army of Northern Virginia was fragmented that spring, with most of the commands going to the Peninsula to aid Magruder or with General Jackson to the Shenandoah Valley. Jackson's orders were to prevent the forty-five thousand federals in the Valley from sending reinforcements to McClellan. In April Confederate officials ordered Ewell's division to join him there, giving Jackson a total of fifteen thousand men to carry out his mandate.

The division's march to Swift Run Gap in the Blue Ridge Mountains was even more trying than the terrible Manassas evacuation. Marching orders stipulated that each man carry only the barest of necessities, but this was hardly necessary because most soldiers possessed very little following the Manassas withdrawal. Taylor took only one change of underwear and a tent fly, and most of his Tigers carried one blanket, two pairs of socks, and an extra shirt and pair of drawers and shoes. Typical among the Louisianians was Ser-

9. Handerson, *Yankee in Gray*, 40.

geant Edmond Stephens, who complained, "I have but one suit of clothes & them now on my back and have been for a month."[10]

When the division left its Gordonsville campground on April 18, a few fortunate soldiers were put aboard a train. Most, however, were forced to walk to the Valley. In a scene reminiscent of Manassas, a steady, soaking rain set in, turning the Virginia roads and fields into bottomless morasses. Eighteen miles were covered the first day in a pouring rain that soon turned to sleet, then snow. The freezing precipitation continued to lash the men for the next ten days and caused much grumbling among them. "We have nothing," wrote one disgruntled Tiger, "but march, march, and halt and sleep in wet blankets and mud." On the third night, an early spring blizzard blanketed the Louisianians as they camped in an open field. In exasperation, T. A. Tooke told his wife, "I thought that I knowed something about Soldiering, but I find that I had never soldiered it this way."[11]

When the majestic Blue Ridge Mountains were finally reached, Taylor's Louisianians led the division through steep, winding Swift Run Gap. After hours of struggling up the mountain, the division was lashed again by a violent storm when it passed through the clouds. The air grew heavy and dark, lightning crashed all around, and thunder reverberated across the mountain's rocks and hollows. The weary men were strangely subdued, some scared senseless by the titanic storm. Each peal of thunder brought a "moan and groan" from Taylor's brigade. Then as suddenly as it began, the storm subsided and the brigade emerged above the clouds into brilliant sunlight. Spirits lifted as the regimental bands began playing "Listen to the Mockingbird," and jokes and good-natured ribbings were spun at the expense of those who were frightened. After twelve torturous hours, Swift Run Gap was behind them and the division bivouacked at the western base of the mountains at Conrad's Store.[12]

For nearly a month Ewell's division remained around Conrad's

10. Stephens to parents, May 12, 1862, in Stephens Collection, NSU.

11. T. A. Tooke to wife, April 26, 1862, in T. A. Tooke Letter, NSU.

12. Stephens to parents, May 12, 1862, in Stephens Collection, NSU; Oates, *Fifteenth Alabama*, 92–93; Taylor, *Destruction and Reconstruction*, 32–37; Reed, *Private in Gray*, 14–15.

Store awaiting orders to join Jackson. While there, Wheat's Tigers came close to losing their laurels when they engaged the 13th Indiana and some federal cavalry near Somerville. With two of his companies, one company from the 9th Louisiana, and part of the 6th Virginia Cavalry, Wheat was picketing the Shenandoah River when he was attacked by the Yankees. The Hoosiers were driving Wheat's men back in confusion when Major Davidson Penn came running to the rescue at the head of several of his 7th Louisiana companies. The reinforced Confederates then drove the Yankees back to the river and forced the Union cavalry to swim across to escape. In the skirmish, the Tigers inflicted about thirty casualties on the Hoosiers at a loss of two dead, four wounded, and one deserter. The lone deserter was a "crazy Greek," who took several Yankees prisoner and fought gallantly until the enemy broke and ran. At that point, one of his comrades claimed, he threw down his musket and "ran off after them as hard as he could go [and] has not been heard from since."[13]

Ewell finally received orders to join Jackson at New Market. Jackson had defeated Union General Robert Milroy at McDowell and sent him fleeing to Franklin, where General John C. Frémont's army was garrisoned. Jackson was now heading for General Nathaniel Banks's army at Strasburg and Front Royal to try to defeat him before he became aware of the extent of Milroy's rout. Ewell was to join Jackson at New Market and take part in the attack on Banks.

Marching rapidly, Taylor's brigade was able to catch up with Jackson on May 17. Jackson's entire Valley Army was camped in a large field along either side of the road Taylor's men came marching in on. At first, individuals, then small groups and companies of Jackson's men began lining up alongside the road to catch a glimpse of the famous Louisiana Tigers. Leading Taylor's brigade and playing "The Girl I Left Behind" was the band of Wheat's Battalion, with the Zouaves of the Tiger Rifles keeping step close behind. The rest of the brigade marched smartly behind them, with their blue pelican and green Irish flags flapping lazily in the breeze. With arms at

13. C. Brown to mother, May 9, 1862, in Folder 9, in Polk, Brown, and Ewell Family Collection, SHC; Stephens to parents, May 12, 1862, in Stephens Collection, NSU; Handerson, *Yankee in Gray*, 40–41; *OR*, Vol. XII, Pt. I, 458–60; *ibid.*, Pt. III, 882; *Southern Historical Society Papers*, n.s., V (1920), 199; Brown, "Reminiscences of the Civil War," I, 35, in Brown Collection, SHC.

right shoulder shift the brigade looked as if it was on parade, although it had covered twenty-six miles that day. "It was," remembered Taylor, "the most picturesque and inspiring martial sight that came under my eyes during four years of service." In silent tribute, the hundreds of soldiers lining the road snapped to "present arms" as the Tigers marched by.

No sooner had the Tigers made camp than the 8th Louisiana's band began playing lively polkas and waltzes. The men grabbed partners and danced exuberantly around the campfires as the astonished Virginians watched. Taylor remembered the murmurs of disapproval from the pious Virginians, who frowned upon "the caperings of my Creoles, holding them to be 'devices and snares.'" The Virginians of one of Jackson's artillery batteries certainly held the Tigers in contempt, although for reasons other than their dancing. The artillerymen had a pet dog named Stonewall Jackson that could do an array of tricks, such as sitting up at roll call and holding a small pipe between its teeth. The gifted canine caught the eye of Taylor's Tigers, and they tried unsuccessfully to "liberate" him from the battery. But at last, one artilleryman sadly wrote, "the cunning thieves succeeded in hiding him," and the dog passed permanently to Taylor's brigade. A love of pets seemed to be universal among the Tigers. Later, when the 2d Louisiana Brigade was formed, it had a mascot named Sawbuck. The dog followed the men into battle until it was wounded in the foreleg. Thereafter it fell behind when the shooting began—playing "old soldier," the men quipped.[14]

After bivouacking his men, Taylor dismounted and went in search of the commanding general, whom he had never met. Taylor was somewhat apprehensive of this first interview, for Jackson had not yet earned his fighting reputation and was known to be eccentric. Taylor and Ewell had even tried to avoid being attached to Jackson's army. When Ewell's division was ordered to join the Valley Army, Taylor hurriedly traveled to Richmond with Ewell's blessings to per-

14. Taylor, *Destruction and Reconstruction*, 41; Nisbet, *Four Years on the Firing Line*, 41; John H. Worsham, *One of Jackson's Foot Cavalry*, ed. James I. Robertson, Jr. (1912; rpr. Jackson, Tenn., 1964), 41; Clifford Dowdey, *The Land They Fought For: The Story of the South as the Confederacy, 1832–1865* (Garden City, 1955), 176–77; Stiles, *Four Years Under Marse Robert*, 170–72; John Overton Casler, *Four Years in the Stonewall Brigade* (1906; rpr. Marietta, Ga., 1951), 201.

suade his presidential brother-in-law to countermand the order. Taylor apparently left Richmond with Davis' assurances that Ewell's division would be put under General James Longstreet. He was therefore thunderstruck when he returned to Gordonsville and found the division gone. Without bothering to notify Richmond, Jackson had wired Ewell to join him immediately. Wandering about the deserted campground, Taylor found David F. Boyd, one of his officers, and asked where Jackson's army was. When the soldier said he had no idea, Taylor exclaimed, "Well, this is strange! Nobody at Richmond knows anything about it. But there is one consilation. We won't be under this damn old crazy fool long. Gen. Longstreet is coming up here to take command." Taylor was mistaken, however, for he, too, was ordered to join Ewell's division on its march to the Valley. Boyd remembered years later that Jackson was not only skilled in outflanking Union armies but was also adept at slipping around "two of his own best Generals and the 'folks' back at Richmond."[15]

Now at New Market, Taylor was about to face his odd commander for the first time. Jackson was found perched atop a rail fence thoughtfully sucking on a lemon as he watched the Tigers make camp. With his best military bearing, Taylor stepped up to the fence, snapped off a crisp salute, and spat out his name and rank. While awaiting a response, the Louisianian had a chance to size up the general. "A pair of cavalry boots covering feet of gigantic size, a mangy cap with visor drawn low, a heavy, dark beard, and weary eyes" caught his attention. Eyeing the Louisiana camp, Jackson asked in a low, gentle voice how far the brigade had come that day. Twenty-six miles, Taylor proudly replied. "You seem to have no stragglers," Jackson responded. "Never allow straggling," Taylor remarked, thinking how well the brigade's training during the Manassas evacuation had paid off. "You must teach my people," the general said, "they straggle badly." As Taylor nodded politely, a Louisiana band suddenly came alive with a waltz that drew Jackson's attention back to the dancing Tigers. Sucking slowly on his lemon, Jackson silently watched the brigade for a minute and then commented pensively, "Thoughtless fellows for serious work." Coming to the defense of his men, Taylor responded that he hoped their

15. New Orleans *Times-Democrat*, January 31, 1897, in Scrapbook, Boyd Papers, LSU.

gaiety would not affect their performance, but no reply came from Jackson, who quietly sat staring at the Tigers' camp.

Taylor took his leave from Jackson and returned to camp, but late that night Jackson appeared unexpectedly at his campfire and stayed several hours with the Louisianian. Before lapsing into a prolonged silence, Jackson told Taylor the army would move out at daybreak and asked more questions about the Tigers' marching ability. He apparently was greatly impressed with them.[16]

Like Taylor, the Louisiana Brigade was not overly impressed with the new commander. One soldier recalled, "The remark was made by one of us after staring at him a long time, that there must be some mistake about him, [for] if he was an able man, he showed it less than any of us had ever seen."[17] The Tigers' suspicions of Jackson deepened before they recognized his brilliance, for Jackson confided in no one, and his apparently aimless marching enraged many. "I don't know!" was Ewell's response to Taylor's inquiry of the meaning of one of Jackson's marches. "If Gen. Jackson were shot down I wouldn't know a thing of his plans!" "What!" exclaimed Taylor in disbelief. "You, second in command, and don't know! If I were second in command, I would know!" "You would, would you?" Ewell smilingly asked in his peculiar way of cocking his head to one side "like a sap-sucker peeping around a tree." "No, you wouldn't know any more than I do now. You don't yet know the man." It was such frustration of trying to decipher the meaning of Jackson's maneuvers that prompted Ewell once to exclaim to Taylor that he "was certain of [Jackson's] lunacy, and that he never saw one of Jackson's couriers approach without expecting an order to assault the north pole."[18]

All questions about Jackson's ability as a commander were about to be laid to rest. In the next month he dazzled the world with a classic campaign of maneuver and battle, a campaign made successful by the performance of the Louisiana Brigade. Milroy's army had already been defeated and chased to Franklin, where a second army was garrisoned under Frémont. General Banks's third Union

16. Taylor, *Destruction and Reconstruction*, 41–42.

17. Quoted in Burke Davis, *They Called Him Stonewall: A Life of Lt. General T. J. Jackson, C.S.A.* (New York, 1954), 27.

18. New Orleans *Times-Democrat,* January 31, 1897, in Scrapbook, Boyd Papers, LSU; Taylor, *Destruction and Reconstruction*, 30.

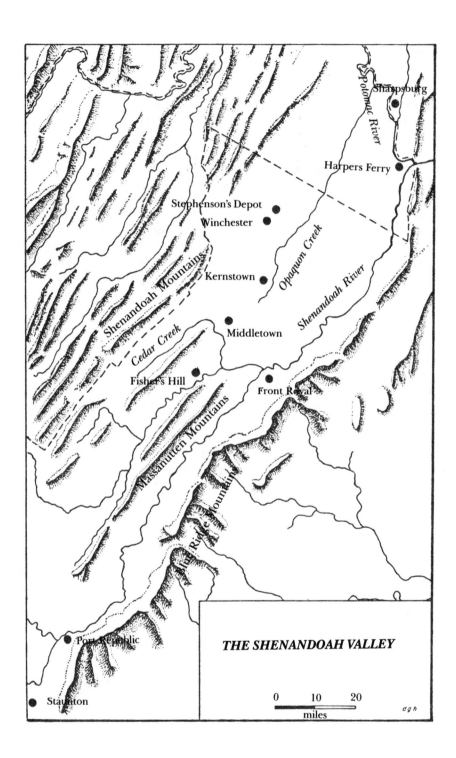

Sharpsburg

Potomac River

Harpers Ferry

Stephenson's Depot

Winchester

Opaquon Creek

Kernstown

Shenandoah River

Shenandoah Mountains

Middletown

Cedar Creek

Fisher's Hill

Front Royal

Massanutten Mountains

Blue Ridge Mountains

Port Republic

Staunton

THE SHENANDOAH VALLEY

0   10   20
miles

d g h

army at Strasburg and Front Royal was north of Jackson and was next on his list of victims. Using cavalry to screen his movements from Banks, Jackson left New Market on May 21 and headed east over the Massanutton Mountains to Luray. There he turned north and rapidly closed in on Front Royal, with Taylor's men in the lead setting a pace of thirty miles a day.

Following the east bank of the Shenandoah's East Fork, Jackson's army approached Front Royal on May 23. Outside town, Jackson and Taylor were met by Belle Boyd, a local woman, who told Jackson the enemy had artillery covering the wagon bridge across the East Fork but none at a nearby railroad bridge. Eager to display his men's ability, Taylor was delighted when Jackson turned and ordered him to advance his brigade toward town. Emerging from a narrow belt of woods, the Louisianians startled the Union pickets, who hurriedly scampered over the wagon bridge to sound the alarm.

In plain view of the enemy camps across the river, Taylor deployed his men in line of battle and then rashly rode alone to the river's edge for a closer look at the Union defenses. Exhausted from the long day's march, Taylor's horse stepped into the stream to drink and instantly drew the enemy sharpshooters' fire. The shower of balls sent geysers of water splashing up all around Taylor's thirsty horse, but the Louisianian was reluctant to beat a hasty retreat. "I had not yet led my command into action," Taylor wrote, "and, remembering that one must 'strut' one's little part to the best advantage, sat [on] my horse with all the composure I could muster. A provident camel, on the eve of a desert journey would not have laid in a greater supply of water than did my thoughtless beast." Finally getting his fill, Taylor's horse raised its head, looked around nonchalantly, and slowly ambled up the bank back toward the Louisiana Brigade. The Tigers wildly cheered their plucky leader, but their chorus was answered by a volley of Yankee musketry that knocked over several soldiers.[19]

Taylor found Jackson deep in thought, apparently oblivious to the preceding drama. His spirit up, the Louisianian suggested taking his brigade across the unguarded railroad bridge to hit the federal line. Jackson nodded his consent, and Taylor ordered Colo-

19. Taylor, *Destruction and Reconstruction*, 45.

nel Henry Kelly to send his 8th Louisiana across. With Kelly in front, the regiment rushed down to the bridge and began tiptoeing across the railroad ties under a brisk fire. Two men tumbled off into the turbulent water below and drowned after being shot or losing their footing. The rest of the regiment made it over without incident and forced the Yankees to set fire to the wagon bridge and retreat back into town.

Taylor realized that if the wagon bridge was lost it would take all day for the army to cross this railroad bridge. Looking inquisitively at his commander, Taylor again received an approving nod. He immediately called upon Wheat's men and the Moore Fencibles, a 9th Louisiana company attached to Wheat's Battalion as sharpshooters, to follow him across the burning span. One of Ewell's aides recalled years later: "I shall never forget the style in which Wheat's Battn. passed us, as we stood in the road. [Wheat] was riding full gallop, yelling at the top of his voice—his big sergeant-major [Jennings] running at top speed just after him, calling to the men to come on—& they strung out according to their speed or 'stomach for the fight,' following after—all running—all yelling—all looking like fight. Their peculiar zouave dress & wild excitement made up a glorious picture." [20]

While Wheat's Tigers ran across the burning bridge, some of Kelly's men stopped at the river's edge and scooped up water in their slouch hats before continuing down the opposite bank to help. With Wheat and Taylor in the lead, the Tigers reached the other side and began throwing the burning pieces into the river while Kelly's men doused the flames with their water-filled hats. The bridge was saved, "but it was rather a near thing," Taylor recalled. The clothing of Wheat, Taylor, and the rest of the Tigers was singed and scorched by the flames, and "smoke and fire had decidedly freshened up [Jackson's] costume"; he had ridden across the clogged bridge close behind Taylor. [21]

Wasting no time, Jackson had Wheat's Battalion and the 1st Maryland deploy and chase the stunned federals through Front Royal. Taylor's commissary officer, Major Aaron Davis, also gathered up a number of mounted orderlies and pursued the enemy until a

20. Brown, "Reminiscences of the Civil War," I, 38, in Brown Collection, SHC.
21. Taylor, *Destruction and Reconstruction*, 46.

sudden return volley unhorsed him with a fatal ball through his chest. Darkness and increased resistance from the Union troops finally ended the chase. The jubilant Louisianians then took count of their losses. During the three-hour battle, eight men had been wounded, with Davis and the two luckless Tigers who fell from the railroad bridge being the only fatalities. Jackson had liberated Front Royal and captured seven hundred prisoners and a large quantity of badly needed supplies at a small loss to himself. A few additional prisoners were seized early the next day when some of Wheat's more daring men donned captured federal uniforms and commandeered a train for Markham, where a small Union outpost was unaware of Front Royal's capture. Upon their arrival, the Tigers mingled with the Yankees and even persuaded a few to return with them to Front Royal for an extended "visit."

As the tired but victorious Louisianians settled in for the night, Jackson showed his appreciation of the Tigers by again coming to Taylor's sputtering campfire. After a lengthy silence, Jackson muttered that Taylor's brigade would accompany him in the morning but gave no hint of their objective. Taylor knew it was useless to try to pry out more details, so he and Jackson spent the rest of the night in silence.

Rising well before daylight on May 24, Jackson had the army in pursuit of Banks's men by 6:00 A.M. Banks was retreating rapidly down the Valley from Strasburg toward Winchester, where he hoped to concentrate his forces and make a stand. Jackson, in turn, was trying to outmarch Banks on the parallel Front Royal–Winchester road to intercept his fleeing column midway between Strasburg and Winchester at Middletown.[22]

Taking one hundred of Wheat's Tigers, a detachment of General Turner Ashby's cavalry, and the Rockbridge Artillery as an escort, Jackson personally led the chase while the rest of Taylor's brigade followed. Jackson ordered Wheat's men to stick close to the artillery, so they "trotted along with the horses and artillery at Jackson's

22. Dufour, *Gentle Tiger*, 176; Taylor, *Destruction and Reconstruction*, 43–47; *OR*, Vol. XII, Pt. I, 701–703, 778, 800–801; Oates, *Fifteenth Alabama*, 96–97; Compiled Service Records, War Record Group 109, Microcopy 320, Roll 201, NA; McHenry Howard, *Recollections of a Maryland Confederate Soldier and Staff Officer Under Johnston, Jackson and Lee* (1914; rpr. Dayton, Ohio, 1975), 106.

heels" like a pack of devoted hounds despite the fast pace set by the horse-drawn pieces. While the rest of the Valley Army continued on to Winchester, Jackson veered westward off the road with his escort and Taylor's and Elzey's brigades at 8:00 A.M. to hit Middletown.[23]

At 2:00 P.M. Jackson topped a ridge overlooking Middletown and was greeted by the sight of federal wagons filling the pike as far as the eye could see. Jackson quickly deployed his escort and began raking the clogged road with shot and shell. In minutes, he wrote, "the turnpike, which had just before teemed with life, presented a most appalling spectacle of carnage and destruction. The road was literally obstructed with the mingled and confused mass of struggling and dying horses and riders."[24]

Riding at the head of his brigade some distance behind, Taylor heard the shooting and double-quicked his men toward the battle. The brigade arrived at Middletown just as a squadron of federal cavalry came charging down the road in an attempt to cut through Jackson's small band blocking the way. The Tiger escort quickly overturned a wagon in the middle of the road and together with the lead elements of the brigade took shelter behind a stone fence alongside the pike. With sabers flashing, the Yankee troopers thundered down the road in a cloud of dust but were blasted out of their saddles as they rode past the Tigers' fence. The Louisiana volley decimated the center of the charging column, and the rear element "plunged on, in, over, upon the bleeding pile, a roaring, shrieking, struggling mass of men and horses, crushed, wounded and dying. It was," this witness claimed, "a sickening sight."[25]

The head of the column continued down the road while the riders in the rear retreated back to Strasburg. Some Tigers gleefully jumped over the fence to examine the carnage but were cut down in the road by a sudden volley from a Union regiment hiding behind a distant fence. But these Yankees immediately withdrew and allowed the Tigers a chance to reap the spoils of victory. When Taylor rode up, he found "the gentle Tigers were looting right merrily, diving in and out of wagons with the activity of rabbits in a

23. Taylor, *Destruction and Reconstruction*, 47.
24. *OR*, Vol. XII, Pt. I, 703.
25. Henry Kyd Douglas, *I Rode with Stonewall* (Chapel Hill, 1940), 54.

warren; but this occupation was abandoned on my approach, and in a moment they were in a line, looking as solemn and virtuous as deacons at a funeral."[26]

While gathering up prisoners, the Louisianians let out whoops of laughter when they found a number of apparently inexperienced troopers strapped to their saddles. Other Tigers were surprised to find some of the Yankees wearing antiquated breastplates, including some federal dead with neat, round bullet holes drilled through the armor. While the Louisianians examined these odd relics of war, several shells came shrieking into the road from a Union battery that had set up unnoticed on a hill to the south. One shell exploded in the midst of the 7th Louisiana and injured several soldiers. Another buried deep into the ground directly beneath Taylor's horse and nearly smothered mount and rider with earth when it exploded. Taylor was unhurt by the round and sent out a skirmish line that easily forced the battery to withdraw back to Strasburg.[27]

Jackson had cut Banks's army in two when he boldly struck the federal column at Middletown. Part of the enemy army continued on to Winchester while the rest had to escape by marching westward out of the Shenandoah Valley. At the loss of only three dead and twelve wounded, Taylor helped capture or destroy several hundred Union supply wagons and take nearly one hundred prisoners. In addition, two Union battle flags were taken by the 6th Louisiana and four guidons by Hays's 7th Louisiana.

This lopsided victory, however, should have been an even greater success. As soon as Middletown was secure, Jackson began pursuing the federals as they fled toward Winchester. His artillery soon brought the Yankees to bay and began lobbing shells into them, but Jackson's chief of artillery found he had no infantry within reach to press the attack. Riding back toward Middletown, the artilleryman found a hundred or so of Hays's men, but they were "much broken down by fatigue and heat." He urged them to join his artillery and

26. Taylor, *Destruction and Reconstruction*, 47.

27. *Ibid.; OR*, Vol. XII, Pt. I, 704–707, 726, 779, 800–801; Bound Volume 9 in Association of the Army of Northern Virginia, LHAC; Compiled Service Records, War Record Group 109, Microcopy 320, Roll 201, NA; Stephens to parents, June 14, 1862, in Stephens Collection, NSU; Freeman, *Lee's Lieutenants*, I, 387; Dufour, *Gentle Tiger*, 176–77; Davis, *They Called Him Stonewall*, 44–45; Robert L. Dabney, *Life and Campaigns of Lieut.-General Thomas J. Jackson* (New York, 1866), 371–72.

then continued on until he found the Confederate cavalry and a group of Tigers busily looting the captured wagons. Threats and pleas failed to dissuade them from their task, and Banks made good his escape to Winchester.[28]

Taylor's men had played the key role in the battles at Front Royal and Middletown, but Jackson was furious over their failure to pursue the enemy. On May 27, he issued General Order No. 54 stating that "the shameless pillaging practised by numbers of cavalry and infantry, who were intrusted with the advance in pursuing the enemy . . . so reduced [Ashby's] command as to render it necessary to discontinue the pursuit." On the same day Jackson ordered Ewell to investigate the pillaging conducted by his men, "especially by members of General Taylor's command," but there is no record of anyone being punished for the incident.[29]

Despite Jackson's slow pursuit, his army continued moving toward Winchester until late in the night. Taylor's brigade finally halted just outside Winchester while the rest of the army bivouacked slightly east of them on the Front Royal road. Some of the Tigers had received only an hour's rest when they were aroused early on May 25 to begin preparing for battle. A dense fog enveloped the hills, and heavy skirmish fire began building along Ewell's line to the east as Taylor led his men down the road to get into position. Suddenly one of Jackson's aides came galloping wildly out of the fog and told the Louisianian to hurry on with his brigade. Taylor rode ahead and found the general with the artillery, which at that moment was being pounded in a duel with federal guns placed on a hill anchoring the Union right. Shouting over the roaring guns, Jackson pointed to the enemy battery and told Taylor he must circle around to the left and silence the guns before they decimated the Confederate artillery.

Hugging the base of a ridge, Taylor was leading his men toward the hostile battery when Jackson overtook him to make sure all was well. Upon seeing their general, the Tigers let out a spontaneous cheer to greet him, but Jackson instantly hushed them lest they give away their position. With this mild rebuke, the men silently lifted their hats in an impromptu salute, and Jackson responded likewise.

Jackson caught up with Taylor just as the brigade filed across a

28. *OR*, Vol. XII, Pt. I, 726; Freeman, *Lee's Lieutenants*, I, 390.
29. *OR*, Vol. XII, Pt. I, 252.

slight depression within view of the federal guns. One veteran recalled that shells came screaming toward them and "almost took
our hats off." Taylor tried to get Jackson to leave the dangerous
position, but Jackson ignored him. Several men were hit by the
shrieking missiles, and the rest ducked involuntarily as the shells
whizzed overhead. Furious and embarrassed that Jackson was witness to this cowardice, Taylor screamed, "What the hell are you
dodging for? If there is any more of it, you will be halted under this
fire for an hour." The men quickly straightened up "as if they had
swallowed ramrods." But Jackson was unimpressed. He leaned
over to Taylor and with a sorrowful look clasped his shoulder and
said, "I am afraid you are a wicked fellow." When Jackson turned
and rode away, he was again cheered by the Tigers and responded
with a rare smile.[30]

Screened by the ridge and fog, Taylor was able to deploy his men
unobserved at the base of the Union-occupied hill. In a steady walk
the brigade advanced up the hill just as the sun broke brilliantly
through the fog. Like the opening curtain of a drama, the lifting
fog suddenly thrust the Louisiana Brigade into view of both armies. Led by Taylor, who occasionally turned in his saddle to check
his men, the brigade advanced without firing a shot. Halfway to the
enemy artillery, a squadron of federal cavalry charged Colonel
Kelly's 8th Louisiana on the left flank but was quickly broken up by
one volley. At that moment Taylor yelled, "Charge!" and the line
leaped forward.

The charge of the Louisiana Brigade was one of the most spectacular of the Civil War and the first ever witnessed by Jackson's
men. It was a picture-book assault that was forever etched into the
minds of those soldiers who witnessed it. "There was," wrote one
Virginian, "all the pomp and circumstance of war about it that was
always lacking in our charges." Ewell's men far to the east watched
as the Union defenders suddenly realized they were being flanked.
One of them wrote, "We could see a sudden commotion on that
end of their line" as the federals desperately tried to bend back
their line to meet the assault. But there was no stopping the Louisianians. The Irishmen of the 6th Louisiana swept forward in a
wave behind the aging Colonel Seymour. The colonel was flushed

30. Taylor, *Destruction and Reconstruction*, 51; James Huffman, *Ups and Downs of a
Confederate Soldier* (New York, 1940), 47; Douglas, *I Rode with Stonewall*, 57.

with excitement as he ran toward the enemy waving his sword in one hand, hat in the other, and yelling above the battle, "Steady men! dress to the right!" "I have rarely seen a more beautiful charge," wrote another witness. "This full brigade, with a line of glistening bayonets bright in that morning sun, its formation straight and compact, its tread quick and easy as it pushed on through the cloves and up that hill was a sight to delight a veteran." [31]

Over a stone ledge and two fences the Tigers ran under heavy fire, urged on by the encouraging cheers of their comrades to the east. "They moved with the most beautiful precision," said one Confederate, "although their trail was marked by dead and wounded men at every step." Slowly at first, then in a flood, the entire right flank of Banks's line gave way before the charging Tigers. Ewell's men to the east then joined in a general advance that pushed the rest of the Union line out of Winchester. For the first time the Valley Army heard the high-pitched, hair-raising yelp of the rebel yell echo over the battlefield. [32]

Winchester was bedlam as the Confederates chased the defeated Yankees through its streets. One rebel remembered that the civilians "shouted to our men from their doors and windows and cheered them on." Another wrote, "The pavement was crowded with women, children and old men, waving their handkerchiefs, weeping for joy and shouting as we passed at double-quick." One woman, however, greeted Taylor's men in agitation, upset that so many Yankees were escaping. "Oh!" she shouted to them. "You are too late—too late!" But a tall, lanky Creole of the 8th Louisiana broke ranks, swept her up in his arms, and planted a resounding kiss upon her lips. "Madame!" he exclaimed, "*Je n'arrive jamais trop tard!*" He then swaggered back to his cheering regiment and left the woman "with a rosy face, but [a] merry twinkle in her eye." [33]

31. Worsham, *One of Jackson's Foot Cavalry*, 46; Taylor, *Destruction and Reconstruction*, 51–52, 78; *OR*, Vol. XII, Pt. I, 404–407; Davis, *They Called Him Stonewall*, 52; Howard, *Recollections of a Maryland Confederate*, 111; Douglas, *I Rode with Stonewall*, 58.

32. W. W. Goldsborough, *The Maryland Line in the Confederacy, 1861–1865* (Baltimore, 1900), 45; Davis, *They Called Him Stonewall*, 53.

33. Oates, *Fifteenth Alabama*, 98; see also Huffman, *Ups and Downs of a Confederate Soldier*, 47; Rev. Philip Slaughter, *A Sketch of the Life of Randolph Fairfax . . . Including a Brief Account of Jackson's Celebrated Valley Campaign* (Baltimore, 1878), 28–29; Taylor, *Destruction and Reconstruction*, 52.

Once again Taylor's Louisiana Brigade was the toast of the army. Immediately following the grand charge, Jackson galloped up to Taylor and gratefully shook his hand in a silent gesture, which the Louisianian claimed was "worth a thousand words from another." G. P. Ring, one of Taylor's officers, claimed that Jackson told Taylor "he never saw or read of such a charge made by us at Winchester. . . . All the Virginia troops in this Army say that we beat any body they ever saw at a charge and now they say we can stand as long under a murderous fire as any troops in the World." [34]

The victory was not without cost. Fourteen Tigers were dead, including the 6th Louisiana's Major Arthur McArthur, and eighty-nine wounded. Among the latter was Lieutenant-Colonel Francis T. Nicholls of the 8th Louisiana, who lost his left arm by amputation after his elbow was shattered by a minié ball halfway up the hill. There is also some evidence that the Confederate victory was marred by acts of atrocity on the Tigers' part. One Union report claimed that Taylor's men "glutted their vengeance for the loss of New Orleans" by giving no quarter in the fight. Ordinarily such a charge would be dismissed as wartime propaganda, but one Louisianian wrote home a few weeks after the battle that some of the Tigers' wounded were bayoneted or clubbed to death at Winchester. In the future, he vowed, "Jackson's army will . . . take few prisoners." [35] Although it is hard to conceive that the fleeing Union soldiers had an opportunity to kill any wounded Confederates, it is possible the reverse could have occurred.

After Banks's defeat at Winchester, the Union army retreated toward the Potomac River and safety. Ewell's division continued the pursuit but eventually gave it up after the federals took refuge in the heavily fortified stronghold of Harpers Ferry. The campaign so far had been a brilliant success, with Jackson's fifteen thousand men besting three times their number in marching and fighting. Now, however, his army was in mortal danger of being trapped in the Valley. Frémont's army was en route from Franklin to cut off Jackson at Strasburg, and General James Shields was bringing a large

34. Taylor, *Destruction and Reconstruction*, 52; G. P. Ring to wife, June 14, 1862, typescript copy, in Army of Northern Virginia Papers, Part I, LHAC.
35. George M. Morgan to Joe, June 18, 1862, in Francis Warrington Dawson Letters, DU; *OR*, Vol. XII, Pt. I, 780–81, 800–801; *ibid.*, Pt. III, 251; Lathrop (ed.), "Autobiography of Francis T. Nicholls," 250–51.

detachment into the Valley from the east for the same purpose. On May 30, elements of Shields's force recaptured Front Royal deep in Jackson's rear, along with 156 men of the 8th Louisiana and 12th Georgia who were guarding the captured supplies there. In addition to this double threat was the remnant of Banks's army now regrouping at Harpers Ferry. Jackson was caught in the middle of a triangle, with Banks at the apex and Frémont and Shields at the base angles.[36]

On May 31 Jackson began retreating back to Strasburg in an attempt to escape before the two converging Union armies closed the back door. Taylor's brigade and the rest of Ewell's division in camps north of Winchester marched more than thirty miles that Saturday before camping with Jackson near Strasburg. Several badly wounded Louisianians, including Colonel Nicholls, had to be left behind in Winchester and were captured. Persistent rumors circulated in the following weeks that Nicholls was arrested as a spy while dressed as a civilian and that he was not being treated as a prisoner of war. These stories, however, proved to be without basis.[37]

The exhausted Taylor immediately searched out Jackson and found his commander in a rare talkative mood huddled by a smoky campfire. Staring into the flickering flame, Jackson informed Taylor between long pauses that Frémont's army was only three miles west of them and Shields was to the south threatening to cut the army's escape route. The only way to safety, Jackson said, was to prevent Shields and Frémont from linking up. To do this, Ewell's division would hold back Frémont in the morning while Jackson personally led the precious booty-laden wagon train to the south before Shields could cut the road. To help keep Shields on the opposite bank of the Shenandoah, Jackson sent his cavalry as far south as Port Republic to burn the bridges on the river.[38]

By the time the sun peeped over the Blue Ridge on Sunday, June 1, Jackson was on the road with his wagons and Ewell's men were deploying on the hills west of Strasburg to meet Frémont. Soon

36. *OR*, Vol. XII, Pt. I, 682, 694–95, 707–709; *ibid.*, Pt. III, 299; Taylor, *Destruction and Reconstruction*, 53–54.

37. *OR*, Series II, Vol. IV, 812; Francis R. T. Nicholls to Robert Carter, October 14, 1889, in Francis R. T. Nicholls Letters, LSU.

38. Taylor, *Destruction and Reconstruction*, 53–54.

Ewell's entire line was engaged in heavy skirmishing, but Ewell was puzzled by the superior Union army's lack of aggressiveness. Reluctant to prod the skittish Yankee line, Ewell pondered what to do. Taylor finally suggested that the Louisiana Brigade be allowed to circle around the Union left flank to gain information on the Yankees' plans. Ewell readily consented, and Taylor led his men to the Confederate right, where he soon found a Mississippi colonel, who told him the Union flank opposite him seemed to be very weak.

Taylor quickly deployed his troops and struck out at the federal left flank. When the Yankees immediately broke and ran, Taylor wheeled down the Union line and began scooping up prisoners by the score when the Yankees simply laid down their arms in surrender. "Sheep," Taylor claimed, "would have made as much resistance as we met." Taylor's only casualties were a few men mistakenly shot by other Confederates who thought the Tigers were a Union brigade maneuvering on the Yankee flank. The rest of Ewell's division joined in the chase, but Ewell finally called a halt after he realized he had fulfilled Jackson's instructions to delay Frémont's advance. The Confederates pulled back to the road and were soon marching after Jackson's wagon train. Upon reaching it, Taylor received orders to pull his brigade off the road and set up as a rear guard to make sure Frémont posed no further threat. Jackson did not appear overly concerned about Frémont. He told Taylor the Yankee general would not advance until morning and that Banks's rattled men would not get within striking distance until the next day. Taylor was making a mental note of this when Jackson suddenly turned and rode off without telling him how long he was to remain on the side of the road or if there were any cavalry further back to notify him if Banks should beat Jackson's timetable. With these questions racing through his mind, Taylor watched over his men as they prepared to camp fireless in the cool spring night.[39]

A few hours after he retired, Taylor awoke and sat up, thinking he heard the sound of distant gunfire drifting in from the north. In a few minutes the sound was unmistakable—and getting closer. Wondering if Banks was moving in faster than Jackson had anticipated, he mounted his horse and rode out of the sleeping camp to investigate. On the dark road, Taylor met a squadron of Confeder-

39. *Ibid.*, 58–60.

ate cavalry who informed him that the Yankees were indeed approaching fast and that only one squadron of cavalry separated
them from the sleeping Tigers. Galloping back to camp, Taylor
quickly aroused his sleeping soldiers and managed to get the drowsy
men out to the road after much kicking, grumbling, and cursing.
Taking two Irish companies of Colonel Seymour's 6th Louisiana,
Taylor formed a hasty rear guard and sent the rest of the brigade
trotting down the pike to try to catch up with Jackson. This was
barely done when several Tigers were knocked hard to the ground
by a confused mass of screaming, shooting, saber-hacking Confederate and Union cavalry that came crashing into the Irishmen.
The Yankee troopers were soon beaten back, and one of the badly
bruised Louisianians was allowed to ride the horse of the lone prisoner taken during the clash.

To keep a better watch over his Irishmen, Taylor dismounted and
stayed with them for the remainder of the long march. The night
was so dark, Taylor remembered, that "owls could not have found
their way across the fields." Out of this blackness came an occasional cavalry charge and rounds of searching artillery fire, but
little damage was inflicted. The Irishmen remained cheerful despite the rigors of the miserable night and passed the time joking
about their predicament. It was a "fine night intirely for divarsion,"
they laughed, and many talked eagerly of meeting Shields's Irishmen at the end of their march. Frémont's Germans "is poor creatures," they told Taylor, "but Shields' boys will be after fighting."
Taylor laughed at this and told his men he would bet on them in
any upcoming fight. "You may bet your life on that, sor," they
shouted.[40]

Not by chance had Taylor picked these two Irish companies for
the arduous task of protecting the rear that dark night. Despite
their drinking, fighting, and general rowdiness in camp, few could
match these sons of Ireland when it came to marching and fighting.
The Irishmen of the 6th Louisiana had already earned a reputation for endurance. One officer who accompanied them on a particularly hot, dusty march at Manassas was astonished to watch
them so completely outstrip their comrades that two halts were necessary to allow the rest of the regiment to catch up. They again

40. *Ibid.*, 60, 61; *OR*, Vol. XII, Pt. I, 730–31.

proved themselves by marching cheerfully all night, once even hooting down Taylor when he mused aloud of perhaps bringing back another regiment to relieve them.[41]

At dawn the footsore Tigers came upon General Charles Winder's Stonewall Brigade drawn up across the road to relieve them. Winder had heard the shooting during the night, realized the Louisianians were holding the rear alone, and took his brigade out of line to wait for them. Winder held the rear and skirmished with Banks's cavalry throughout the morning until Ashby's cavalry finally arrived to take over that post. With only an hour's rest, Taylor's brigade marched all day until finally crossing the Shenandoah's West Fork at Mount Jackson late that afternoon in a drenching rain. With the rain-swollen Shenandoah between it and the pursuing Yankees, Jackson's small army was safe for the moment.[42]

After a thirty-six-hour rest, Jackson continued the retreat and reached Harrisonburg on June 5. There the intrepid band turned eastward toward Port Republic and the only standing bridge across the Shenandoah River. Behind them Frémont and Banks had joined forces, crossed the West Fork, and were pressing the Confederate rear guard. On June 6 most of the Valley Army took refuge between the North and South rivers, two tributaries that met at Port Republic to form the Shenandoah's East Fork. To prevent Banks and Frémont from following, Ewell's division camped just west of North River at Cross Keys to burn the bridge once all of Jackson's men had crossed. It appeared that Jackson had positioned himself in the jaws of a trap. Ewell's division, on the same side of the river as Frémont and Banks, was separated from the main army, and Shields was rapidly approaching Port Republic from the north to cut off Jackson.[43]

On the morning of June 8, Frémont hit Ewell's division at Cross Keys and drove in his pickets. As Ewell attempted to make a stand, he received urgent orders from Jackson to dispatch Taylor's brigade to Port Republic. While Ewell held off Frémont, the Louisianians rapidly marched toward Jackson, thinking he must be under attack by Shields. After covering two miles, however, one of Jackson's aides

41. Taylor, *Destruction and Reconstruction*, 60–61; Brown, "Reminiscences of the Civil War," I, 7–12, in Brown Collection, SHC.
42. Taylor, *Destruction and Reconstruction*, 61–63.
43. *OR*, Vol. XII, Pt. I, 711–12.

stopped Taylor and sent him back to Ewell because the threatening force at Port Republic turned out to be only a small detachment of Union artillery. The Tigers reversed themselves and hurried back to Cross Keys, to find the enemy already defeated there.[44]

Upon reaching Cross Keys, Taylor's brigade halted next to General Isaac Trimble's Georgia brigade. The men were told to be prepared to move out in a few minutes and not to wander off, but Seymour's Irishmen broke ranks and shocked the Georgians by scurrying through the woods and fields in search of dead Yankees to loot. While busily going through the pockets of one dead soldier, an Irishman was asked by one Georgian if he and his comrades were prepared to fight Shields's army, which contained a large number of Irish soldiers. Of course, came the distracted reply. The Tiger then straightened up and complained of how little booty the fallen Germans of Frémont's army yielded. He hoped the Yankee Irishmen would prove more profitable.[45]

On the morning of June 9, Jackson left two brigades near Cross Keys to watch Frémont and sent Winder's men across South River to look for Shields. Taylor's brigade and the rest of the army crossed over North River by the lone bridge and South River by a rickety footbridge built during the night by Union prisoners. The Tigers halted for breakfast when finally across this last river but were cut short by the sudden sound of heavy gunfire in the direction Winder had taken. After leaving orders for the brigade to follow, Taylor jumped onto his horse and rode toward the battle. He soon found Jackson calmly astride his horse watching the fight develop between Winder and Shields. The terrain was decidedly with the Yankees. The lush green Blue Ridge to the east sloped down to within a thousand yards of the river before leveling out into an open plain. Shields skillfully deployed his men perpendicular to the river along a rift where the plain rose abruptly to form a plateau overlooking Winder's position. With his flanks solidly anchored on the river and mountain, it was a formidable line, and Winder's brigade was being badly shot up trying to dislodge Shields from it.

A six-gun battery posted on the federal left near the mountain was wreaking havoc on Winder's men. Taylor and Jackson agreed

44. *Ibid.*, 781–84; Stephens to parents, June 14, 1862, in Stephens Collection, NSU; Taylor, *Destruction and Reconstruction*, 66–67.
45. Nisbet, *Four Years on the Firing Line*, 53–54.

that the battery had to be silenced. Jackson called on his engineer to guide Taylor's brigade along the base of the mountain to a position from which the Tigers could attack. Without bothering to tell Taylor, Jackson jerked Hays's 7th Louisiana out of line as the brigade filed off toward the mountain and sent it to reinforce Winder's brigade.[46]

While the rest of the brigade followed Taylor on the circuitous route to the right, Hays led his men out onto the broad plain to join Winder. Hays was given command of the Confederate left, with his own 7th Louisiana and the 5th and 27th Virginia under his direction. No sooner had he established a defensive position than the federals began advancing across the plain to finish off the outnumbered Confederates. Knowing well that his thin gray line stood little chance against the attacking bluecoats, Hays tried to throw the enemy off balance by ordering his regiments to charge. With a yell, the Virginians and Louisianians jumped to their feet and ran across the plain under a murderous fire of artillery and musketry. Unfortunately, the bold assault was totally ineffective against the Yankees. Hiding behind tall spires of wheat, the 7th Ohio opened fire on the rebels from a very close range. "This shower of lead," wrote the historian of the 7th Ohio, "made a fearful gap in the lines of the advancing column."[47]

Seeing Hays's line staggered by this fire, the Yankees renewed their charge, and "an awful scene of carnage" took place as the two lines collided. A bitter struggle raged around the regimental flags, with the 29th Ohio finally shooting down the color-bearer of the 7th Louisiana and making off with his battle flag. Colonel Hays was knocked out of action by a ball, and Lieutenant-Colonel Charles de Choiseul collapsed mortally wounded. The Confederates were dropping at a fearful rate before Major Penn took over and managed to place the men behind a fence that afforded them some protection. But even here the Tigers were subjected to a concentrated fire that splintered the rails and sent showers of wooden missiles into their faces. At first in small groups, then in a rush, the regi-

46. *Ibid.*, 67–69; *OR*, Vol. XII, Pt. I, 713–16, 741–42, 785–87; James I. Robertson, Jr., *The Stonewall Brigade* (1963; rpr. Baton Rouge, 1977), 108–109; Howard, *Recollections of a Maryland Confederate*, 126; Dabney, *Life and Campaigns of Jackson*, 419–20.

47. George L. Wood, *The Seventh Regiment: A Record* (New York, 1865), 117.

ment finally broke and ran to escape the slaughter. The Virginians had no choice but to follow the Tigers, and soon the entire Confederate line was bolting for the rear, where Ewell was forming his division.

Major Penn succeeded in rallying some of the men around two Confederate fieldpieces, but it was obvious that this handful of defenders stood no chance against the blue line rolling toward them. Suddenly, one Virginian recalled, there was heard "a mighty shout on the mountain side . . . and in a few minutes I saw General Dick Taylor's Louisianians debouching from the undergrowth, and like a wave crested with shining steel rush toward the . . . deadly battery with fixed bayonets, giving the Rebel yell like mad demons." Another Virginian recalled that at the crucial moment the Tigers pounced on the battery "like a hawk on a chicken."[48]

Taylor had quietly followed a long, winding forest trail along the base of the mountain to get into position on the federal left flank. Arriving unobserved, the Tigers found that a deep gorge still separated them from the Yankee artillery and that Union pickets were posted above them on the side of the mountain. Through whispered orders, the brigade deployed in the brush just as the cheers of Shields's victorious soldiers rose over the plain. When Taylor ordered the charge, there was still some confusion among his companies as they tried to align themselves in the thicket, but there was no time to attend to such details. Screaming at the top of their voices, the Tigers burst out of the brush. Racing into and over the ravine, they were upon the startled artillerymen before the Yankees could wheel the guns around. A young Virginia officer serving as Taylor's aide was the first to reach the battery, but he was killed by the federals before the rest of the brigade arrived to chase them off. All organization was lost during the headlong flight over the gorge, and the mass of men climbed on top of the captured guns like children. Laughing hysterically, they straddled the tubes, slapped each others' backs, and cheered their victory.

Suddenly, scores of Taylor's men were cut down in heaps by artil-

48. Dufour, *Gentle Tiger*, 185; Huffman, *Ups and Downs of a Confederate Soldier*, 50; *OR*, Vol. XII, Pt. I, 713–16, 741–42, 750–53; Freeman, *Lee's Lieutenants*, I, 454–60; Robertson, *Stonewall Brigade*, 108–12; Slaughter, *Randolph Fairfax*, 32; J. Hamp SeCheverell, *Journal History of the Twenty-Ninth Ohio Veteran Volunteers, 1861–1865, Its Victories and Its Reverses* (Cleveland, 1883), 46–47.

lery fire from another federal battery, which had turned its guns on the brigade from only 350 yards away. Sergeant Stephens, whose musket was shot in two in his hands, wrote that the Yankees "poured grape into us like smoke." Seeing Union infantry massing for a counterattack behind this new battery, William "Big" Peck, the 9th Louisiana's huge, six-foot, six-inch lieutenant-colonel, yelled for the men to kill the artillery horses of the captured guns to prevent them from being recovered by the enemy. Major Wheat drew out his knife and began slashing the throats of the horses nearest him. Blood spurted over the major as he carried out the grisly task, making him "as bloody as a butcher." Others reached out, placed their muskets against the poor creatures' heads, and fired. The horses were still shrieking and jerking in their death throes when the Yankees charged into the battery and began clubbing Taylor's men. "It was a sickening sight," one Tiger said of the resulting carnage, "men in gray and blue piled up in front of and around the guns and with the horses dying and the blood of men and beasts flowing almost in a stream."[49]

These Yankees were the brave Buckeyes of General Erastus Tyler's Ohio brigade. After breaking up Hays's attack across the open plain, the brigade struck out at Taylor and in a matter of minutes overpowered his men and kicked them out of the battery. Refusing to abandon the guns, Taylor fell back to the ravine, regrouped his men, and charged the Yankees a second time. Again there was fierce hand-to-hand fighting as bayonets crossed and muskets became clubs. Around the cannons five color guards of the 5th Ohio were shot down in rapid succession and the regiment's battle flag was wrenched away and captured by the Tigers. Despite such losses, however, the Buckeyes managed to hold on and again succeeded in prying Taylor's men from the battery and in bludgeoning them back to the ravine.

Back in the gorge the Tigers were in disarray. Never had such resistance been offered by the enemy, and doubts were racing through each soldier's mind as to the wisdom of having to test the Yankees' mettle a third time. Taylor, however, did not hesitate. He quickly reassembled the men and even threw the regiments' musicians and drummers into his line. Suddenly the brigade wavered as

49. Quoted in Dufour, *Gentle Tiger*, 187; Stephens to parents, June 14, 1862, in Stephens Collection, NSU.

the forgotten Union pickets on the side of the mountain behind them began taking pot shots at the formation. Taylor was forced to pull two companies of Colonel Leroy Stafford's 9th Louisiana out of line and dispatch them to silence the sharpshooters before he could launch his third attack on the battery.

Tyler's men had begun dragging the fieldpieces back to their lines by hand and had succeeded in saving one gun when the Tigers rushed upon them for the third time. The day's fighting had cost the Buckeyes more than two hundred men thus far, and they were too weak to stop the Tigers' charge. For a few desperate moments the battle raged around the guns, but the Yankees finally broke and pulled back to their lines. No cheering accompanied the capture of the battery this time, for across the field could be seen new federal brigades veering away from Jackson's line and charging toward Taylor. The Louisianian knew he could not hold out against any more attacks and silently resolved to pull back to the gorge and make a stand. Luckily, Ewell came crashing through the underbrush at that moment, leading two Virginia regiments. By now Shields's line was in total confusion as a result of his left flank being smashed by Taylor, and a renewed advance by Jackson's entire army put the Yankees to flight.[50]

The carnage around the battery proved the Louisiana Irishmen's prediction that Shields's boys were looking for a fight. After witnessing four years of bloody warfare, Taylor wrote, "I have never seen so many dead and wounded in the same limited space." More than 300 Buckeyes and Tigers lay jumbled together among the dead artillery horses. In the short contest, Taylor had 165 men shot and beaten down at the battery, while Hays lost another 123 on the open plain. The 19 officers and 269 men that the Louisiana Brigade lost during the two-hour Battle of Port Republic was the highest casualty rate among Jackson's brigades.[51]

Despite Taylor's heavy losses, Jackson had again emerged the win-

50. *OR*, Vol. XII, Pt. I, 693–97, 801–803; Wood, *Seventh Regiment*, 117–22; New Orleans *Daily Item*, August 25, 1896, in Scrapbook, Boyd Papers, LSU; John M. Paver, *What I Saw from 1861 to 1864* (1906; rpr. Ann Arbor, 1974), 81–82; John D. Imboden, "Stonewall Jackson in the Valley," in Johnson and Buel (eds.), *Battles and Leaders*, II, 295–96.

51. Taylor, *Destruction and Reconstruction*, 70; *OR*, Vol. XII, Pt. I, 690, 787; Wood, *Seventh Regiment*, 117–27.

ner from the two days' fighting around Cross Keys and Port Republic. With a loss of a little over 1,000 men, Jackson had inflicted more than 1,700 casualties upon Shields and Frémont and had captured thousands of muskets and an abundance of other equipment. More important, he had succeeded in making his escape from the Valley and was now in position to aid in the defense of Richmond.

Jackson knew who to thank for this success. Riding up to the battery "with an intense light in his eyes," Jackson looked over the bloody ground surrounding the guns and told the members of the Louisiana Brigade that the five captured pieces would be presented to them as a tribute. "I thought the men would go mad with cheering," Taylor wrote, "especially the Irish." One huge Irishman in the 6th Louisiana, "with one eye closed and half his whiskers burned by powder," straddled the barrel of one gun and began yelling to Taylor, "We told you to bet on your boys!" [52]

Ewell wrote in his official campaign report that to the Tigers belonged "the honor of deciding two battles—that of Winchester and [Port Republic]." A more accurate statement would be that the Louisiana Brigade played a key role in almost every engagement of Jackson's famous Valley Campaign. Taylor's men saved the crucial bridge at Front Royal, cut the federal column at Middletown, pushed the enemy out of Winchester, and broke the Union flank at Port Republic. Much of the credit for Jackson's success in capturing or tying down thousands of federal troops in the Valley, plus taking ten thousand muskets, nine artillery pieces, and thousands of dollars worth of supplies belongs to the Tigers. [53]

G. P. Ring pointed out to his wife that the Louisiana Brigade's contribution came at a high price. During the campaign, only one meal of meat and bread was received per day, and usually a scant five or six hours of sleep was all that was allowed after a day's march. Two-thirds of the time was spent in pouring rain, and when the weather cleared, it was too cold for a restful sleep because most of the blankets were kept with the wagons in the rear. These cruel conditions broke the health of many Tigers and the morale of others. Desertions within the Louisiana Brigade increased dramatically during the campaign as soldiers found the warmth of Union

52. Taylor, *Destruction and Reconstruction*, 69–70.
53. *OR*, Vol. XII, Pt. I, 786.

encampments strongly appealing. The Pemberton Rangers, a foreign-dominated company in the 6th Louisiana, had eleven men, or
about 10 percent of its complement, desert during the month of
May, 1862.[54]

Despite the desertions, the Tigers were aware of their contribution to the campaign and proudly claimed that Jackson was refer-
ring to them as his "Iron Brigade." The Louisianians now wor-
shiped the man who only a month before they had considered
crazy. Ring wrote, "It will be something to boast of hereafter that I
was one of Stonewall Jackson's Army. . . . I had rather be a private
in such an Army than a Field Officer in any other Army. Jackson is
perfectly idolised by this Army, specially this brigade and he is as
much pleased with us as we are with him."[55]

This was not an idle boast, for Jackson proved his feelings when
he recommended Taylor's promotion to major-general the day
after the Battle of Port Republic. "The success," he wired Richmond, "with which he has managed his Brigade in camp, on the
march, and when engaged with the enemy at Front Royal, Middletown, Winchester, and yesterday near Port Republic makes it my
duty as well as my pleasure to recommend him for promotion."[56]

Jackson permitted his army to take a well-deserved rest following
the fatiguing campaign, but on June 17 he once again put the men
on the road. This time the destination was Richmond; rumors
spread down the column that a large offensive was being planned
against McClellan on the Peninsula.

54. Ring to wife, June 14, 1862, in Army of Northern Virginia Papers, Part I,
LHAC; Bound Volume 6 in Association of the Army of Northern Virginia, LHAC.

55. Ring to wife, June 24, 1862, in Army of Northern Virginia Papers, Part I,
LHAC; Ben Hubert to Letitia, June 13, 1862, in Hubert Papers, DU.

56. T. J. Jackson to Gen. Samuel Cooper, June 10, 1862, in Compiled Service
Records of Confederate General and Staff Officers, and Nonregimental Enlisted
Men, War Record Group 109, Microcopy 331, Roll 243, NA.

Chapter   V

I HAVE GOT MY FILL
OF FIGHTING

While Taylor's brigade was marching to glory in the Valley, the Tigers on the Peninsula were engaged in several less spectacular but bloody clashes near Richmond. Following the Battle of Williamsburg, Colonel Theodore Hunt's 5th Louisiana served as rear guard when Johnston withdrew his army closer to the embattled capital. After days of constant skirmishing with the pesky Union cavalry and infantry, Hunt's weary men finally crossed the Chickahominy River at New Bridge and encamped for a well-deserved rest. On May 24, however, the 4th Michigan Volunteers discovered Hunt's camp while on a reconnaissance foray. While part of the Union regiment traded shots with three companies of Tigers posted at New Bridge, the rest of the 4th Michigan silently waded across the river upstream and moved down upon the unsuspecting Confederates. When the Union troops assailed the Tigers, the Louisianians hurriedly set fire to the bridge and fell back through their camp in confusion, leaving numerous dead and wounded behind. The fleeing Tigers soon met the 10th Georgia coming to their aid, rallied, and finally forced the Yankees to withdraw across the river. McClellan proudly shot off a wire to President Abraham Lincoln claiming that the 4th Michigan had "about finished [the] Louisiana Tigers." He was not far wrong, for at a loss of only ten men the Michigan boys had killed or wounded fifty Tigers and captured forty-three.[1]

Only a week after this humiliating defeat, other Louisiana commands were thrown into a savage fight along the Chickahominy River. While pursuing Johnston up the Peninsula, McClellan split his army across the sluggish Chickahominy, posting three of his army corps north of the stream and two south of it around Seven

1. *OR,* Vol. XI, Pt. I, 31, 651–54, 664–66.

Pines and Fair Oaks. Seeing a chance to smash these two isolated corps, Johnston ordered the divisions of Generals A. P. Hill and Magruder to demonstrate against the three Union corps north of the river while Longstreet led his own and the divisions of Generals D. H. Hill, Benjamin Huger, and Gustavus Smith against the two Union corps south of the Chickahominy.[2]

The battle opened at approximately 2:00 P.M., May 31, when Longstreet's men advanced against General Erasmus Keyes's IV Corps. The battle raged all afternoon, but Longstreet's commands became confused in the unfamiliar territory and the fight quickly deteriorated into a series of uncoordinated attacks by individual Confederate brigades. As the sun was setting over the dark and bloody field, General R. H. Anderson galloped up to Coppens' Battalion and St. Paul's Foot Rifles as they lay in the woods under a heavy fire. A Tennessee brigade had just been repelled by the federals, who were strongly posted on a hill fronting the Tigers. Anderson calmly rode down the length of the prone gray line and shouted over the din of battle that the Louisianians must take that hill. "Remember Butler and New Orleans," he yelled, "and drive them into hell!" The Louisianians sprang to attention as excited officers yelled out commands in French and dressed the line. In the growing darkness, a nearby band struck up "Dixie" as the Zouaves and Foot Rifles silently crept through a belt of timber to within fifty yards of the first Union line. Shouting "Picayune Butler," the Tigers suddenly broke into a run and routed two Pennsylvania regiments with a sudden volley of musketry from only fifteen yards. But when the surprised Yankees discovered just how few Confederates there actually were, they halted their retreat, turned, and cut down the first line of Tigers with a well-aimed barrage of minié balls. The outnumbered Louisianians were being severely thrashed by the Pennsylvanians when more Confederates arrived to help push the Yankees back again.[3]

2. *Ibid.*, 933–35.

3. An English Combatant, *Battlefields of the South, from Bull Run to Fredericksburg, with Sketches of Confederate Commanders, and Gossip of the Camps* (New York, 1864), 253; *Confederate Veteran*, XIV (1906), 521; Aurelia Austin, *Georgia Boys with "Stonewall" Jackson: James Thomas Thompson and the Walton Infantry* (Athens, 1967), 27; Mills Lane (ed.), *"Dear Mother: Don't Grieve About Me, If I Get Killed, I'll Only Be Dead." Letters from Georgia Soldiers in the Civil War* (Savannah, 1977), 130; *OR*, Vol. XI, Pt. I, 939–41.

When darkness ended the battle, both sides began strengthening and rearranging their lines in preparation for the next day's clash. Many of Coppens' men used the cover of darkness for more rewarding endeavors. One witness wrote, "These Louisianians seem to be great epicures, for scarcely one came off the field without having a well-filled haversack, and a canteen of liquor." While making the rounds of his battle line early on June 1, General George Pickett blundered upon several of these Zouaves, "who had evidently been on a plundering expedition." Loaded down with booty, the surprised Tigers tried to outmaneuver the irate officer by riding around him on their awkward mules. Pickett, however, was able to grab the reins of one mule and demanded an explanation from the cornered Zouave. The Tiger blurted out in fright that the Yankees were right behind them and begged Pickett to let go of his mule. The general reluctantly obliged so he could alert his superiors of the approaching enemy.[4]

Soon after Pickett's surprise encounter, D. H. Hill's division opened the second day's battle by fiercely assaulting the federal line. The stubborn Yankees held, however, and then counterattacked the stunned rebels. The 14th Louisiana took an active part in beating back this last Union advance before the battle finally ground to a halt.

Both sides lay battered and bruised from the two-day struggle, with little accomplished strategically to justify the 6,000 Confederate and 5,000 Union casualties. Unquestionably severe, the losses within the Louisiana commands are difficult to verify because of conflicting claims. Coppens, who was seriously wounded in the battle, entered the fight with 225 men and left more than half of them dead or wounded on the field, including 11 of his officers. A contemporary newspaper claims that St. Paul lost approximately 100 of his 196 men, although another paper puts the casualty figure for his three companies at 57. This latter account indicates that Coppens' and St. Paul's battalions were consolidated in the battle and notes that 310 of the 380 Louisianians engaged were casualties.[5]

Although no major action took place for several weeks following

4. English Combatant, *Battlefields of the South*, 254; *OR*, Vol. XI, Pt. I, 982.
5. Unidentified newspaper clipping in New Orleans Civil War Scrapbook, Part I, TU; unidentified newspaper clipping in Army of Northern Virginia Papers, Part I, LHAC; Wallace, "Coppens' Louisiana Zouaves," 279.

the fight at Seven Pines, the Louisiana commands continued to man the front lines and engaged in frequent skirmishing with the enemy. Lieutenant-Colonel Edmund Pendleton, the thirty-eight-year-old Virginian commanding the 3d Louisiana Battalion, wrote his daughter that on June 17 four of his men walked beyond the picket line and unexpectedly encountered five Yankees bathing in the Chickahominy. A quick exchange of gunfire left two Union soldiers dead. "So you see," he told her, "we are not on very neighborly terms with them."[6]

This unfriendliness was soon to worsen, for the Army of Northern Virginia now had a new commander who had very unneighborly plans for "those people," as he called the enemy. General Robert E. Lee was thrust into command of the army after Johnston was severely wounded at Seven Pines. Always the aggressor, Lee saw an opportunity to cripple McClellan's Army of the Potomac and send it reeling back down the Peninsula. Following the Battle of Seven Pines, McClellan had shifted all of his army south of the Chickahominy with the exception of Fitz-John Porter's corps, which was strongly dug in behind Beaver Dam Creek near Mechanicsville. In a maneuver similar to Johnston's, Lee planned to concentrate two-thirds of his men north of the river to smash Porter's corps, while Magruder and Huger remained to the south to hold the bulk of McClellan's army in place. After the destruction of Porter, McClellan would be forced to retreat and could be overwhelmed while in motion.

It was to participate in this maneuver that Jackson's veterans were recalled from the Valley. Jackson would force Porter's corps out of its Beaver Dam Creek line by assaulting the Union right flank from the north while Longstreet, A. P. Hill, and D. H. Hill struck out from the west and southwest. Lee planned to strike his knockout blow on June 26 but was beaten to the punch by McClellan, who sent forward the left of his army on June 25 to secure an area from which to launch his own assault. The picket line of Huger's isolated division was thrown back by the advancing bluecoats, and A. P. Wright's brigade was rushed forward with others to shore up the line. Wright deployed Lieutenant-Colonel W. R. Shivers' 1st Louisi-

6. Lieutenant-Colonel Edmund Pendleton to daughter, June 18, 1862, in Elizabeth P. Coles Collection, SHC.

ana and the 22d Georgia along the Williamsburg Road. When the federals were seen emerging from thick woods in front, Wright hurled his men forward and drove the Yankees back through a cornfield before the Union troops halted and made a stand in a second patch of woods. The Louisianians and Georgians fell back to the far edge of the field, regrouped, and then charged through the corn again. The advancing rebel line was badly thinned by accurate volleys of federal musketry that rattled through the cornstalks. Colonel Shivers fell out with a ball through his arm, leaving Captain Michael Nolan to lead the Tigers onward. Crouching as they braved the flying lead, the Confederates finally made it across the deadly field and drove the Yankees back.[7]

The Tigers were ecstatic, for in this their first fight they had captured the battle flag of General Daniel Sickles' famed Excelsior Brigade. In the midst of backslapping congratulations, however, the regiment was suddenly showered by minié balls as a new Union charge came crashing through the timber. As Wright's men were driven back across the cornfield, they were raked by a federal battery that belched a deadly fire of shell and canister into their backs.

This fighting raged near a small school for some time before finally sputtering out as darkness fell. Captain Nolan's Louisianians were then able to ease back out with some Georgians and Tar Heels and restore the original picket line. The 1st Louisiana's initiation into combat had been a harsh experience. Among the perforated cornstalks lay 16 of the regiment's 27 officers and 128 of the 328 enlisted men who took part in the fight. But the regiment's performance had not gone unnoticed. In his report of the fighting, General Wright wrote his superiors, "I beg leave to bring to your notice the gallant conduct of the First Louisiana Regiment in their charge" across the cornfield. With the general's blessings, the Tigers had "King's School House" emblazoned across their battle flag to show that they were now tested veterans.[8]

Despite McClellan's bloody probe, Lee went ahead with his plans to pounce on Porter's exposed corps at Beaver Dam Creek. Lee's in-

---

7. Clifford Dowdey, *The Seven Days: The Emergence of Lee* (Boston, 1964), 152–53.

8. *OR*, Vol. XI, Pt. II, 787–91, 804–808; Bartlett, *Military Record of Louisiana*, 4; Bound Volume 1 in Association of the Army of Northern Virginia, LHAC; unidentified newspaper clipping in Army of Northern Virginia Papers, Part I, LHAC; Samuel Huey Walkup Journal, June 25, 1862, in DU.

structions were simple—when A. P. Hill heard Jackson open the fight on Porter's right flank, he was to begin the western attack by clearing the federals out of Mechanicsville and then assault the Beaver Dam Creek line. All through the morning of June 26 Hill waited, straining to catch the sound of gunfire to the north. All was ominously quiet, however, for Jackson was uncharacteristically slow in getting into position. When 3:00 P.M. came and there was still no sign of Jackson, Hill decided to advance on his own lest the day be wasted. Mechanicsville was quickly cleared of the enemy and Beaver Dam Creek was reached. Scanning the frowning cannon and musket barrels jutting out from behind the Union breastworks, Hill decided the only chance for a breakthrough was to send J. R. Anderson's brigade circling to the left to try to turn the federal right flank.

After slowly snaking through a dense wood, Anderson's men finally emerged on the Union right flank. A formidable obstacle faced Anderson. The federals were well dug in behind earthen and rail breastworks with several batteries of artillery posted on the crest of a hill behind them. In addition, the federals had dammed up the creek at this point, turning the normally ten-foot-wide stream into a fifty-yard pond. Despite the odds, Anderson silently deployed the 14th and 35th Georgia and Pendleton's 3d Louisiana Battalion along a densely covered creek bank. Under a devastating fire, the Georgians and Tigers rushed through a near impassable briar thicket and tumbled down the slippery five-foot creek bank into the water. Many of the men were shot down in midstream or as they struggled up the muddy bank, but at last a sizable portion of the attacking column made it across the pond. Bleeding and torn from the briars, the Confederates were still able to root out the Yankees and seize a segment of their breastworks. A frantic plea for reinforcements was sent back to Anderson by the colonel of the 35th Georgia, but the rest of the brigade was being pounded by federal artillery and was in near chaos along the far edge of the pond. No help came, and the men had to hold on alone until they could safely recross the water under the cover of darkness.[9]

Porter withdrew his corps from Beaver Dam Creek that night and fought a series of delaying actions throughout the morning of

9. *OR*, Vol. XI, Pt. II, 834–40, 877–81; *ibid.*, Vol. LI, Pt. I, 117–18; Dowdey, *Seven Days*, 176–80.

June 27. Roger Pryor's brigade, which included the 14th Louisiana and Coppens' and St. Paul's consolidated battalions, was thrown against one of Porter's lines early that morning. In dense smoke and fog that hid objects thirty yards away, these Tigers loaded and fired as fast as they could into the enemy they thought was across a deep gully blocking their advance. Men were dropping rapidly from the fire of the unseen foe when screaming rounds of artillery suddenly began exploding along the gray line. Major David Zable of the 14th Louisiana realized that a friendly battery atop a hill in the rear was shelling the brigade by mistake in the fog. The major dispatched a courier to silence the guns, but the messenger was dropped by a bullet before getting far. Zable then spurred his horse and galloped back to the battery himself. Upon reaching the cannons, he pointed out his brigade to the artillerymen and quickly corrected the error. While up above the fog, Zable was astonished to see that the previously unseen Yankees who were decimating his regiment were posted far up a slope and not directly ahead of his men as thought. For an hour the Tigers had been subjected to a murderous fire while harmlessly pumping round after round into the side of a hill. Zable hurriedly rode back down into the shrouded valley and ordered the men to aim higher. Cadmus Wilcox's brigade arrived soon after and got the advance rolling again by throwing a makeshift bridge across the gorge fronting the brigade.[10]

By midafternoon Porter had skillfully set his men in two lines along a series of ridges overlooking a boggy creek bottom known as Boatswain's Swamp. Taking cover behind log breastworks and with batteries of artillery higher up the hill behind them, the Yankees would be able to slaughter Lee's men as they crossed the bottom. The Confederates were being forced to attack from a position Longstreet claimed "the enemy wished us to attack from." At 2:30 P.M., A. P. Hill made contact with Porter and sent his brigades charging against this new defensive position. After an hour and a half of savage bloodletting, however, Hill called a halt to the futile attacks and withdrew to let Longstreet and Jackson give it a try.[11]

Pryor came trotting down the length of his brigade at 4:30 P.M., halted before the 14th Louisiana, and ordered it to follow him to-

10. David Zable, "The Battle of Gaines' Mill," in Reminiscences, Executive and Army of Northern Virginia, LHAC.
11. *OR*, Vol. XI, Pt. II, 757.

ward the Union lines. The brigade followed Pryor across a wide
field, first walking, then breaking into a run down a gentle slope
toward Boatswain's Swamp. Federal gunners sprang to their pieces
and pounded Pryor's line for several minutes before the Confederates got within range of the Union infantry. When the Yankee muskets opened fire, the bullets tore ragged holes through the Louisiana line. Lieutenant Robert Miller had one ball pass through his
sword scabbard and kill a man running beside him. "The bullets
came so thick," he wrote, "that I felt a desire to see how many I
could catch with my open hand stretched out." [12]

As the brigade neared a gully formed by the creek that ran
through Boatswain's Swamp, the shrill rebel yell rose over the roar
of battle. Jumping and clawing their way across the gorge, the
Louisianians had to reform their line on the other side while under
a heavy fire. They then sent a volley crashing back at the Yankees
and charged once again. The Tigers quickly reached a federal battery and in ten minutes killed half its crew before wheeling the big
guns around to fire salvos at the now retreating Yankees. After a
few shots the guns were left behind and the chase was renewed.
When darkness ended the fighting, the Confederates held the
field, but Pryor's brigade had lost 860 men out of 1,400 engaged.
The fighting around the Union battery had been among the fiercest
of the day. The 14th Louisiana counted 51 dead and 192 wounded,
with one company of 45 men losing 29 members shot down. Coppens' and St. Paul's battalions fared little better with 5 dead and 46
wounded. [13]

Such carnage quickly took the fighting spirit out of the Tigers.
Lieutenant Miller lamented after the battle, "I have got my fill of
fighting, I want no more of it." Miller blamed poor tactics on Pryor's
part for the heavy losses suffered by the brigade at Gaines' Mill.
Pryor had resigned from the House of Representatives in 1861 to
throw in his lot with the South and turned down his election to the
Confederate Provisional Congress to become colonel of the 3d Virginia Volunteers. The caustic Miller declared: "He is a *politician*-
general and merits the contempt of all *soldiers*. He hoped by displaying the largest number of men killed and wounded in his

12. Conner (ed.), "Letters of Lieutenant Robert H. Miller," 88.
13. *OR*, Vol. XI, Pt. II, 779–81, 973–84; Zable, "Battle of Gaines' Mill," in Reminiscences, Executive and Army of Northern Virginia, LHAC.

Brigade to obtain a promotion. He succeeded, by placing us in exposed positions and by getting his regiments confused in producing the longest list of killed and wounded. . . . It is not necessary to say that in all the fight, Brig. Gen. Pryor was at a distance to the rear which precluded the possibility of an accident to him."[14] In all fairness to Pryor, the confusion Miller referred to was found in nearly all of the Confederate brigades, and there are numerous mentions by others of his often exposing himself to enemy fire. How much of Miller's complaints was shared by other Louisianians and how much was personal spitefulness may never be known.

Soon after Longstreet began his advance on Porter's left, Jackson sent forward his own brigades against the Union right. There a breakthrough was effected that disorganized Porter's line and presented the opportunity Pryor needed to capture the federal battery on the Union left flank. Jackson's "slows" had prevented his men from becoming engaged before the Battle of Gaines' Mill. Fresh from their Valley victories, Jackson's "foot cavalry" was eager to mete out the same treatment to McClellan's boys that the federals along the Shenandoah River had received. But tension mounted within the brigades throughout June 26 as the long, rolling thunder of artillery and musketry came from their right. It was obvious that A. P. Hill was meeting stiff resistance at Beaver Dam Creek. That night Jackson's troops became uneasy as they came to realize that the general's slowness had prevented them from aiding Hill.

The Louisiana Brigade had further cause to worry, for a new officer was guiding it through this campaign. Taylor had fallen ill with an attack of paralyzing pain in his head, back, and loins only a few days earlier and had to be transported in an ambulance. Colonel Isaac Seymour, the venerable commander of the Irish 6th Louisiana, was senior officer in the brigade so Taylor turned command over to him temporarily.[15]

The night of June 26 was dark, and tension ran high in the Louisiana Brigade as the men lay on their arms. Around midnight the jittery command was jolted awake by "the most unearthly and terrible shriek that ever greeted mortal ears." As the jumpy soldiers leaped to their feet, fumbled with their muskets, and tried to form

14. Conner (ed.), "Letters of Lieutenant Robert H. Miller," 88; Warner, *Generals in Gray*, 247–48.

15. Dowdey, *Seven Days*, 230–31; Taylor, *Destruction and Reconstruction*, 76–77.

a line in the pitch blackness, a crazed mule came braying through the camp. Muffled laughter and irate curses spread down the line as word was passed that the screams were from the horses of Colonels Stafford and Peck, which had suddenly started fighting and sent the frightened mule bolting through camp.[16]

After a restless night, Ewell's division resumed the march and followed the path of the battling A. P. Hill. Cautiously the Louisiana Brigade picked its way through abandoned federal camps littered with discarded equipment, dead horses, and shattered bodies. Many Tigers passed time by picking up letters from the shambles and reading them aloud to their amused comrades. Major Wheat, however, was not amused. Since the preceding day, when the brigade lay listening to the rumble of battle along Beaver Dam Creek, he was strangely subdued—even melancholy. His friends attributed this mood to the earlier deaths of his brother at Shiloh and a cousin in the Valley. But this was not the cause of the major's depression— Wheat was about to die, and he knew it.

To all who would listen, the major talked of his impending death and made them promise to bury him where he fell. When he awakened on June 27, Wheat passed his brandy flask to Major David F. Boyd and Colonel Stafford and read aloud a prayer from a small prayer book given him by his mother. Then, Boyd recalled, Wheat would "cry like a child, take another drink and read from his little book again." Later, while riding beside Lieutenant-Colonel Peck, Wheat declared emphatically that he would die before sunset and talked at length about his parents, especially his mother. Throughout the day's march, Wheat pulled out his prayer book and read aloud from it. One in particular seemed to hold special meaning for him. Entitled "Joyful Resurrection," it began, "Lord, I commend myself to Thee. Prepare me for living, prepare me for dying." At first, the Tigers made light of Wheat's tearful farewells, but as they saw his growing seriousness and dismay, they, too, began to feel an oppressiveness.[17]

16. Henderson, *Yankee in Gray*, 44; Taylor, *Destruction and Reconstruction*, 76–77; Brown, "Reminiscences of the Civil War," I, 62, in Brown Collection, SHC.

17. New Orleans *Daily Item*, August 25, 1896, in Scrapbook, Boyd Papers, LSU; Dufour, *Gentle Tiger*, 172, 190–93; Henderson, *Yankee in Gray*, 44–45; Oates, *Fifteenth Alabama*, 81–82; *Confederate Veteran*, VII (1899), 54–55; Dowdey, *Seven Days*, 230–31; *Southern Historical Society Papers*, XVII (1899), 57.

By 2:00 P.M., Ewell's division was in position to attack the right flank of Porter's line around Gaines' Mill. As the Tigers began falling into line, heavy firing erupted to the right, where Hill's men were beginning their assault. Soon Jackson came riding down his line to make sure all was ready. Seeing him, Wheat spurred his horse out to greet his commander, having apparently snapped out of his despondent mood as soon as he heard the battle begin. Approaching Jackson, Wheat told him the front was no place for the commander to be and begged Jackson not to expose himself in this battle as he so often had done in the Valley. Leave the fighting to Wheat's Tigers, the major exclaimed. Clearly touched by the major's concern, Jackson reached out, grasped Wheat's hand, and told him he appreciated the thought, but that it was Wheat who would be in the most danger and he hoped the major would not be hurt. But Wheat apparently was no longer concerned about himself. Riding up to Major Boyd, he exclaimed with pride as he scanned his ragged wharf rats, "Major, just look at my Louisiana planters! I'd like to see any 5,000 button makers stand before them this day.[18]

Heavy firing continued to build on Jackson's right, clearly indicating that Hill's attack was running into stiff opposition. To relieve some of the pressure, Jackson ordered his brigades forward against the Union right flank anchored on a hill across Boatswain's Swamp. With his officers prodding the troops past tempting Union encampments, Seymour quickly pushed the Louisianians across an open field and into a thick wood. Sweeping through the timber, the brigade became the target of searching artillery shells that shattered tree tops and rained branches and shrapnel on top of the line. Smoke hung heavy in the foliage, and brush impeded the advance, but the Tigers trotted down into the knee-deep water filling the swamp. Many officers became confused in the acrid smoke and thick brush and were not sure if they were still on course after sloshing through the swamp to the base of a hill. They quickly found they were, however, when a hailstorm of bullets ripped through the formation. Seymour pitched over dead from bullets in his head and body. For awhile the leaderless Tigers drifted on the

18. New Orleans *Daily Item*, August 25, 1896, in Scrapbook, Boyd Papers, LSU; Dufour, *Gentle Tiger*, 193.

side of the hill under the murderous fire. Confronting an unseen enemy and unsure what to do, a few Tigers fell back into the swamp but most simply halted on the hillside.[19]

Major Wheat became furious when he saw his Tigers falling back. Alone, he rode beyond the Tigers and threaded his way through the brush toward the Union line. Suddenly, both horse and rider collapsed in a heap only forty yards from the smoking enemy works. Caught in the open, Wheat was killed instantly by a ball that tore through one eye and out the back of his head. As at Manassas, the Tigers became demoralized after seeing their beloved major fall and began running back down the deadly slope. Major Boyd cut off one Tiger and demanded to know why he was running. "They have killed the old Major," the Tiger sobbed, "and I am going home. I wouldn't fight for Jesus Christ now!" Wheat's biographers claim that the tale of the major crying out, "Bury me on the field, boys!" just as he died is true. It is pure legend, however, for eyewitnesses state that Wheat died instantly and was alone at the time of his death. The story probably originated from Wheat's asking earlier in the day during his despondent mood that he be buried where he fell.[20]

Having never encountered such a fire in the Valley, the entire Louisiana line was in confusion and ready to bolt for the rear. Yet no one stepped forward to take command while the smoke-enshrouded enemy knocked scores of Tigers out of line. In fifteen minutes, Henry Handerson wrote, four men fell dead and four more severely wounded within ten steps of him, and another bullet ripped through his slouch hat. Unable to stand under the fusillade any longer, the brigade finally broke and fled back down the slope to the swamp below. Desperate comrades dragged and carried as many of the wounded with them as possible, but a number of the injured were left between the lines.

With federal bullets kicking up mud and water all around, the Tigers splashed back across the stagnant swamp just as Trimble's

19. Handerson, *Yankee in Gray*, 45; New Orleans *Commercial Bulletin*, July 30, 1862, in New Orleans Civil War Scrapbook, Part II, TU.

20. New Orleans *Daily Item*, August 25, 1896, in Scrapbook, Boyd Papers, LSU; Dufour, *Gentle Tiger*, 195; Handerson, *Yankee in Gray*, 46; Douglas, *I Rode with Stonewall*, 102–103; Reid, *History of the Fourth S.C.*, 102; Edward Porter Alexander, *Military Memoirs of a Confederate* (New York, 1907), 34.

brigade came charging through to plug the gap left by their retreat. Now forty-five minutes after Seymour's death, Colonel Stafford took command of the brigade, unaware of the colonel's death until after the retreat. His 9th Louisiana and part of the 7th and 8th Louisiana were in fair order and formed behind a slight crest on Trimble's flank. But finally Trimble ordered them to withdraw further back out of fire because, as one Confederate officer wrote, they were still "somewhat confused." General John B. Hood's Texas brigade then came whooping through the swamp and in thirty minutes accomplished what the Tigers had failed to do. With a yell and a volley, the Texans broke through the federal breastworks and precipitated the Union withdrawal which Pryor's and other brigades capitalized on further to the right.[21]

As other commands pressed Porter in the growing darkness, Stafford went to work pulling his disorganized command back together. Darkness came quickly in the timbered swamp, and lanterns were lit to search out the 142 wounded who lay propped up out of the water against stumps and logs, moaning and crying for help. For the 29 dead, there was no hurry—they could be found and buried in the morning.[22]

June 28 was a day of skirmishing and maneuvering as Porter pulled back to the south side of the Chickahominy to join the rest of McClellan's army. When Lee's troops resumed the pursuit on Sunday, June 29, a new federal line was encountered near Savage Station, where General Edwin Sumner's corps covered McClellan's withdrawal across White Oak Swamp. Magruder was the first to advance against the Union line, but he was bloodily repulsed. McLaws then deployed and sent in the brigades of Paul Jones Semmes and Joseph Brevard Kershaw along the Savage Station railroad. Advancing through a dense wood, Colonel Hunt's 5th Louisiana suddenly halted after hearing someone issuing commands to an unseen force hidden in the undergrowth ahead. Hammers clicked and muskets were brought up, but several of Semmes's officers

21. Brown, "Reminiscences of the Civil War," I, 66, in Brown Collection, SHC; *OR*, Vol. XI, Pt. II, 552–59, 563, 605–607, 619–20; Dowdey, *Seven Days*, 229–32; Handerson, *Yankee in Gray*, 96; *Confederate Veteran*, VII (1899), 54–55; Oates, *Fifteenth Alabama*, 116–21; New Orleans *Commercial Bulletin*, July 30, 1862, in New Orleans Civil War Scrapbook, Part II, TU.

22. *OR*, Vol. XI, Pt. II, 609–10.

stayed the nervous men, thinking the command was a stray Confederate brigade. Hunt, however, could see the mysterious soldiers forty yards ahead and was not certain they were friendly. General Semmes sent Private John Maddox of the 5th Louisiana out to investigate. "Who are you?" yelled Maddox. "Friends!" came the reply. "What regiment?" Maddox inquired. When the unidentified soldier yelled back, "Third Vermont!" Semmes ordered the brigade to open fire, and a roaring battle broke out in the dark woods.[23]

The 3d Vermont was part of the Vermont brigade that had battled Colonel Levy's 2d Louisiana so furiously at Dam Number One ten weeks earlier. This fight was no different. In the growing twilight, the Tigers and Yankees sent thousands of minié balls tearing through the brush. Hunt's men used "buck and ball," a combination of a minié ball and two buckshot, in their smoothbore muskets. With a scant forty yards of brush and timber separating the lines, this load was particularly deadly. When darkness finally ended the fight twenty minutes later, the Vermont brigade had lost a staggering total of 358 men—a full half of its effective force. Semmes counted a mere 64 casualties among his brigade. The 5th Louisiana lost only 6 men, but the Confederates claimed to have counted 100 federal bodies in front of Hunt's position.[24]

Again the Yankees withdrew during the night, but the Confederates found yet another Union line formed around Glendale and Frayser's Farm on June 30. Once again Lee's brigades were thrown into the attack piecemeal and were chewed up by the entrenched federals. Pryor's brigade was lying along the edge of a field suffering under a heavy artillery barrage when the general came riding down the line to prepare for the advance. Pryor's presence seemed to attract even more shells—one exploded in the midst of the 14th Louisiana, taking out a half dozen men, and another cut off the leg of Pryor's horse. When the charge was finally sounded, the brigade surged across the field into a heavy barrage of artillery and musketry. The 14th Louisiana's color bearer fell dead, but the flag was snatched up by another and the advance continued. The suicidal charge accomplished little, however, for the few breakthroughs

23. *Ibid.*, 720–25.
24. *Ibid.*, 715–25; Benedict, *Vermont in the Civil War*, I, 140, 290–98; Dowdey, *Seven Days*, 260–81.

achieved by the Confederates were only temporary and the rebels paid a staggering price for their *élan*. The 14th Louisiana began the advance with 900 soldiers and left 243 littered across the field when it was over. One Tiger wrote of a company entering the fight with 42 members, but "only nine men came out without bullets in their hides." Such losses prompted the Tigers to dub Frayser's Farm the "Slaughter House."[25]

The Battle of Frayser's Farm ended as had those on each of the preceding five days—thousands of Confederates were lost in the clash, but McClellan's army was left intact and withdrew during the night to establish a strong position on Malvern Hill near the James River. Lee's weary command approached this new line cautiously and spent most of July 1 encircling it in an arc, preparing for still another assault. The Union defenses were as strong as any seen by the Army of Northern Virginia. Several lines of blue infantry were arranged along the hill's slope, with battery upon battery of artillery positioned behind them with a clear view of any approaching rebels. Lee planned to throw most of his army into the attack, but again poor staff work and confusion resulted in only individual brigades advancing against the near impregnable line.

At 4:45 P.M. Huger's division ran out of the woods surrounding the hill and began ascending the slope. "Remember Beast Butler and our women!" cheered the 1st Louisiana as it trotted toward Union General George W. Morell's position. Federal gunners touched off their pieces and tore gaps through the gray line with canister, while the Yankee infantry took out a number of men with long-range volleys of musketry. When three hundred yards from the enemy line, Wright's brigade found cover in a shallow depression. While the men were regrouping for the final phase of the assault, a detachment of federal infantry suddenly came swarming down the hollow on Wright's left, and it took forty-five minutes of fierce fighting to beat them off. It was almost dark when Wright's brigade and the other Confederate units emerged from the hollow for the final charge. The three hundred yards of open ground were quickly covered, and the ragged gray line smashed into the

25. Bartlett, *Military Record of Louisiana*, 44; John W. T. Leech, "Frazier's Farm," in Reminiscences, Executive and Army of Northern Virginia, LHAC; *Southern Historical Society Papers*, XXI (1893), 163–64; Dowdey, *Seven Days*, 282–302.

Union infantry posted in front of the artillery. In the savage fighting the Confederates cut down the 62d Pennsylvania's flag five
times, the 12th New York's four times, and killed the colonel of the
4th Michigan. The Tigers thereby gained some revenge for this
latter regiment's rough handling of the 5th Louisiana six weeks earlier at New Bridge. The 22d Massachusetts rushed in to help, and
each of its men quickly fired his allotted sixty rounds before the
battle ended. Wright's brigade was finally able to push the Yankees
back to their artillery, but then collapsed, too exhausted and shot
up to continue any further. Fewer than 300 of Wright's original
1,000 men were left to man the battle line when darkness finally
enveloped the hill. Casualties claimed 362, and the rest were scattered in confusion among other brigades.[26]

On Wright's left several brigades in Magruder's command were
also being slaughtered. Before the battle began, the 10th Louisiana
in Semmes's brigade had been eagerly awaiting the opportunity to
enter the fray. Eugene Waggaman, the likable, devoutly religious
colonel of the 10th, had been marking time for six days while his
regiment was kept in reserve during each of the preceding battles.
Now on the last day of the campaign, his regiment was again left
in the woods as a reserve. The Tigers were bitter and openly expressed their anger when one of Semmes's couriers galloped up to
Waggaman and handed him a note. "Fall in!" the colonel roared as
he scanned the order. The men's spirits lifted as they realized they
were to be part of the charge and that Hunt's regiment was to be
the reserve.

After advancing for some distance, Waggaman halted his men at
a fence skirting a large field. Five hundred yards in the distance the
Yankee line was visible; the only protective cover for a charging column was a shallow ravine halfway to the enemy. The first two hundred yards were covered in a rush but not before numerous men
were hurled out of line by the Yankees' accurate artillerymen. Taking cover in the ravine, Waggaman regrouped his shaken line, had
his men fix bayonets, and then walked to the center of the regiment. "Men," he shouted, "we are ordered to charge the cannon in
our front and take them. The Tenth Regiment has been in reserve
all week, and every other Louisiana regiment has been in action.

26. *OR,* Vol. XI, Pt. II, 99, 266–67, 315, 329; *Southern Historical Society Papers,*
XXXVIII (1910), 211.

Not a shot must be fired until we get to the guns. Now, men, we are going to charge. Remember Butler and the women of New Orleans. Forward, charge!" [27]

Out of the hollow they ran, taking a full five minutes to cover the last three hundred yards because of a heavy fire from thirty-six artillery pieces. Those Tigers who survived the murderous fire and still had heart for the fight closed in on the 69th New York and 12th United States Regulars. Watching from the woods, one member of the 5th Louisiana saw the Tigers approach the federal position and then disappear into its flame and smoke as if swallowed by hell itself. Waggaman and a handful of his men penetrated the Union line and engaged the Yankees with bayonets. Surrounded by bluecoats, one of Waggaman's Irishmen was bayoneted through the neck beside the colonel, and Waggaman knocked a Yankee's musket out of his own face before it could be fired. Cries of "Bayonet him!" and "Kill him!" rose all around as Waggaman continued hacking his way through the enemy line. In a short time, however, the colonel and sixteen of his men were overwhelmed and captured, but not before Waggaman was able to throw away his sword to prevent it from falling into enemy hands. On many occasions, Waggaman led his men into battle carrying only a cane, but at Malvern Hill he wielded his family's 150-year-old sword. Unknown to him, a Union soldier picked up the discarded sword from the battlefield, and it was returned to Waggaman by order of General Winfield Scott Hancock when the colonel was exchanged some weeks later. [28]

Waggaman and his 10th Louisiana were the only elements of the brigade that managed to penetrate the federal line. But the Tigers paid dearly for this honor. Of the 318 men engaged in the fight, 18 were dead, 35 wounded, and 18 missing. To the left, Waggaman's sister regiment, the 2d Louisiana, suffered even greater losses. Lieutenant-Colonel J. T. Norwood led it against the deadly batteries

27. Edward Pinkowski, *Pills, Pen and Politics: The Story of General Leon Jastremski, 1843–1907* (Wilmington, Del., 1974), 40.

28. Anonymous address on the Battle of Malvern Hill in Reminiscences, Executive and Army of Northern Virginia, LHAC; Buckley, *A Frenchman, a Chaplain, a Rebel*, 121, 123; Pinkowski, *Pills, Pen and Politics*, 37–41; *OR*, Vol. XI, Pt. II, 720–25; Bartlett, *Military Record of Louisiana*, 13, 24–30; *Southern Historical Society Papers*, XXV (1897), 183–84; *ibid.*, I (1876), 75; Eugene Waggaman to Louis Janin, July, 1862, in Box 56, Folder 9, Janin Family Papers, HL; New Orleans *Times-Picayune*, May 16, 1862, in Melrose Scrapbook #230, NSU.

on Malvern Hill and was mortally wounded in the charge, along with Major R. W. Ashton, who was killed when he seized the regiment's colors after three color bearers were shot down. After losing 182 men, the most of any of Lee's regiments, the 2d Louisiana finally halted and withdrew without reaching its objective. Taylor's brigade was never ordered to take part in the deadly assaults, but several of his regiments mistakenly joined in the attack and lost 24 dead and 92 wounded.[29]

Although the Battle of Malvern Hill cost the Tigers more than four hundred men, it also enhanced their reputation as fighters and added to the legend that was growing around their name. In General Thomas Meagher's New York brigade, the 88th New York clashed either with the 1st or 10th Louisiana, although they mistakenly thought it was Wheat's "desperadoes." After the battle, the regiment was licking its wounds and searching for new muskets to replace the ones destroyed during the hand-to-hand fight. General Sumner, its corps commander, at first refused to issue new weapons, thinking the men had discarded them during the lengthy retreat. He changed his mind, however, when he was shown a "pile of muskets with cracked and splintered stocks, bent barrels and twisted bayonets"—evidence of the fierce clash with the Tigers. The general was told by the regiment, "The boys got in a scrimmage with the Tigers, and when the bloody villains took to their knives, the boys mostly forgot their bayonets, but went to work in the style they were used to, and licked them well, sir."[30]

The Battle of Malvern Hill ended the Seven Days' Campaign. McClellan was bottled up at the end of the Peninsula and no longer seriously threatened Richmond, but his position was too strong to be assaulted. In the campaign Lee lost some 20,000 men and inflicted about 16,000 casualties upon the enemy. Just how many men the Tigers lost during that bloody week is uncertain, but their casualty rate was among the highest of any state. The official returns for the campaign list 179 dead, 797 wounded, and 73 missing among the Louisiana troops. These records, however, do not mention the

29. *OR,* Vol. XI, Pt. II, 601, 609, 659–74, 748–50, 973–84; Taylor, *Destruction and Reconstruction,* 86; *Southern Historical Society Papers,* X (1882), 217; Handerson, *Yankee in Gray,* 48–50.

30. Michael Cavanagh, *Memoirs of Gen. Thomas Francis Meagher . . . Including Personal Reminiscences* (Worcester, Mass., 1892), 450–51.

3d Louisiana Battalion and do not always coincide with losses for particular battles listed elsewhere in the official records. Whatever the exact numbers, the Louisianians' initiation into combat was frightening. Father Louis-Hippolyte Gache spoke for many Tigers when he wrote, "I do love to see an army in battle array. I thrill to the thunder of artillery cannon and to the crack of infantry rifles; my blood tingles when I watch cavalry manoeuvers. . . . But alas, the events of Monday, Tuesday, Wednesday and Thursday have surfeited my appetite for war. I have now seen enough carnage to last me for life." [31]

Losses were so heavy during the Seven Days' Battle that the Army of Northern Virginia had to be reorganized. In compliance with Jackson's recommendation, Taylor was promoted to major-general and transferred to the Trans-Mississippi Department. The Louisiana Brigade wanted to go with Taylor and petitioned Davis for permission to accompany him. Taylor supported the idea but failed to get approval. The 5th and 14th Louisiana Volunteers were then added to the Louisiana Brigade, and the 9th Louisiana was taken out. Wheat's famous Tiger Battalion was disbanded on Taylor's recommendation, probably because heavy losses had made it so small as to be useless as a separate command. The Louisiana Brigade in Ewell's division now consisted of the 5th, 6th, 7th, 8th, and 14th Louisiana Volunteers and the Louisiana Guard Battery. The brigade was placed under Harry Thompson Hays, the 7th Louisiana's commander, who was promoted to brigadier-general on July 25, 1862. The forty-two-year-old Hays had proven himself an able commander while leading the 7th Louisiana through numerous engagements and was recommended for the position by Taylor. Hays was a native of Tennessee and a lawyer, who had moved to New Orleans in his youth. After distinguished service in the Mexican War, the prominent attorney entered politics and became an active member of the Whig party. A hard drinker and tough fighter, he was respected by all and proved to be an excellent choice for the command. [32]

31. Buckley, *A Frenchman, a Chaplain, a Rebel*, 117; *OR*, Vol. XI, Pt. II, 502–10, 973–84.

32. *OR*, Vol. XII, Pt. III, 917–18; *ibid.*, Vol. LI, Pt. II, 597; Stephens to Tom Stephens, August 3, 1862, and Stephens to sister, August 15, 1862, in Stephens Collection, NSU; Warner, *Generals in Gray*, 130; Compiled Service Records, War Record

Because Lee believed that morale would be strengthened if brigades were composed of regiments from the same state, a 2d Louisiana Brigade was formed and placed in Jackson's old division, now commanded by General William Taliaferro. A new regiment, the 15th Louisiana, was first formed by adding two companies of St. Paul's Foot Rifles to the 3d Louisiana Battalion. Then it was brigaded with the 1st, 2d, 9th, and 10th Louisiana Volunteers and Coppens' Battalion. This 2d Louisiana Brigade was placed under the command of General William E. Starke, a native of Virginia, who had moved to New Orleans and become a prominent cotton dealer. Although Starke had resided in Louisiana for years before the war, he left the state to become colonel of the 60th Virginia Volunteers once fighting broke out. Because of his background, the Louisianians viewed his appointment with hostility, for they felt one of their own colonels should have been chosen to lead the new brigade. Starke would have to win the confidence of the Tigers through a show of courage and ability. He quickly received the opportunity to demonstrate both, for as soon as the army was reorganized, Lee resumed the offensive.[33]

Group 109, Microcopy 320, Roll 100; Handerson, *Yankee in Gray*, 99, 132; James McDowell Carrington to Eliza Henry Carrington, October 16, 1862, in Carrington Family Papers, VHS.

33. Eugene Janin to John McLean, August 18, 1862, in Folder 2, Janin Collection, SHC; *OR*, Vol. XI, Pt. II, 648–49, 656; Warner, *Generals in Gray*, 289.

Chapter VI

DARK AND DISMAL FIELDS

After several weeks of rest following the Seven Days' Battle, Lee's mangled army was ready to strike the federals another blow. McClellan's force remained inactive on the Peninsula, but General John Pope was bringing a large army across the Rappahannock River north of Richmond. To counter this threat, Lee began shifting his men to Gordonsville on July 13. Since Harry Hays was still recuperating from the wound he received at Port Republic, his brigade was temporarily commanded by Colonel Henry Forno of the 5th Louisiana. Forno, an elderly veteran of the Mexican War and former New Orleans police chief, was not a popular officer, but he proved to be a skillful fighter.[1]

On August 9 Jackson severely mauled Pope's men when he pounced on them at Cedar Run, near Slaughter Mountain. The two Louisiana brigades saw only limited action in this fight, but they sustained moderate losses from the Union artillery. Forno had only eight men wounded, but Starke's brigade counted six dead and twenty-eight wounded. One Tiger reported that the 14th Louisiana lost six soldiers from one shell that tore through the regiment and "scattered the brains and blood of poor Ralph Smith all over a dozen of us."[2]

The Tigers seemed more intent on scouring the field for booty than winning the battle. Father Gache of the 10th Louisiana saw numerous members of Starke's brigade robbing Yankee dead and

1. Alison Moore, *The Louisiana Tigers, or the Two Louisiana Brigades in the Army of Northern Virginia, 1861–1865* (Baton Rouge, 1961), 163; Buckley, *A Frenchman, a Chaplain, a Rebel*, 48, 57.

2. Conner (ed.), "Letters of Lieutenant Robert H. Miller," 89; See also *OR*, Vol. XII, Pt. II, 176–85, 214–15, 223–24, 226–28; Jedediah Hotchkiss, *Make Me a Map of the Valley: The Civil War Journal of Stonewall Jackson's Topographer*, ed. Archie P. McDonald (Dallas, 1973), 126, 295.

wounded. He wrote a friend, "These wretched men (and their number was greater than you might suppose) were not concerned with bringing help to the wounded, but in emptying their pockets and stealing their clothes. . . . There were some who went so far as to strip a dead man of every last piece of clothing to leave his body lying naked in the dust. I came upon two of these ghouls kneeling on either side of a corpse they had just despoiled fighting about who should keep the poor man's canteen."[3]

Jackson's victory effectively halted Pope's southward movement and forced him to pull back north of the Rappahannock. Since the Yankee general was still being reinforced, however, Lee became convinced that Pope was the greater threat and began pulling the remainder of the Army of Northern Virginia away from McClellan's front so as to follow up Jackson's victory. Lee left Longstreet's corps to watch the Yankees across the Rappahannock, while Jackson crossed the river upstream and swept into Pope's rear. To divert Pope's attention from Longstreet, Jackson planned to cut the Orange and Alexandria Railroad deep in the federals' rear at Bristoe Station and then fight a holding action until Lee and Longstreet could reinforce him and, he hoped, crush the Yankees.

After covering fifty-five miles in thirty-six hours, Jackson's "foot cavalry" approached Bristoe Station at sunset on August 26. The gray horsemen leading the advance flushed out a handful of Union defenders and called on Forno to hurry up his Tigers to help rout them. From three miles away the Louisianians double-quicked into the station and managed to capture the few Yankees who had not already fled. While the exhausted Tigers lay gasping for breath, the shrill whistle of a train was heard down the double-tracked rails to the right. Before they had a chance to hide, the train came chugging out of a belt of timber and began picking up speed as the engineer spotted the rebels and opened the throttle. When the cars rumbled past Forno's position, the brigade fired a volley of musketry that killed the engineer and riddled the locomotive. But the train failed to slow up and disappeared down the line to spread the alarm in Washington.[4]

3. Buckley, *A Frenchman, a Chaplain, a Rebel*, 132–33.
4. Rev. Joseph Durkin (ed.), *Confederate Chaplain: A War Journal of Rev. James B. Sheeran, c.s.s.r., 14th Louisiana, C.S.A.* (Milwaukee, 1960), 9; *OR*, Vol. XII, Pt. II, 551–55; Compiled Service Records, War Record Group 109, Microcopy 320, Roll 148, NA.

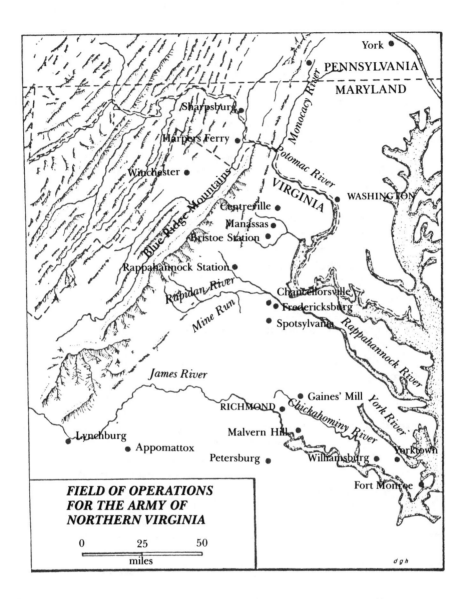

**FIELD OF OPERATIONS
FOR THE ARMY OF
NORTHERN VIRGINIA**

0   25   50

miles

York

PENNSYLVANIA

MARYLAND

Sharpsburg

Harpers Ferry

Momocacy River

Potomac River

Winchester

VIRGINIA

WASHINGTON

Blue Ridge Mountains

Centreville

Manassas

Bristoe Station

Rappahannock Station

Rapidan River

Mine Run

Chancellorsville

Fredericksburg

Spotsylvania

Rappahannock River

James River

Gaines' Mill

RICHMOND

Chickahominy River

York River

Malvern Hill

Lynchburg

Appomattox

Petersburg

Williamsburg

Yorktown

Fort Monroe

d g h

As soon as the train was gone, Jackson called on the 21st North Carolina to aid the Tigers in barricading the track in case another train approached. No sooner had a barrier of crossties been erected than a second train was heard coming from Pope's base at Warrenton. While the Tar Heels and Tigers concealed themselves along the track, Jackson strolled along the rails instructing the men to hold their fire until the train hit the barrier. The engineer was slowly approaching the station when the excited Louisianians rose prematurely and peppered the train with musket balls. The locomotive's boiler and stack were perforated by the bullets, and steam hissed through a score of holes. Smoking and wheezing, the engine smashed into the crossties with a roar and careened with its twenty cars into a muddy ravine.

The Tigers swarmed down into the ravine to inspect their prize. They cheered with delight upon seeing that the locomotive, which bore the name "Abe Lincoln," had a bullet hole drilled through the likeness of the president painted on it. Then, suddenly, off in the distance was heard a third train, and the troops scrambled back up to the track to hide. This locomotive also hit the barrier and tumbled off the track with its load of cars. The steam had barely cleared when yet a fourth train approached the cluttered station. This engineer, however, managed to halt his locomotive out of musket range upon seeing the deserted station and twisted wreckage. He sensibly ignored the "all clear" signal tooted by the whistle of one wrecked locomotive by a Tiger and refused to budge. The frustrated Louisianians fired at the distant train and sent it chugging back to Warrenton to inform Pope of the gray-clad raiders.[5]

Knowing that Pope would soon be in pursuit, Jackson left Ewell's division at Bristoe Station to watch for the Yankees while he took the rest of his corps to capture Pope's supply depot at Manassas Junction. Early on the morning of August 27, Ewell dispatched Forno's brigade, with the 60th Georgia and one cannon, down the

5. Durkin (ed.), *Confederate Chaplain*, 9–11; *OR*, Vol. XII, Pt. II, 650–51, 747–48; Brown, "Reminiscences of the Civil War," I, 91–92, in Brown Collection, SHC; Jubal A. Early, "Jackson's Campaigns Against Pope in August, 1862," in Pamphlets, Part II, LHAC; Compiled Service Records, War Record Group 109, Microcopy 320, Roll 148, NA; Freeman, *Lee's Lieutenants*, II, 90–92; Oates, *Fifteenth Alabama*, 133–35; W. B. Taliaferro, "Jackson's Raid Around Pope," in Johnson and Buel (eds.), *Battles and Leaders*, II, 503; Dabney, *Life and Campaigns of Jackson*, 518.

track to destroy the bridge across Kettle Run. When the Tigers met a detachment of federals coming to investigate, they unlimbered the cannon and with several well-placed shots sent the Yankees scampering back aboard the train. The 6th Louisiana, commanded by Colonel Henry B. Strong, a native of Ireland, was then deployed as pickets while Major Trevanion Lewis' 8th Louisiana destroyed the bridge. After issuing orders for these two regiments to retire if attacked, Forno led the rest of the command back to Bristoe Station.

That afternoon Pope sent General Joseph Hooker's division to drive off the troublesome Confederate "raiders." The 6th and 8th Louisiana retired before this large force and withdrew to within four hundred yards of Ewell's main line. The 8th Louisiana took cover in a pine thicket next to the track and watched as Hooker advanced with two brigades in column on either side of the track. Expecting nothing more than Confederate cavalry, the Yankees were taken by surprise when the Tigers suddenly opened fire from a range of fifty yards and charged from the thicket. The 5th Louisiana, 6th Louisiana, and 60th Georgia joined in the shooting and soon had the Yankees running "like Turkeys," one rebel claimed. The brief encounter was bloody, but the four Confederate regiments managed to hold back Hooker's fifteen regiments before breaking off the engagement and rejoining Ewell's line. The two Union brigades that bore the brunt of the fight lost 408 men in the ambush, but the Louisianians tallied only 90 casualties and the Georgians 42.[6]

Under orders to rejoin Jackson if hard pressed, Ewell quickly disengaged from Hooker and hurried his men on to Manassas Junction. When they tramped into the station well past dark, many of the men were incensed to find that most of the supplies had already been snatched up by Jackson's soldiers. Having lived off roasted corn since crossing the Rappahannock, the rebels had made the most of the occasion and spent the better part of the day ransacking the vast Yankee warehouses. One Confederate wrote, "To see a starving man eating lobster salad & drinking rhine wine, barefooted & in tatters

6. Brown, "Reminiscences of the Civil War," I, 93, in Brown Collection, SHC; *OR*, Vol. XII, Pt. II, 443–52, 455, 457, 461–62, 708–709, 716; Taliaferro, "Jackson's Raid," 506; Early, *War Memoirs*, 114–18; Frederick Phisterer (comp.), *New York in the War of the Rebellion, 1861 to 1865* (Albany, 1890), 376, 428–32.

was curious; the whole thing is indescribable." "We got any amount of sugar and coffee, bacon and salt," declared Sergeant Stephens of the 9th Louisiana. "Though we could not take anything off except what little we could put in our haversacks."[7]

Despite their late arrival, Forno's men found that a mile-long supply train still remained untouched. Father James Sheeran of the 14th Louisiana wrote of the scene when Ewell's men were turned loose on this train: "I had often read of the sacking of cities by a victorious army but never did I hear of a railroad train being sacked. I saw the whole army become what appeared to be an ungovernable mob, drunk, some with liquor but the others with excitement. . . . Just imagine about 6,000 men hungry and almost naked, let loose on some million dollars worth of [supplies]. . . . Here you would see a crowd enter a car with their old Confederate greys and in a few moments come out dressed in Yankee uniforms; some as cavalry; some as infantry; some as artillerists; others dressed in the splendid uniforms of Federal officers."[8]

At midnight the train was fired to destroy what could not be carried off, but some die-hard rebels still searched the burning cars for booty. "It was a very dark night," wrote one of Ewell's aides, "& the scene as wild & grand as I ever imagined. Many of the men were gathered around the burning cars & buildings, examining their contents—throwing back into the flames what they did not want—looking dark & strange against the fiery background." When the order was given to fall in, however, the mob became an army once again and moved out to take up new positions around the hamlet of Groveton.[9]

Knowing that Pope would soon move against his force, Jackson chose to wait in ambush for the foe beside the Alexandria-Warrenton pike near the community of Groveton. Late in the afternoon of August 28, General Rufus King's division casually marched past Jackson's position, unaware of the rebel trap. When General

7. C. G. Chamberlayne (ed.), *Ham Chamberlayne—Virginian: Letters and Papers of an Artillery Officer in the War for Southern Independence, 1861–1865* (Richmond, 1932), 100; Edmond Stephens to parents, September 7, 1862, in Stephens Collection, NSU; *OR*, Vol. XII, Pt. II, 554–55; Bartlett, *Military Record of Louisiana*, 30–31; Oates, *Fifteenth Alabama*, 136–37.
8. Durkin (ed.), *Confederate Chaplain*, 11–12.
9. Brown, "Reminiscences of the Civil War," I, 95, in Brown Collection, SHC.

John Gibbon's brigade passed the waiting Confederates, Taliaferro's division swept over a rise to the Yankees' left and savagely assailed the blue column. For several hours the brigades of W. S. H. Baylor, Alexander Taliaferro, Isaac Trimble, A. R. Lawton, and William Starke struggled unsuccessfully to overwhelm Gibbon's "Iron Brigade." Taliaferro wrote in his official report that it was "one of the most terrific conflicts that can be conceived." As a blood-red sun slowly set, the two lines stood erect in an open field beside the road and blasted each other from a range of less than one hundred yards. At dusk Taliaferro's line rushed across the field and pushed Gibbon's men back toward the road, but the stubborn Yankees refused to break. The battle raged well into the night, with only the muzzle flash of thousands of muskets revealing the opposing line. Soon Taliaferro fell wounded and then Ewell dropped out with a shattered kneecap. Starke took command of the battered division and turned the Louisiana Brigade over to Colonel Stafford, who fought to maintain his position in front of the scrappy 7th Wisconsin and 56th Pennsylvania. Not until 9:00 P.M. did the federals slowly withdraw back to the turnpike and the firing finally died out.[10]

The bloody clash at Groveton was Starke's initiation as a brigade commander, but his actions were highly praised by his superiors. Taliaferro later wrote that the Louisiana Brigade's "gallantry was conspicuous, and the ability of its commander, Brig. Gen. W. E. Starke, was a guarantee that it did all that the gallant Louisianians . . . were required to perform." It is not known how many Tigers fell during this twilight fight, but it had to be many judging from the losses sustained by the federals. General King lost 751 men, or more than one-third of his effective force, and the 7th Wisconsin lost every one of its field officers in front of the Tigers' position.[11]

During the night and early morning of August 29, Jackson placed

10. *OR*, Vol. XII, Pt. II, 657.

11. *Ibid.*, 378, 554–58, 658, 668–69; Taliaferro, "Jackson's Raid," 510–11; John Pope, "The Second Battle of Bull Run," in Johnson and Buel (eds.), *Battles and Leaders*, II, 469; Rufus R. Dawes, *Service with the Sixth Wisconsin Volunteers*, ed. Alan T. Nolan (1890; rpr. Madison, 1962), 59–68; Early, *War Memoirs*, 119–21; Brown, "Reminiscences of the Civil War," I, 102, in Brown Collection, SHC; Oates, *Fifteenth Alabama*, 137–38; Freeman, *Lee's Lieutenants*, II, 110, 138; Alexander, *Military Memoirs of a Confederate*, 199.

his three divisions along the cuts and embankments of an unfinished railroad grade that lay in a thick forest near the old Bull
Run battlefield. It was here, Jackson decided, that he would wait
for the inevitable Union assault and tie down Pope's army until Lee
arrived with reinforcements. Retaining acting command of the division, Starke placed Taliaferro's division on the right of the Confederate line, while Lawton, who had replaced the wounded Ewell,
put his division in the center. A. P. Hill's men anchored Jackson's left
near Bull Run.

Pope soon had most of his army on hand and began preparing
for an assault by pounding the railroad grade with artillery fire at
10:00 A.M. Throughout this bombardment Forno's brigade lay in
reserve, calmly waiting to be called into action. A young Virginian,
lost from his command, stumbled across these Tigers and was told
by a Louisiana major, "Better stay with us, my boy, and if you do
your duty I'll make it right with your company officers when the
fight's over. They won't find any fault with you when they know
you've been in with the 'Pelicans.'" The young soldier did remain
awhile with the Tigers and marveled at their unique appearance.
"Such a congress of nations," he recalled, "only the cosmopolitan
Crescent City could have sent forth, and the tongues of Babel
seemed resurrected in its speech. English, German, French, and
Spanish, all were represented, to say nothing of Doric brogue—
and local 'gumbo.'" The Virginian remembered how the Tigers,
bored with waiting, passed the time by quietly playing cards "with a
greasy, well-thumbed deck, and in smoking cigarettes, rolled with
great dexterity, between the deals." Before leaving the Tigers, the
young soldier was shocked to see the Louisianians cheerfully play a
hand of cards—with the loser having to fill his mates' canteens by
running to a nearby spring across a bullet-swept field.[12]

At 2:00 P.M. Pope threw his blue infantry against General Maxcy
Gregg's brigade on the far left of Jackson's line. For an hour and a
half these South Carolinians held out against overwhelming odds,
but they were finally forced to fall back from the railroad grade
after exhausting their ammunition. Forno's brigade was summoned
and came crashing through the timber at 3:30 P.M. Running at top

12. Allan C. Redwood, "Jackson's 'Foot-Cavalry' at the Second Bull Run," *Battles
and Leaders*, II, 535–36.

speed, the Tigers slammed into General Cuvier Grover's brigade—
one of the commands Forno had faced earlier at Bristoe Station—
and sent it reeling back to the grade in confusion. With the screaming Tigers nipping at their heels, Grover's men stumbled across the
railroad and fell back onto General Nelson Tyler's brigade. Charging
after the confused blue-coats, the Louisianians wildly bayoneted and
clubbed the federals and captured several officers by leaping onto
their horses and dragging them from their mounts. After having
their colors wrenched away by the victorious Tigers, the Yankees
finally withdrew and left the grade to Gregg and Forno.

No sooner had the Confederates rammed new rounds down
their muskets and bellied up to the grade than another blue tide
rolled through the smoky woods and captured a portion of Jackson's line to Forno's right. Forno staunchly held his position and
prevented the Yankees from turning his right flank, thus partially
sealing the break-through. But at the same time another federal
brigade advanced out of the timber, fired a deafening volley, and
battled its way up to the embankment before being broken up by
point-blank volleys of rebel musketry. The Tigers' muskets were
fouling from the rapid fire and almost too hot to handle, but they
received no respite. Still more Union soldiers surged forward over
the shattered bodies of their comrades and planted their battle
flags ten feet from the Tigers before falling back. With ammunition exhausted and casualties mounting, Gregg and Forno were
near the breaking point. Then, one of Gregg's men recalled, "a
shout behind [us] paralyzed us with dread." The Confederates
whirled around in fright to face the expected flank attack but
saw instead Early's brigade charging through the underbrush to
their aid.[13]

In the rear, when he received word of the Union penetration on
Forno's right, Early snatched up the 8th Louisiana, which was gathering ammunition for Forno, put it into line with his Virginians,
and hurried toward the front. Early's charge jolted the Yankees
from the railroad grade on Forno's right and sent them tumbling
back toward their own lines. Out of ammunition and shot to pieces,
Forno's command was in too poor shape to offer Early much aid.
When Early rolled past the Louisianians, Forno was flattened by

13. Richard Wheeler, *Voices of the Civil War* (New York, 1976), 167.

a sharpshooter and taken to the rear, as was Colonel Zebulon York
of the 14th Louisiana. Command of the brigade fell to Colonel
Strong, but by then the fighting on this part of the field was mostly
over. Early, Gregg, and Strong were relieved from duty that night
and withdrew to rest and count their losses. For the Louisianians
this grisly task took most of the night; they had suffered thirty-
seven dead, ninety-four wounded, and four missing in the day's
action.[14]

Far to the right of Forno's position lay Starke's brigade. Placed in
the woods behind a deep cut in the railroad grade, Starke's soldiers
quietly rested until Pope's men charged the Confederates that afternoon and seized a portion of the line to the left of the Louisianians. Galloping up to his brigade, Starke yelled for the men to fix
bayonets and then led the Tigers out to join Colonel Bradley Johnson's Virginia brigade in a counterattack. A chorus of rebel yells rose
from the line as the two brigades charged into the Yankee-filled
woods opposite them. Following Colonel Johnson, who placed his
hat on the tip of his sword and vigorously waved the men onward,
the Louisianians and Virginians collided violently with the first federal line and rolled it back upon a battery of artillery. In the charge,
Johnson's men trampled General Daniel Sickles' color-bearer but
continued on without picking up the trophy. Running close behind
the Virginians, several members of the 1st Louisiana stopped to
pick up the abandoned colors of the famed Excelsior Brigade and
claimed them for the Tigers.[15]

The federal artillerymen furiously rammed their charges and
blasted the rebels when the Confederates halted to dress their line
only one hundred yards from the deadly battery. Such action, recalled one Tiger, "might have been heroic, but it certainly was not
wise," for numerous men were cut down by the artillery fire while
the two brigades regrouped. But when the advance renewed, the
open ground was quickly covered and the Union gunners driven

    14. *Ibid.*, 165–67; *OR*, Vol. XII, Pt. II, 258, 445–46, 555–59, 645–47, 671–72,
710–14, 812; Alexander, *Military Memoirs of a Confederate*, 204, 206; Pope, "Second
Battle of Bull Run," 476–77; Freeman, *Lee's Lieutenants*, II, 116–18, 142; Early,
"Jackson's Campaign," in Pamphlets, Part II, 36, 37, LHAC; anonymous account of
Forno's brigade at the Second Battle of Bull Run, in Reminiscences, Executive and
Army of Northern Virginia, LHAC.
    15. Bartlett, *Military Record of Louisiana*, 31.

from their pieces. Lieutenant Thomas Mills of the 10th Louisiana was the first to reach one gun and claimed it for the Tigers, while Johnson's men overran another. When the Louisianians tried to take their trophy back to the railroad cut, however, they found all the artillery horses were dead. Undaunted, the 15th Louisiana forced fifty federal prisoners into the harnesses and to the cheers of the Confederate line prodded them with bayonets back to the cut.[16]

The morning of August 30 was greeted by the sound of heavy skirmishing and thunderous artillery duels. Although Lee and Longstreet had arrived on the battlefield the day before, Jackson's men continued to bear the brunt of the fighting as Lee held Longstreet's corps back until the most opportune moment. Starke's brigade held the embankment to the right of the railroad cut under orders from Jackson to hold that position at all costs. At 3:00 P.M., wave after wave of blue infantry was hurled against Jackson's line. The Louisianians' position lay along the top of a sharp hill, which the advancing Union lines had to scale to reach the Confederates. The federals remained mostly out of sight until they suddenly popped into view over the crest of the hill only fifty yards from the Tigers. "We cut them down as they threw themselves in sight," wrote Sergeant Edmond Stephens, "until they gave it up for a bad job & retreated, what was left of them." The Tigers managed to beat back every assault on their embankment, but losses were heavy. Lieutenant-Colonels W. H. Spencer of the 10th Louisiana and R. A. Wilkerson of the 14th Louisiana were counted among the dead.[17]

After successfully breaking up three Union assaults, the Tigers found themselves dangerously short of ammunition. Two men of the 9th Louisiana were dispatched to the rear for more, but a fourth Union attack was mounted before they returned. The ensuing clash was "the ugliyst fight of any," claimed Sergeant Stephens. Groping frantically for ammunition among the dead and wounded, the Louisianians were barely able to beat off the determined Yankees, who threw themselves up to the very muzzles of the Tigers'

16. *Confederate Veteran*, II (1894), 13; *OR*, Vol. XII, Pt. II, 664–68; Bartlett, *Military Record of Louisiana*, 4, 31; Durkin (ed.), *Confederate Chaplain*, 15; Stephens to parents, September 7, 1862, in Stephens Collection, NSU.
17. Stephens to parents, September 7, 1862, in Stephens Collection, NSU.

muskets. When the Tigers fired their last round, "the flags of the opposing regiments were almost flapping together," remembered one Alabaman. In desperation Lieutenant-Colonel Michael Nolan shouted for the men to make use of the numerous rocks that lay scattered around the embankment. Sensing that the rebels were at the end of their rope, the Yankees were charging up to the base of the embankment when suddenly fist- and melon-size stones arched out of the smoke that hung over the grade and rained down upon them. "Such a flying of rocks never was seen," claimed one witness, as the Tigers and other nearby Confederates heaved the heavy stones at the surprised federals. Numerous Yankees on the front line were killed by the flying rocks, and many others were badly bruised.[18]

The unexpected "battle of rocks" briefly confused the blue line, but within minutes the Union soldiers were regrouping to finish off the rebels. Fortunately, General D. H. Hill had placed his artillery on a rise to the right of the Louisianians and was able to enfilade the advancing federal lines. Soon after the Tigers began throwing their rocks, the federal charge was broken by Hill's artillery. As the Yankee attack collapsed, Pope's entire line began falling back, and Lee sent Jackson's and Longstreet's corps pressing after them in a massive counterattack.

The Second Battle of Manassas ended with a federal rout just as had the first battle fought along the small stream. But the victory had been costly for Lee, for among his 10,000 casualties were 5 generals and 10 colonels. Starke's share of the bloodletting in the savage fighting around the railroad cut was a staggering 110 dead, 269 wounded, and 6 missing.[19]

The Tigers' fierce defense of the railroad grade became well known throughout the South and made Starke's brigade something of a legend. As the rock-throwing incident was retold over the years, the Louisianians' stand on the bloody embankment was seen as the epitome of southern bravado. Their heroism cannot be denied—the stoic Tigers did, indeed, hold onto their position long

18. Oates, *Fifteenth Alabama*, 144–45.

19. Anonymous letter, November 26, 1862, in Folder 2, Janin Collection, SHC; *OR*, Vol. XII, Pt. II, 666–69, 812, 814; Handerson, *Yankee in Gray*, 98; *Confederate Veteran*, XIV (1906), 498; Chamberlayne (ed.), *Ham Chamberlayne*, 101; Durkin (ed.), *Confederate Chaplain*, 16; Freeman, *Lee's Lieutenants*, II, 142.

after others might have fled, and their reliance on the rocks is well documented. But it was not their strong arms and keen aim that broke up the last federal charge, as is often claimed. The barrage of stones surprised the Yankees, but it is inconceivable that the Union soldiers could have been beaten back with rocks after they had clung so tenaciously to the crest of the hill under deadly volleys of musketry. The fire that finally broke the federal assault came from Longstreet's corps, of which Hill's artillery was a part. When the federals seemed about to break through the Tigers' position on August 30, Longstreet shattered the blue lines with an enfilading fire from Hill's artillery.[20]

Father Sheeran left a vivid description of the effect this artillery had on the Union troops. After walking over the field on September 1, he wrote: "Oh! May I never again witness such scenes as I saw this day. . . . The Yankees in front of the R[ail] R[oad] occupied by the La. troops were lying in heaps. Those in front of the R. R. had something of the appearance of men, for they were killed with rocks or musket balls and with their face to our men. But those scattered throughout the woods and fields presented a shocking spectacle. Some with their brains oozing out; some with the face shot off; others with their bowels protruding; others with shattered limbs. . . . They were almost as black as negroes, bloated and some so decomposed as to be past recognition."[21]

On the same day Sheeran examined the ghastly battlefield, another clash was in progress a short distance away. Hoping to crush Pope, Lee sent Jackson in pursuit of the federal army and forced the Yankees to fight at Ox Hill, near Chantilly. After deploying his divisions, Jackson advanced his line toward the Yankees just as a thunderstorm drenched both armies at 5:00 P.M. In Lawton's division, Colonel Strong's Louisianians and Trimble's brigade held the front line while Lawton's and Early's brigades waited in support. Just as contact was made with the enemy, however, Starke called on Early to move his men to the far left to prevent a threatened flanking movement by the Yankees. Early was filing past the rear of Strong's position when the Louisianians were routed by the Yankees

20. *Confederate Veteran*, II (1894), 13; James Longstreet, "Our March Against Pope," in Johnson and Buel (eds.), *Battles and Leaders*, II, 520, 521; Douglas, *I Rode with Stonewall*, 139–41.

21. Durkin (ed.), *Confederate Chaplain*, 18–19.

and fled through Early's brigade. Early, who had to deploy his men to fight off the federals, felt the rout was attributable to Strong's "being entirely inexperienced on the management of a brigade." He claimed that when the federals charged the Tigers, Strong so confused his command while trying to deploy it that the men could not present a front to the enemy. Others upheld Early's assessment of the brigade's performance, but Father Sheeran claimed a Georgia regiment precipitated the rout after "some *Greenhorn,* acting as Adjutant" came running down the line screaming that they had been flanked. Major Lewis' 8th Louisiana was able to retire in good order, but the rest of the Tigers quickly rallied and returned to the front to hold Early's left.[22]

After a short, sharp clash the federals withdrew and left the field to the rebels. For the Tigers the humiliating encounter was as gory as a major battle. The 5th, 6th, 8th, and 14th Louisiana suffered the highest number of casualties in Jackson's corps. Strong's brigade lost a total of thirty-nine dead, ninety-nine wounded, and three missing. The balls flew so thick in the fight that many men wondered how they came out of the battle uninjured. Charles Behan of the 5th Louisiana had a bullet splinter his musket stock as he took aim, four balls rip through his clothing, and most of his pants blown off by a shell. Nevertheless, he emerged unscathed—only to be killed a short time later at Antietam.[23]

Having forced most of the enemy out of Virginia, Lee made the momentous decision to take the war to the North by invading Maryland. Lee hoped that his ragged army would find badly needed supplies and recruits in this border state and a major victory on northern soil would win the Confederacy sorely needed foreign aid. The Tigers were excited over the prospect of entering virgin territory and anxiously looked forward to liberating Maryland's abundant food supplies. The invasion began on September 5, when the tattered rebels waded across the Potomac River after an exhausting twenty-six-mile march. Although hungry and tired, the men were in good spirits as they sloshed across the shallow river while nearby bands played "Dixie." Since Strong's brigade had not

22. Early, *War Memoirs,* 130; Durkin (ed.), *Confederate Chaplain,* 22–23; *OR,* Vol. XII, Pt. II, 555–59, 647, 714–15; Oates, *Fifteenth Alabama,* 150.
23. William Behan to father, October 14, 1862, in Behan Family Papers, TU; *OR,* Vol. XII, Pt. II, 717.

eaten all day, his Tigers were dismissed briefly on the Maryland side to gather a meager meal from a cornfield before marching on to Frederick.[24]

Huge crowds of curious onlookers lined the road to watch the rebels march by. Some earnestly waved and cheered the brigades, but most were either openly hostile or indifferent toward their "liberators." While passing by one farm, an inebriated member of Starke's brigade discovered one of these fiercely loyal civilians when he stopped at the front gate to secure some bacon from the farm's mistress. During the exchange, the woman became irate and accused the soldier of not paying for the bacon. The entire column was halted by the wailing woman, who declared she was a staunch Unionist "and must not be imposed on by any Confederate rebel." After much haranguing, the woman found that she was mistaken and the Tiger had gained the bacon honestly. After watching this entertaining affair, Father Sheeran stepped forward and admonished the woman to be more careful in her accusations but said the Tigers would forgive her if she gave three hearty cheers for Jeff Davis. Although the woman adamantly refused his suggestion, Father Sheeran claimed her ruffled feathers were somewhat smoothed by the time the brigade departed.[25]

In Frederick the largely sympathetic populace crowded the streets and balconies to watch as the rebels passed through and tore down the town's federal flags. Although most of the Confederates were well behaved, some ran amuck, breaking into liquor stores and roughly handling the townspeople. When a civilian delegation confronted Jackson and accused "foreign" soldiers in his command of being the culprits, the general immediately ordered Starke's brigade to return to town for an identification. Starke, however, was incensed at Jackson's singling out his troops and refused to obey the order unless the other brigades were also sent back. Jackson placed Starke under arrest, but a subsequent investigation proved the perpetrators were actually members of Jackson's own Stonewall Brigade. Starke had earned a reputation as a strict disciplinarian and sometimes arrested his own officers when they failed to keep the men in ranks. He probably refused to obey Jackson's order because

24. *OR*, Vol. XIX, Pt. I, 144–48; Compiled Service Records, War Record Group 109, Microcopy 320, Roll 163, NA; Durkin (ed.), *Confederate Chaplain*, 23–24.
25. Durkin (ed.), *Confederate Chaplain*, 25–26.

he was confident his officers had kept a close watch on the men as they passed through Frederick. Starke was killed before he was brought to trial for defying Jackson, and Jackson's Virginians seem to have escaped any punishment for their deeds.[26]

Once in Maryland, Lee dispatched Jackson's corps to capture the federal garrison at Harpers Ferry while the rest of the army continued its northern penetration. Jackson recrossed the Potomac, encircled Harpers Ferry, and with relative ease forced its surrender on September 15. Although the town yielded 11,000 prisoners, 73 cannon, 13,000 small arms, and an abundance of supplies, Jackson cordoned it off, Captain G. P. Ring complained, "to secure the spoils from the soldiers." This disappointment was compounded by Jackson's exhausting forced marches. "If Jackson keeps on at it," Ring told his wife, "there will be no army left for him to command." Ring's company carried 112 men on its rolls four months earlier but now reported only 11 for duty. One company in the 6th Louisiana had 2 officers commanding 2 men by the time Harpers Ferry fell, and the entire 1st Louisiana had only 121 men.[27]

Although Jackson's envelopment of Harpers Ferry went smoothly, Lee's maneuvers in Maryland hit a snag. General McClellan had been resurrected by Lincoln after Pope's fiasco at Bull Run and was now once again pressing down on Lee with the Army of the Potomac. After a copy of Lee's campaign orders fell into federal hands, McClellan became privy to the Confederates' plans and began chasing Lee with uncharacteristic speed. To meet the Yankee threat, Lee chose to concentrate his forces along Antietam Creek near Sharpsburg and ordered Jackson to rejoin him there. Jackson left A. P. Hill at Harpers Ferry to parole the federal prisoners and put the rest of his corps on the road to Sharpsburg on the night of September 15.

As Jackson was leaving Harpers Ferry, Harry Hays finally rejoined his brigade and led it back across the Potomac into Maryland. Jackson's old division, now under General J. R. Jones, and Ewell's division, commanded by General A. R. Lawton, arrived at

26. *Ibid.*, 27; Bartlett, *Military Record of Louisiana*, 31; Freeman, *Lee's Lieutenants*, II, 159; Pinkowski, *Pills, Pen and Politics*, 42.

27. G. P. Ring to wife, September 15, 1862, typescript copy, in Army of Northern Virginia Papers, Part I, LHAC; *OR*, Vol. XIX, Pt. I, 144–48, 952–55, 965, 1007, 1016; *ibid.*, Pt. II, 669.

Antietam Creek on the afternoon of September 16. For the remainder of the day both armies exchanged skirmish and artillery fire as they jockeyed for positions along the sluggish stream. The heavy cannonading claimed a number of casualties in Starke's brigade before the firing finally subsided after dark.[28]

At dawn of September 17, Jones's division was positioned west of the Hagerstown Road facing north, with Taliaferro and Starke in support of Winder's and Jones's brigades on the front line. Across the road to Jones's right was Lawton's division. Lawton had his own brigade, under Colonel Marcellus Douglass, and Trimble's brigade stretched through a cornfield, supported by Hays's men, who were lying three hundred yards to Douglass' rear. At first light, federal batteries far to the east opened a deadly enfilading fire upon Lawton's brigades as General Hooker's crack division advanced down the Hagerstown Road from the north. When the approaching Yankees came into sight, they were greeted by a chorus of rebel yells that rattled the cornstalks. Seeing the cornfield glistening with polished bayonets, Hooker halted and deployed his artillery to rake the field. "In the time I am writing," he penned, "every stalk of corn in the northern and greater part of the field was cut as closely as could have been done with a knife, and the soldiers lay in rows precisely as they had stood in their ranks a few minutes before. It was never my fortune to witness a more bloody, dismal battlefield."[29]

Lawton's division was cut to pieces as the men lay in the cornfield and open ground to the rear. "I thought, Darling," wrote Ring to his wife, "that I heard at Malvern Hill heavy cannonading, but I was mistaken." The exploding rounds quickly enshrouded the woods and fields with a thick grayish haze, giving the advancing Yankee lines a ghostly appearance as they emerged through the smoke.[30]

By 6:45 A.M., Douglass was dead and his men overpowered and falling back before the advancing enemy. Called on to help, the Ti-

28. James V. Murfin, *The Gleam of Bayonets: The Battle of Antietam and the Maryland Campaign of 1862* (New York, 1965), 209; Stephens to parents, September 21, 1862, in Stephens Collection, NSU; Early, *War Memoirs*, 139; *OR*, Vol. XIX, Pt. I, 967, 1007.

29. *OR*, 218, 955–57; Murfin, *Gleam of Bayonets*, 211–23; Alexander, *Military Memoirs of a Confederate*, 252.

30. G. P. Ring to wife, n.d., in Army of Northern Virginia Papers, Part I, LHAC.

gers quickly crossed the three-hundred-yard gap under a heavy artillery barrage and rushed past Douglass' men to the edge of the cornfield. There the 550 Louisianians collided with General George Hartsuff's brigade and chased it through the corn to Hooker's next line drawn up in a patch of woods. The Tigers advanced to within 250 yards of the timber but were then riddled by musketry and artillery. Colonel Strong and his milky-white steed made easy targets and were quickly knocked down by the whistling balls. Captain Ring rushed to the slain colonel's side to recover his personal effects but in seconds was shot through the knee and arm and caught two bullets in his sword as he knelt beside the body. Henry Richardson, also in the 6th Louisiana, was shot on his horse during the deadly fusilade and was dragged helplessly around the bloody field by his foot until another bullet killed the frightened animal. The Tigers bravely stood their ground for a few minutes but were overwhelmed by the hail of lead and forced to retreat. Hays yelled for the remnants of the brigade to withdraw to a small Dunker church in the rear of Jackson's line. With a shout, the federals stormed across the field and through the corn in pursuit, one Yankee stopping to pick up Colonel Strong's gloves and wave the trophies triumphantly over his head. Just as Hays made it safely to the church, Hood's Texans charged past and drove the Yankees back through the corn once again.

While trying to regroup the command, Hays realized how heavy his losses had been during the thirty-minute engagement. Over 60 percent of the brigade had fallen, with 45 dead, 289 wounded, and 2 missing. Every staff officer and regimental commander had been shot down, including Colonel Gaston Coppens, who was reportedly killed while serving with a Florida regiment. The 6th Louisiana entered the fight with 12 officers and had 5 killed and 7 wounded. Such losses destroyed the brigade's organization, leaving only 40 or so men still grouped around the colors when Hays reached the church. In addition to the Tigers' losses, Douglass' brigade lost more than half of its men and Trimble's suffered a casualty rate of over 30 percent.[31]

31. *OR*, Vol. XIX, Pt. I, 813, 923–28, 974, 978–79; Ring to wife, n.d., in Army of Northern Virginia Papers, Part I, LHAC; *Tensas Gazette*, October 24, 1935, in Melrose Scrapbook 231, NSU; Wallace, "Coppens' Louisiana Zouaves," 280; William A. Frassanito, *Antietam: The Photographic Legacy of America's Bloodiest Day* (New York,

Starke's brigade was called into action along the Hagerstown
Road the same time as Hays. From daybreak until 6:45 A.M., these
Tigers lay in reserve but were subjected to the same artillery barrage that raked Hays's men. One shell instantly killed the 5th Louisiana's Charles Behan on this his eighteenth birthday, and another
put General Jones out of action after it exploded directly over his
head. Starke then turned his brigade over to Colonel Stafford and
took command of the division just as Winder's and Jones's brigades
began falling back before Hooker's juggernaut. Under a furious
fire of musketry, Stafford and Taliaferro advanced to take the place
of these two shattered brigades. Although directing the actions of
the entire division, Starke grabbed the Tigers' flag and led the brigade out toward the enemy. Sweeping down the west side of the
road, the gray line quickly moved through a patch of woods and
charged into the Yankee brigades. A terrific roar filled the air as each
side cut loose with long, rolling volleys of thunderous musketry.
Colonel Jesse M. Williams of the 2d Louisiana fell badly wounded
with a bullet through his chest, and Starke was hit almost simultaneously with three balls that sent him tumbling from his horse mortally
wounded. Despite Starke's death, the brigade pushed the federals
across the road and charged after them through a "murderous fire
which thinned our ranks at every step."[32]

After helping crush Hays's brigade, General John Gibbon's "Iron
Brigade," which had stood up to Starke at Groveton, made a stand
along the eastern side of the road and pumped a deadly fire into
the Tigers' right flank. Stafford immediately wheeled the brigade
to the right to face this new menace. Scarcely fifty yards apart, blue
and gray faced each other across the chest-high rail fences that
lined the narrow road and traded volleys that splintered and mutilated both fence and men. Two regiments of federal sharpshooters
joined in the fight and began picking apart Stafford's left flank
while a Union battery unlimbered seventy-five yards from the road

---

1978), 103, 112–15, 119–20; Murfin, *Gleam of Bayonets*, 223–41; Early, *War Memoirs*,
150, 152; Alexander, *Military Memoirs of a Confederate*, 252, 254; John Bell Hood,
*Advance and Retreat: Personal Experiences in the United States and Confederate States Ar-
mies*, ed. Richard N. Current (1880; rpr. Bloomington, 1959), 42–43; Milo M.
Quaife (ed.), *From the Cannon's Mouth: The Civil War Letters of General Alpheus S.
Williams* (Detroit, 1959), 130; Dawes, *Sixth Wisconsin*, 95.

32. *OR*, Vol. XIX, Pt. I, 1017.

and shattered the gray line with canister. Still, Stafford's men stood under this murderous fire for fifteen minutes before the Virginia brigades on their left "run and left our Brigade alone." Within minutes, the federals poured into the gap created by the Virginians' retreat and forced the Tigers to pull back. Scores of dead and wounded had to be left jumbled up along the pike, but the Louisianians remained defiant, fighting stubbornly as they sullenly retired toward the Dunker church.[33]

At the church Stafford was forced to relinquish command of the brigade because he had received a painful foot bruise from shell fragments. Choosing a successor was a problem, for every field officer in the command had been hit. Colonel Edmund Pendleton finally took over even though his ankle had been badly bruised when a shell passed between his legs. The brigade's losses came to 81 dead, 189 wounded, and 17 missing. Some companies almost ceased to exist. Sergeant Stephens reported that the 9th Louisiana "is almost destroyed." The regiment's Bienville Blues lost 20 of 32 men, and a company from Claiborne Parish had 10 killed and 8 wounded among its 18 members.[34]

In less than an hour both Louisiana brigades had been shattered by McClellan's tough Yankees. While reforming around the Dunker church, some Tigers joined Early's brigade when it later rushed into the battle. But most of the Louisiana survivors were too scattered and exhausted to rejoin the fray. The battle soon ended on this part of the field, as the fighting drifted further to the south. The Tigers had been instrumental in holding off Hooker's vicious attacks but had paid a heavy price. The carnage along the Hagerstown Road, where Starke's brigade traded volleys with the Yankees, was particularly horrifying. One Yankee wrote that "the piles of dead . . . were frightful" and added that after the battle, a path had

33. Stephens to parents, September 21, 1862, in Stephens Collection, NSU; Frassanito, *Antietam*, 126–29, 131–39; *OR*, Vol. XIX, Pt. I, 230, 233, 1008, 1012–13, 1016–18; Dawes, *Sixth Wisconsin*, 87–92; Henry Kyd Douglas, "Stonewall Jackson in Maryland," in Johnson and Buel (eds.), *Battles and Leaders*, II, 628; C. A. Stevens, *Berdan's United States Sharpshooters in the Army of the Potomac, 1861–1865* (St. Paul, 1892), 202–203; Worsham, *One of Jackson's Foot Cavalry*, 87; Daugherty, "W. E. Moore in the Civil War," in Moore Papers, UT.

34. *OR*, Vol. XIX, Pt. I, 813, 1014–18; Stephens to parents, September 21, 1862, in Stephens Collection, NSU; Behan to father, October 14, 1862, in Behan Papers, TU.

to be made through the road by dragging the bodies off it and placing them along the fences.[35]

Although the terrific battle waged along Antietam Creek ended in a draw, Lee withdrew back into Virginia on September 19 because his army was too decimated to continue the invasion. Lee's 10,291 casualties suffered in the campaign again made it necessary to reorganize a number of his brigades. Colonel Francis T. Nicholls, temporarily on duty in Texas, was promoted to brigadier-general and succeeded Starke as commander of the 2d Louisiana Brigade, although Colonel Pendleton led the brigade until Nicholls rejoined his command in January, 1863. In addition, the 9th and 14th Louisiana exchanged places within the two Louisiana brigades, although the reasons why are unclear. The seventeen men remaining in Coppens' Battalion were redesignated as the Confederate States Zouaves Battalion and were detached for garrison duties for the remainder of the war.[36]

The two Louisiana brigades were now mere skeletons of their former selves. On September 22, for example, Hays's brigade had only 693 officers and men present for duty, with 480 absent without leave and 1,401 on sick or wounded furlough. So many noncommissioned officers absented themselves for "frivolous excuses" in Colonel Penn's 7th Louisiana that he issued orders that any noncom who left his post without permission would be reduced to the ranks. By the middle of October the number present for duty in Hays's brigade increased to around 1,500, but an astonishing 2,310 men were listed as being absent sick or wounded. The Louisiana brigades were allowed a few months' rest to recuperate from the bloody summer's campaigns, but the cold winds that were beginning to howl through the rebel camps ushered in new hardships.[37]

35. Dawes, *Sixth Wisconsin*, 94.

36. *OR*, Vol. XIX, Pt. II, 669, 683–84; Wallace, "Coppens' Louisiana Zouaves," 280–82; Lathrop (ed.), "Autobiography of Francis T. Nicholls," 251.

37. Trimonthly report of Ewell's division, in General Jubal A. Early Papers, 1861–1865, War Record Group 109, Entry 118, NA; Louisiana Troops, 7th Regiment Orderly Book, 1862–64, NYPL.

THE SCOURGE OF THE CONFEDERACY
Coppens' Louisiana Zouaves
Courtesy Southern Historical Collection

WHARF RATS OF WHEAT'S TIGER BATTALION
Courtesy Library of Congress

COLONEL CHARLES D. DREUX
Louisiana's first casualty
Courtesy Confederate Memorial Museum

GENERAL RICHARD TAYLOR
Jackson's right-hand man in the Shenandoah Valley
Courtesy Louisiana Office of State Parks, Mansfield State Commemorative Area

HOLDING THE LINE WITH ROCKS
Starke's Louisiana Brigade at Second Manassas
From R. U. Johnson and C. C. Buel (eds.), *Battles and Leaders
of the Civil War*

ANTIETAM'S DARK AND DISMAL FIELD
Louisiana dead of Starke's Brigade
Courtesy Library of Congress

GENERAL HARRY T. HAYS
He would become one of Lee's premier lieutenants.
Courtesy Confederate Memorial Museum

GENERAL LEROY A. STAFFORD
One of three commanders to die while leading the
Second Louisiana Brigade
Courtesy Confederate Memorial Museum

Chapter VII

FIGHTING THE GOOD FIGHT

Following the Maryland campaign the Army of Northern Virginia destroyed the Baltimore and Ohio Railroad near Martinsburg and then settled in for a long-needed rest. Father Sheeran reported that Nicholls' brigade was in excellent condition that fall and winter as many of the wounded and stragglers returned to camp. In addition, ranks left vacant from the past five months of campaigning began to be filled with conscripts. Hays's brigade, however, was in poor shape to meet the chilling October winds. "The Boys are shivering & huvering around their little chunk fires," wrote Sergeant Stephens. "Though as meny as black birds, we are sadly in need of clothing & Piticularly in Blankets & Shoes." So few men could afford the five-dollar "Confederate shoes" sold by the regimental quartermaster that by November, Stephens claimed, "our whole Army is very near Shoeless."[1]

Arms and food were in as short supply as shoes among Hays's Tigers. Hays reported that during the first week of November only 39 of his 783 men were fully equipped, with 344 having only their weapons and 400 completely unarmed. The brigade's supplies were also woefully inadequate; beef and flour were about the only commodities available. In November the brigade's rations consisted of ten pounds of wheat per one hundred men issued once a week and only a small quantity of beef handed out the other six days. When the brigade was stationed in the Valley for awhile, James Carrington noted that it was impossible to get any bacon. "Nothing can

1. Edmond Stephens to brother, October 12, 1862, and Stephens to sister, November 27, 1862, in Stephens Collection, NSU; Clothing Account, 7th Regiment of Louisiana Volunteers, 1862, War Record Group 109, Chap. V, Vol. 205, NA; Theodore A. Newell to uncle, December 7, 1862, in Box 1, Folder 2, Newell Papers, LSU; Durkin (ed.), *Confederate Chaplain*, 33–34; Handerson, *Yankee in Gray*, 99; Bartlett, *Military Record of Louisiana*, 44.

be bought in this country except sometimes a chicken for which one dollar is the price," he complained. Carrington proudly reported that he did succeed in acquiring nineteen pounds of honey for his company, but at a cost of nineteen dollars. "So you see," he wrote, "how much of our confederate 'money' it took to get anything in this part of the state."[2]

Conditions in Hays's brigade worsened with the weather. For most of the winter of 1862–1863 the Louisianians had no shelter with which to ward off the biting Virginia cold. While at Front Royal Hays's men burrowed into the ground like animals, using blankets and tent flies to cover the holes they dubbed "Camp Hole in the Ground." On December 20, 1862, a member of the 8th Louisiana froze to death after getting drunk and lying exposed to the elements all night.

Food continued to be in short supply as well. By early 1863 weekly rations ranged from one and three-quarter pounds of meat for some men, to one-third pound of bacon, one and one-eighth pounds of flour, and three ounces of sugar for others. Colonel Pendleton wrote that coffee cost him $4.75 per pound and prices for all goods were so high that his food bill was $100 per month. But apparently Pendleton ate rather well, for Captain Thomas G. Morgan of the 7th Louisiana tallied his food bill for April, 1862, at $12.52. With this he purchased six and a half pints of beef, fourteen and a half pints of bacon, fifty-four pints of flour, six pints of rice, nine pints of sugar, two pints of salt, three pints of molasses, and three pints of peas. Lowly privates, of course, could ill afford extra food at any price and were forced to supplement their diets by poaching on neighboring farms.[3]

2. James McDowell Carrington to Eliza Henry Carrington, October 16, 1862, in Carrington Family Papers, VHS; Memorandum from Major W. F. Hawks to Major David F. Boyd, November 7, 1862, in Folder 1, David F. Boyd Selected Papers, LSU; Requisition Papers in Early Papers, War Record Group 109, Entry 118, NA.

3. Durkin (ed.), *Confederate Chaplain*, 37–38; Compiled Service Records, War Record Group 109, Microcopy 320, Roll 163, NA; Bound Volume 8 in Association of the Army of Northern Virginia, LHAC; Major Francis Rawles to Lieutenant Alex Marks, December 10, 1862, in MC-3/MSS. 3, Museum of the Confederacy; Edmund Pendleton to unknown, December 9, 1862, *ibid.*; Pendleton to daughter, February 6, 1863, in Coles Collection, SHC; Stephens to parents, February 25, 1863, in Stephens Collection, NSU; William J. Seymour, "Private Journal During the Confederate War," in Seymour Papers, UM.

The deplorable conditions in Hays's brigade are clearly illustrated in the inspection reports of Hays's assistant adjutant general, John H. New. His inspection for January 10, 1863, lists discipline as "good" in the 5th and 9th Louisiana but "poor" in the 6th, 7th, and 8th regiments. The men's competence in drilling was little better. The 6th and 7th regiments were rated moderately good, the 9th "tolerable," the 8th "miserable," and the 5th was excused from drill for lack of shoes. This shoe shortage was critical among all the commands—the 9th Louisiana listed 103 men without them on January 30—as was the need for underclothing and blankets. No tents were available for a hospital, and brigade prisoners were detained in the open air because there was no guardhouse. The men's weapons were described as being in "sad" condition with hardly any bayonets in camp. There were "not more than three camp kettles" in the entire brigade with which to cook the meager rations, and some companies had only one skillet to share among all the men. To cap off his gloomy report, New exclaimed, "There is a painful apathy and indifference among company officers, [who] understand a few stereotyped movements in the Battalion drill, [but] take them out of them and they are at Sea."[4]

New was so desperate to find relief for the brigade that he wrote Louisiana Representative John Perkins in January, 1863, to ask his help in securing supplies for the men. Of the fifteen hundred men in the brigade, New claimed that four hundred had no footwear whatever and many were without blankets. "There are some," he added, "without a particle of underclothing, having neither shirts, drawers, nor socks; while overcoats, from their rarity, are objects of curiosity." New's plea helped improve conditions, for an order of a thousand shoes was finally forwarded to Hays from the quartermaster in Richmond. Confederate officials, however, blamed the army, not themselves, for the brigade's condition, stating that all requisitions sent to Richmond from the army had been filled.[5]

Apparently Hays and New made a determined effort to improve conditions within the brigade, for each succeeding inspection showed clear gains. A guard tent was erected by February 28 to house the two officers and twenty-one men under arrest, and a few

4. Inspection report by John H. New, January 10, 1863, in Early Papers, War Record Group 109, Entry 118, NA.
5. *OR*, XXI, 1097–99.

log huts were constructed by winter's end. Additional shoes and blankets eventually arrived, and discipline among the officers and men improved as the weather warmed and daily drills were resumed.[6]

Such cruel conditions as were tolerated during the fall and winter of 1862–1863 had a demoralizing effect on the Tigers. Between September 1 and November 23, 1862, nine men deserted from company H of the 15th Louisiana, and Colonel Pendleton claimed that nearly half of Nicholls' brigade was absent without leave in Richmond that December. To make up the losses incurred by this desertion and by battle casualties, both Louisiana brigades became heavily engaged in recruiting that winter. In early 1863, Colonels Waggaman and Forno were dispatched to Louisiana and Mobile, respectively, to gather recruits, and the government unsuccessfully attempted to persuade Lee to send one of the brigades to Louisiana to collect badly needed replacements. Numerous attempts were made to recruit members from Louisiana and Virginia for the Tiger brigades during the war, but the veterans generally frowned on such replacements. "The conscripts of La.," wrote Thomas Newell, "has got a bad name in Virginia, especially among the troops. They say that they run in Bull Run style as soon as attacked."[7]

The Tigers naturally searched for ways to make the dreary winter camps more bearable. Some played in the snow, skated on ice, or turned to religion—others stole. This latter vice became so prevalent in Hays's brigade that on December 20, the following order was issued:

> The Brig. Genl. comdg. painfully regrets having to call the attention of the officers and men of this command to the frequent occurrence of late of theft and robberies committed within the limits of this camp upon unoffending citizens. He had hoped that there was sufficient pride among the soldiers from Louisiana to put down any such disgraceful acts that . . . bring reproach, if not disgrace, on all. . . . The Brig. Genl. comdg. therefore wishes it distinctly understood that the

6. Inspection reports by John H. New, January 17, 30, February 28, March 31, 1863, in Early Papers, War Record Group 109, Entry 118, NA; Seymour, "Journal," in Seymour Papers, UM; Hotchkiss, *Make Me a Map of the Valley*, 135.

7. Newell to uncle, December 7, 1862, in Newell Papers, LSU; Buckley, *A Frenchman, a Chaplain, a Rebel*, 57; *OR*, XXXI, 1093; *ibid.*, Series IV, Vol. II, 416.

next instance of robbing brought before his attention committed by any member of this Brigade will be punished with the severest penalty known to military law.[8]

The Tigers' persistent preying upon the civilian populace brought numerous delegations of irate citizens to General Early's tent because he had temporary command of Ewell's division. Early, in turn, constantly pestered Hays to stop the depredations and probably provoked him to issue the above order. But Hays apparently did not believe his men were responsible for all the crimes attributed to them and finally exploded over Early's unrelenting accusations. Calling his colonels to his tent, Hays told them he was drawing up a petition to send to Lee asking that the Louisiana Brigade be transferred out of Early's command. Colonels William Monaghan, Leroy Stafford, and Trevanion Lewis signed the document with Hays, but Davidson Penn, a native of Virginia and an old friend of Early's, refused to do so.

Hays sent the petition to Early and asked that it be forwarded to Jackson and Lee. Early's famous temper erupted, however, and he ordered the discontented Tigers to his quarters. Eyeing the group sternly as they sat silently around him, Early said, "Gentlemen, this is a most remarkable document that I have had the honor to receive from you; but I am glad to see there is one man of sense among you—Penn didn't sign it." He then cited example after example of the Tigers' misdeeds that had disgraced his division. His voice rising, Early exclaimed that he had patiently borne all of their misbehavior and now was being insulted by a petition asking him to give up his Tigers. Finally, in a shrill voice, he cried, "Who do you think would have such a damn pack of thieves but me? If you can find any Major General in this army such a damn fool as to take you fellows, you may go!" A tense quiet pervaded the tent as the words sank in. Then the keen-witted Stafford exploded in laughter over the ridiculous scene. The tension was broken, and all were soon laughing at themselves over drinks from Early's jug.[9]

The two Louisiana brigades were never heavily engaged with the enemy that fall and winter of 1862–1863. Both were kept in re-

8. Order by General Harry T. Hays, December 30, 1862, in Louisiana Troops, 7th Regiment Orderly Book, NYPL.

9. New Orleans *Times-Democrat*, in Reminiscences Division, n.d., Confederate Veteran Papers, DU.

serve during the December battle at Fredericksburg, although Hays did lose fifty-four men and Pendleton thirty-seven from heavy Union shelling. Remaining in camp along the Rappahannock after the battle, the Tigers were constantly reminded of the grim reality of war. From Hamilton's Crossing, Sergeant Stephens wrote, "It is no trouble to see a half buried Yankee with one arm, leg or head sticking out from under the dirt and any quantity of dead horses." Such sights were so common, Stephens claimed, that the men paid no more attention to them than if "they were so many chunks." [10]

As the weather warmed and the Rappahannock became free of ice, the Tigers frequently engaged in friendly trade with the federals across the river. Truces were arranged while hand-carved boats laden with tobacco and Richmond newspapers—"the only articles of traffic that our poor fellows possessed"—were sailed to the northern bank in exchange for coffee, sugar, and tea. One Tiger even managed to get a letter delivered home in occupied Louisiana by sending it over for a Yankee to mail. The only drawback to such illicit fraternizing was the discovery that the federals were not too adept at sailing and often the return cargo drifted downstream out of sight. [11]

A number of Tigers, like the 9th Louisiana's Ezra Denson, accepted the Yankees' invitation to cross the river for a visit. Upon his return, Denson told his messmates that the Yankees hailed from the old Northwest and were as tired of the war as the Louisianians. "They expressed a hearty desire to witness its termination," Stephens reported Denson as saying, "for they were disgusted, discouraged and dissatisfied and could not digest old Lincoln's actions calling for negro troops. They said they would be willing to meet us in the middle of the river . . . and shake hands with us and never fire another gun." [12]

A New York native in the 6th Louisiana learned that the federal regiment across the river contained some old acquaintances and swam over to see them. Shocked at his emaciated figure, his old

10. Stephens to parents, March 17, 1863, in Stephens Collection, NSU; *OR*, XXI, 674–75, 686–88.

11. Seymour, "Journal," in Seymour Papers, UM; Handerson, *Yankee in Gray*, 34; Durkin (ed.), *Confederate Chaplain*, 41; Charles Moore, Jr., Diary, March 9, 1863, in LHAC.

12. Stephens to parents, March 17, 1863, in Stephens Collection, NSU.

friends urged him to desert and stay with them. William Seymour, the late colonel's son, who was serving as a volunteer aide to Hays, described what happened next:

> The ragged, half-starved "Rebel" drew himself proudly up, his eyes flashing and face all aglow with patriotic fervor, and contemptuously spurned the dishonorable offer; he told his tempters, that he had oftentimes braved danger and death side by side with those dirty, ragged "rebs" over the River, and shared with them the exposure and suffering of the march and privations of the camp—was fully aware of the supreme condition of the Federal troops; but that he would not desert his colors for all the gold that the Federal Government could command. He declared that he had embarked in what he considered a righteous cause, and if it would be the will of God, he would die fighting for it.[13]

Winter slowly released its cold grip on the Virginia countryside, and spring ushered in a new campaign season. General Joseph Hooker, the new commander of the Army of the Potomac, was laying a clever plan to destroy Lee's army. By pushing part of his force across the river in Lee's front at Fredericksburg, he would create a diversion while the bulk of the Union army crossed the Rappahannock far upstream and swept into Lee's rear. Lee would then be cut off from Richmond and forced to fight on ground of Hooker's choosing. On April 29, General John Sedgwick's corps began crossing the river at Fredericksburg, but Lee discovered Hooker's real purpose when Confederate cavalry reported the Union maneuver upstream. Realizing Sedgwick was only a decoy, Lee left Early's division and General William Barksdale's brigade to watch him while the rest of the army marched to meet Hooker at Chancellorsville.

Fighting broke out on May 1 as Lee and Hooker collided in the Wilderness, an immense area of dense thickets that surrounded the small hamlet of Chancellorsville. Neither side won an advantage this first day, but the Confederates discovered Hooker's right flank to be unprotected and open to attack. In a historic conference, Lee and Jackson agreed to leave the divisions of McLaws and Anderson along Hooker's front while Jackson took his entire corps on a circuitous route to the left to strike the federal flank.

It took most of May 2 for Jackson's men to make the long march

13. Seymour, "Journal," in Seymour Papers.

around to the Yankee right, but his divisions were finally in line by 6:00 P.M. Jackson deployed his corps in three lines, with Gen. R. E. Rodes's division in front, General Raleigh Colston, who now commanded Jackson's old division, second in line, and A. P. Hill in reserve. Advancing through dense thickets of blackjack oak, the rebel lines were guided by the Orange Turnpike on their right until they suddenly burst out of the woods onto the unguarded federal flank. The Germans of General Oliver O. Howard's corps were completely surprised and routed by Jackson's charging men. For two miles the federals fled before the onslaught, unable to make any lasting stand against the rebels until the federal artillery around the Chancellor House was reached. There the Yankees put up a stubborn fight until darkness ended the battle.

The three Confederate battle lines had merged into one during the headlong charge and became a confused mass of men milling about on the Orange Turnpike when the fighting ended. As their officers tried to sort them out that night, a Union battery suddenly opened fire eighty yards down the pike. Chaos reigned as the screaming shells raked the road. Men and horses were blown apart, soldiers panicked and began firing wildly, and riderless horses galloped blindly through the regiments. One Virginian recalled that the artillery fire was "the most terrific and destructive shelling that we were subjected to during the war. We could hear someone scream out every second in the agonies of death."[14] Men screamed, sobbed, and prayed aloud as the deafening shells continued to explode all around. Lieutenant-Colonel Ross E. Burke managed to get the men of his 2nd Louisiana to lie on the ground where they were relatively safe from the wild shooting, but others were not so fortunate. Nicholls spurred his horse and was trying desperately to bring order to his confused brigade when a solid shot ripped through his mount's abdomen and tore off Nicholls' left foot. The general managed to throw himself free from his horse when it collapsed in agony, but he lay unnoticed in the littered road while shells whizzed overhead.

When the barrage finally lifted, a search was conducted for the wounded. A half hour after being hit, Nicholls was found by an ambulance crew, but they left him for dead upon noticing his empty left sleeve and missing foot. Fearing he would soon bleed to death,

14. Casler, *Four Years in the Stonewall Brigade*, 146–47.

Nicholls groped in the darkness for his mutilated leg but "found to my utter surprise that the wound did not bleed at all." After a long wait, he was finally discovered by some Tigers, who wrapped him in a blanket and carried him to the rear. Having seen him badly wounded in the only two battles in which he participated, many men began to believe that Nicholls was jinxed. He recovered from this last wound but never returned to the brigade, serving instead in various administrative positions for the remainder of the war. After the war, when Nicholls embarked on a political career, his battle scars proved helpful in acquiring the veterans' votes. Nicholls ultimately became the governor of Louisiana, but because of his missing left arm and leg, it was said in jest that he was "too one sided for a judge." [15]

Although the day's fight had gone extremely well for the Confederates, the loss in field grade officers was high. Besides Nicholls, Hill and Jackson were both wounded, mistakenly shot by their own men at about the same time Nicholls lost his foot. General J. E. B. Stuart took command of Lee's left wing and realigned the divisions to continue the push at daybreak. Colonel Jesse M. Williams, having recovered from the chest wound he received at Antietam, replaced Nicholls as the brigade was put on the far left of Colston's line.

At dawn of Sunday, May 3, Stuart had Hill's division in front, followed by Colston and Rodes. Advancing at 6:00 A.M., Hill quickly made contact with the enemy and brought on a roaring battle. Colston's division was soon called for and advanced past Hill's bloodied men until it, too, was caught in a terrific fire from the Union lines massed around Chancellor's Hill. On the far left, Williams' men were hotly engaged in a close-quarter fight with the 7th New Jersey. Six color-bearers of the 10th Louisiana were killed in the smoke-filled thicket, and the 1st Louisiana's flag was seized by the Yankees when the Union soldiers flanked the Tigers and forced them to fall back two hundred yards to a line of abandoned federal works. Fortunately, the Yankees failed to press their advantage and allowed Williams time to realign his men before launching their next attack.

The Louisianians had just settled in behind their works when they caught glimpses of blue uniforms easing toward them through the underbrush. The woods seemed to explode in smoke and fire

15. Lathrop (ed.), "Autobiography of Francis T. Nicholls," 252; Nichols, "Notes on Francis T. Nicholls," 308–309; Warner, *Generals in Gray*, 224–25.

as the Tigers shot into the thicket and were immediately answered by heavy volleys from the Yankees. The Yankees' musket fire began arching around the Tigers' left as the enemy tried to flank them, but the maneuver was matched by the 2d Louisiana, which protected the brigade's left flank by bending back perpendicular to the main line. The federals were then content to keep their distance and trade long-range volleys with the Tigers. The rapid fire quickly depleted Williams' ammunition, and the brigade was giving way when General A. H. Colquitt's brigade came running through the woods to assist the Louisianians. Despite their lack of ammunition, the Tigers surged forward with Colquitt's men against General Erastus Tyler's Union brigade. The Pennsylvanians put up a staunch defense, killing one Tiger when he grabbed a federal battle flag and shooting off Colonel Pendleton's finger. But they were soon forced back through the forest, which by now was engulfed in brush fires caused by the flaming muskets.

After forcing back Tyler's men, the Tigers were pulled out of line and sent to the rear to replenish their cartridge boxes and eat lunch. But only a few hours of rest were allowed before the division was ordered to advance once again that afternoon. Placed on the far left, Williams found his objective in the assault to be an infantry-supported battery of twelve guns posted atop a hill to his front. When ordered to charge, the brigade gamely leaped forward but was greeted by murderous rounds of artillery fire when it emerged into a field three hundred yards from the enemy lines. "Exposed to a perfect storm of grape and shells," the 10th Louisiana was particularly hard hit, losing fifty men in less than ten minutes and having its sixth color-bearer of the day killed. The regiment's unpopular colonel, John M. Legett, was ripped open by one shell that almost tore him in half. But Legett lived long enough to ask his men for forgiveness of his shortcomings and to receive their assurances that they held no ill-will against him. The decimated regiment began to falter under the deadly fire and would have broken and run if not for the courageous efforts of Colston and the regimental officers who held the men in line. By then, however, Williams realized that to hold his position was suicidal and quickly ordered the brigade to pull back into the woods and entrench.[16]

16. OR, Vol. XXV, Pt. I, 795–801, 943–44, 961–62, 986, 1003–1009, 1037–41; Buckley, A Frenchman, a Chaplain, a Rebel, 173–74, 186; Battle reports of the 1st, 2d, 10th, and 14th Louisiana Volunteers, in Folder 2, Raleigh E. Colston Collection,

After scratching out some makeshift earthworks, the Louisianians examined their clothing and realized just how fierce the federal musketry had been. Charles and J. M. Batchelor both counted five holes in their clothing and skin. The latter brother's belt buckle saved him from death when it flattened a minié ball, but other bullets clipped him on the throat, cheek, and hand. Charles was struck in the back by grape shot during the withdrawal, but after passing through his knapsack the spent ball did no damage. Other Tigers poked fingers through similar holes in their blanket rolls and slouch hats and marveled at their good fortune.[17]

The Tigers remained in their works and skirmished with the federals throughout the night of May 3 and all of May 4. During this lull, the smoke cleared from the woods and they had a chance to view the ghastly fate of many of their comrades. One Virginian who walked through the thickets where the Louisianians faced Tyler's brigade wrote years later:

> I witnessed the most horrible sight my eyes ever beheld. . . . The scene beggers description. The dead and badly wounded from both sides were lying where they fell. The woods, taking fire that night from the shells, burnt rapidly and roasted the wounded men alive. As we went to bury them we could see where they had tried to keep the fire from them by scratching the leaves away as far as they could reach. But it availed not; they were burnt to a crisp. The only way we could tell to which army they belonged was by turning them over and examining their clothing where they lay close to the ground. . . . It was the most sickening sight I ever saw during the war.[18]

Father Sheeran went over the entire eight miles of battle lines and claimed that the area occupied by the Tigers "was the most shocking of all." Raging fires "for nearly half a mile burned the dead bodies and many of the wounded to a crisp."[19]

While the 2d Louisiana Brigade fought its way through the thickets around Chancellorsville, Hays's brigade was holding the precarious line at Fredericksburg. Hays's men were first called to action

SHC; anonymous obituary of Edmund Pendleton in Coles Collection, SHC; Bartlett, *Military Record of Louisiana*, 25, 45; Bound Volume 2 in Association of the Army of Northern Virginia, LHAC; *Southern Historical Society Papers*, n.s., II (1915), 87; Laurence, "North Louisiana Tiger," 145.

17. J. M. Batchelor to father, June 22, 1863, in Folder 6, Batchelor Papers, LSU.
18. Casler, *Four Years in the Stonewall Brigade*, 151.
19. Durkin (ed.), *Confederate Chaplain*, 43–44.

in the predawn twilight of April 29, when Sedgwick's corps began laying pontoon bridges across the Rappahannock in a dense fog. While the rest of the brigade filed into trenches a mile from the river, Colonel William Monaghan took his 6th Louisiana out to the water's edge to aid the 13th Georgia in delaying the crossing. The Georgians, however, soon exhausted their ammunition and left the Tigers to dispute the landing alone. As the skirmish fire increased, Jackson rode out to Monaghan's position to check on the situation. The federal balls whistled through the air, and the Tigers feared the general would be hit, but after calmly looking over the river he cased his binoculars and rode back to the main line unhurt.

Forno's 5th Louisiana was soon sent in alongside Monaghan, and together they hotly contested the laying of the bridges. By 10:00 A.M. the Tigers' wounded filled the rifle pits and eighteen-year-old Nathan Cunningham, color-bearer of the 5th Louisiana, volunteered to return to the rear to bring back fresh water for them. As he departed, the federals effected a landing below the Tigers and moved into their rear. The order to withdraw was yelled over the roaring battle, but the Tigers on the line's extreme ends failed to hear it and remained in the trenches long after the others fell back. Young Cunningham was racing back to the river with his canteens when he met his comrades heading for the rear. When told of the withdrawal, Cunningham found that no one had thought to bring the regiment's flag, which he had left behind. Ignoring his friends' advice, Cunningham ran to the rifle pits, passed the canteens to the wounded, and retrieved his colors. Turning to go back, he found his path blocked by a company of federals who demanded that he surrender. But when the young soldier said he could never give up as long as he carried the regiment's flag, the impressed Union officer waved down his men's muskets and allowed the plucky youngster to continue on his way.[20]

The Tigers lost eighty-nine men along the river but had delayed for two hours the three thousand federals who led the crossing. The Louisianians spent the next two days strengthening their own works and watching the federals "working like beavers on their fortifications." Little firing was done except for opposing batteries that

20. Letter from anonymous Louisianian, n.d., published in an unidentified Mobile newspaper, in Lawrence L. Hewitt Private Collection, Independence, La.

dueled with one another across the river. The only Louisiana casualties came from one federal shell that exploded in the 9th Louisiana's area, knocking two men out with wounds, and a Confederate round that burst prematurely over the regiment and injured three more men.[21]

On May 1, Lee began shifting most of his forces toward Chancellorsville, leaving Early to occupy several miles of works on the hills overlooking Fredericksburg. For two days the thin Confederate line kept up a brave front by constantly shifting units, cheering nonexisting reinforcements, and lighting thousands of campfires at night. On May 2, Hays's brigade was split, with the 6th and 9th Louisiana placed near Barksdale's brigade fronting Fredericksburg, while the 5th, 7th, and 8th regiments dug in on the right at Hamilton's Crossing. As the sun slowly set, a constant rumble could be heard toward Chancellorsville. But at dusk the sound of the distant battle was drowned out by a lively skirmish that developed between the 7th Louisiana and a federal unit.[22]

By daylight of May 3, Early's eight-mile line was manned by one soldier spaced every twenty feet. Soon after dawn, Barksdale reported that the Yankees were moving out of town toward his position on Marye's Heights. To shore up this threatened point, Early ordered Hays to double-quick his men from Hamilton's Crossing to the Confederate left. Following the trench line, the Tigers began the eight-mile jaunt as the sun ushered in a warm spring day. Soon scores of men began falling out from exhaustion and heat stroke, and others were struck down by federal shells that peppered the column when it became visible to the Union gunners across the river. As the brigade passed behind Barksdale's command, the 6th Louisiana was dropped off to take up a position on the Mississippians' right. Only two hundred men were still with Hays when he finally reached the Confederate left. "Breathless, drenched with perspiration and utterly fagged-out," the small band collapsed in the rifle pits just as the federal attack was launched.[23]

21. Seymour, "Journal," in Seymour Papers, UM.

22. *Ibid.;* Charles Moore, Jr., Diary, April 29–May 2, 1863, LHAC; *OR,* Vol. XXV, Pt. I, 1000–1002; Egidius Smulders to Henry B. Kelley, March, 187[?], in Egidius Smulders Papers, Confederate Personnel, LHAC; Compiled Service Records, War Record Group 109, Microcopy 320, Roll 163, NA.

23. Handerson, *Yankee in Gray,* 55.

From atop their hill, the Tigers had a spectacular view of the blue lines as they swept up the slope of Marye's Heights and were broken up against the famous stone wall. The brigade watched intently as the smoke boiled up above the battle and the shouts and firing of the combatants floated over the field. Twice the Union lines were cut down before the wall, but on the third try they rolled in without stopping and clubbed Barksdale's men from behind it. Suddenly the entire Confederate line collapsed. Barksdale's Mississippians were driven up the slope, and Monaghan's Tigers were forced to abandon their position, losing twenty-seven men captured as they fled before the victorious Yankees. Although they were far from the action, Hays's men also had to beat a hasty retreat or else be cut off by the speedy federals. All but a few of Hays's men evaded the Yankees and rejoined Barksdale on the Telegraph Road a few miles from their original line. The road to Lee's rear was now open to Sedgwick, but he chose to follow Early's retreating rebels instead. By the time Sedgwick corrected this error and began moving toward Hooker, he found the road blocked by other Confederate brigades that had been rushed in to reinforce Early.[24]

By nightfall Lee was in control of the Chancellorsville battlefield and dispatched McLaws and Anderson to join Early for an attack against Sedgwick's isolated corps. On the afternoon of May 4, the federal corps was hemmed in by the three Confederate divisions, with the Rappahannock in its rear. On the Confederate right Hays's brigade was in the center of Early's line facing a Union-occupied hill. The Tigers knew Sedgwick was trapped and waited impatiently for orders to attack. When the signal gun for the assault was finally fired, Hays yelled "Charge!" and the brigade sprang forward with "a cheer as Louisianians alone can give." The Tigers clawed their way up the steep slope screaming "like a legion of 50 ton locomotives." "Our boys were so eager to go," wrote Sergeant Stephens, "[they] were more like a pack of pampered negro dogs

24. Compiled Service Records, War Record Group 109, Microcopy 320, Rolls 148, 187, NA; *OR*, Vol. XXV, Pt. I, 800–802, 839–41, 856, 1000–1002; Charles Moore, Jr., Diary, May 3, 1863, LHAC; Bound Volume 8 in Association of the Army of Northern Virginia, LHAC; Seymour, "Journal," in Seymour Papers, UM; Early, *War Memoirs*, 204–11; Freeman, *Lee's Lieutenants*, II, 618; Alexander, *Military Memoirs of a Confederate*, 349–52.

just lost from the halter on a fresh track. They went not at a double quick but as hard as they could run, squalling & hollering as loud as they could ball . . . every man for him self and Old Yank got up and dusted, leaving things behind as they went."[25]

Without firing a shot, the Tigers scrambled to the top of the brush-covered hill. But upon reaching the Yankees' abandoned picket line they were savagely greeted by the main federal force lying behind its works. Thousands of muskets and several batteries of artillery opened fire simultaneously; one shell alone killed or wounded seventeen members of the 9th Louisiana. "Such a scene as ensued never entered my imagination," wrote Stephens. "A wall of fire on three sides. The air was fairly hissing with round shot, shell, grape, canister and minie balls."[26] Watching from the rear, another soldier claimed: "The enemy opened everything they have on us at once. Their missles ploughed the ground in front [of us] as we advanced as though an earthquake [was] about to bury us alive. The shells burst over our heads, and the fire from the thousands of small arms, caused such a cloud of smoke that until the men advanced further nothing could be seen of them. I thought that they [Tigers] had been swept from the face of the earth at one blast, but hearing that unearthly yell, I knew that they had not faltered, and [that] they had no such intention."[27]

Hays's line did not stop to answer the Yankee volleys but kept up the attack. The federal line melted away and fell back half a mile to a sunken road lined by a chest-high brush fence. Jumping over the fence into the eight-foot-deep roadbed, the Yankees clawed and struggled up the other side. The Tigers were so close upon them that scores of federals threw up their hands in surrender as the Louisianians tumbled into the road on top of them. There was no time to escort the prisoners to the rear, so the Tigers ordered them back and continued their scramble up the opposite embankment.

The federals drew up a second line of defense above the road but did not have time to reload and fire. "They did not wait till we got up," one Tiger wrote, "but merely satisfied themselves that we

25. Handerson, *Yankee in Gray*, 102; letter from anonymous Louisianian, in Hewitt Private Collection; Stephens to unknown, n.d., in Stephens Collection, NSU.

26. Handerson, *Yankee in Gray*, 102.

27. Letter from anonymous Louisianian in Hewitt Private Collection.

were really coming, and off they went again." Hays and Forno urged the men onward and "seemed to be everywhere," one soldier recalled. Hays ignored the enemy's artillery fire that swept the road and galloped up and down it on his lathered horse roaring commands to keep the brigade moving. The brigade rushed out of the deep roadbed and swarmed over an open plateau toward a third Union line drawn up on a higher hill covered with felled trees. By now the brigade was so far ahead of its sister units that the Tigers' comrades were actually firing into them from the rear. Hays's men had "walked over the enemy as giants over pigmies," one newspaper claimed. But the brigade had shot its bolt and was about to collide with Colonel Lewis Grant's fresh Vermont Brigade dug in behind strong breastworks of knapsacks and felled trees.[28]

The Vermont boys waited until the Louisianians were within twenty feet before rising up and delivering a staggering point-blank volley of musketry. For the first time, Hays's men halted their advance to fire back. One Tiger recalled that after dragging himself over deep gullies and felled timber to reach this last Yankee line, "to stand and fight was a rest that was truly refreshing." The Tigers had lost all organization in the long charge, Sergeant Stephens claimed, and the brigade now "formed simply a howling, rushing and firing mob."[29] The momentum was lost, and half the men lay in the rear, where they were felled by bullets or dropped from exhaustion. To escape the Yankees' rapid fire some soldiers hugged the ground behind old Union breastworks; others hid in the numerous gullies that crisscrossed the hillside. Scattered all over the field and under a murderous fire from the Vermont soldiers, the Tigers began giving way. Some were shot down as they ran, but many others were so tired they simply collapsed and were captured. Colonel Stafford was so exhausted that he sat down on a log gasping for breath and was surrounded and taken prisoner. Colonel Lewis of the 7th Louisiana was caught by Colonel Grant and sullenly handed over his sword to the opposing commander. In all, some two hundred Tigers were captured when the assault

28. *Ibid.*; Richmond *Enquirer*, May 19, 1863, in Civil War Scrapbook, 1862–64, p. 193.

29. Letter from anonymous Louisianian in Hewitt Private Collection; Edmond Stephens to unknown, n.d., in Stephens Collection, NSU; Handerson, *Yankee in Gray*, 57.

collapsed, but most were exchanged and returned to the brigade within a few months.[30]

Early and Lee, watching the assault from a high hill, became ecstatic as they saw the Tigers break through the first two enemy lines. Early grabbed his hat, threw it to the ground, and cried, "Those damned Louisiana fellows may steal as much as they please now!" Lee simply clasped his hands together and sighed, "Thank God! the day is ours." Their elation turned to dismay, however, when Hays's charge was broken up on the last hill and the other Confederate brigades failed in their attempts to break Sedgwick's line. Early entertained the thought of renewing the advance and rode out to meet Hays as he tried to reform the remnants of his brigade. Darkness and the complete disarray of the Confederate units, however, dashed any hopes of a second assault.[31]

The Chancellorsville campaign was over. Both Sedgwick and Hooker withdrew safely across the Rappahannock, leaving Lee's men to bury the dead and collect the wounded. The two Louisiana brigades accounted for about 1,000 of Lee's 10,281 casualties. In the deadly thickets around Chancellorsville, Nicholls lost 47 dead, 265 wounded, and an unreported number of missing, with 48 officers among those lost. In the six days that Hays confronted Sedgwick's corps, he had 63 men killed, 306 wounded, and approximately 300 captured.[32]

The heavy losses suffered among field grade officers during the campaign once again forced the Army of Northern Virginia to undergo a reorganization. The greatest loss was that of Jackson, who lingered for several days before succumbing to his wounds. To the

30. Reed, *Private in Gray*, 30; *OR*, Vol. XXV, Pt. I, 600, 610, 614, 800–802, 1000–1002; Handerson, *Yankee in Gray*, 56–59, 101–103; Compiled Service Records, War Record Group 109, Microcopy 320, Roll 163, NA; Dr. G. M. G. Stafford, *General Leroy Augustus Stafford, His Forebears and Descendants* (New Orleans, 1943), 39; Benedict, *Vermont in the Civil War*, I, 143, 166, 367–72; Seymour, "Journal," in Seymour Papers, UM.

31. New Orleans *Times-Democrat*, in Reminiscences Division, n.d., Confederate Veteran Papers, DU; letter from an anonymous Louisianian in Hewitt Private Collection.

32. *OR*, Vol. XXV, Pt. I, 226, 809; Bartlett, *Military Record of Louisiana*, 3–11; Seymour, "Journal," in Seymour Papers, UM; Battle report of the 1st Louisiana Volunteers in Colston Collection, SHC; Richmond *Enquirer*, May 19, 1863, in Civil War Scrapbook, 1862–64, p. 192, TU; Stephens to parents, June 1, 1863, in Stephens Collection, NSU.

delight of the Tigers, Ewell was chosen by Lee to replace the fallen
Jackson as that corps' commander. "He was the choice of all the soldiers as well as the officers," claimed Sergeant Stephens. In addition, General Edward Johnson ultimately replaced Colston as commander of Jackson's old division and a new 3d Corps was formed
around the divisions of Richard Anderson, Henry Heth, and William D. Pender and placed under A. P. Hill. Then there was the task
of choosing a successor to Nicholls. Hill recommended Colonel
Forno, but that officer was transferred to Mobile for recruiting
duty. Edmund Pendleton had commanded the brigade temporarily
while at Fredericksburg but apparently had not impressed his superiors. Pendleton, Lee reported, "is not highly considered, and its
[Louisiana Brigade] service, I fear, will be lost to the army" if he
was promoted. Other officers were considered, but the matter was
left unresolved by the time the Gettysburg campaign got under
way. Although a permanent commander was not named until after
the Gettysburg campaign, the 2nd Louisiana's Colonel Jesse M.
Williams was finally designated as the brigade's temporary leader.[33]

Despite the impressive victory won by the Confederates at Chancellorsville, the campaign left the army depressed when the beloved Stonewall Jackson died from complications after his wounded
arm was amputated. "The loss of no one man of our Confederacy
would be more lamented than that of this great and good man,"
wrote W. B. Colbert. Stephens echoed this sentiment when he reported that Jackson's death "cast a gloom throughout this Army and
peticularly in this Corps, for he was our Comd. Gen'l. and we had
every confidence in him." Many Tigers attended a funeral service
that was held within the army for the slain general. Stephens wrote
that the service was a moving one with the text for the sermon coming from verses 6, 7, and 8 of II Timothy, fourth chapter. A fellow
member of Stephens' 9th Louisiana remembered verse 7, in particular, as the theme of the service: "I have fought a good fight, I
have finished my course, I have kept the faith."[34]

But the faith of many Tigers was shaken by the death of Jackson
and the slaughter at Chancellorsville and Fredericksburg. Soon

33. *OR,* Vol. XXV, Pt. II, 810; Buckley, *A Frenchman, a Chaplain, a Rebel,* 182.
34. W. B. Colbert to Mrs. C. M. and M. M. Potts, May 17, 1863, in Folder 59,
North Louisiana Historical Association Archives, CC; Stephens to Mrs. T. E. and
W. E. Paxton, May 18, 1863, in Stephens Collection, NSU.

after Jackson's funeral, Hays and several of his officers sat in a Richmond hotel room discussing with General John Bell Hood and others the likely fate of the Confederacy. When J. H. Cosgrove queried Hays and Lieutenant-Colonel Burke on whether the Confederacy would survive, both "seemed to express a doubt, although they explained that it did not imply ultimate disaster." Chancellorsville had been a great victory, they said, but no military advantage resulted from it. Hays also complained that the civilian government had taken on near despotic power yet still could not rise to the occasion. It could not even make good use of its available manpower, for Longstreet was absent at Suffolk throughout the late campaign. For the first time, the shadow of doubt was creeping into the minds of the Louisiana Tigers.[35]

35. J. H. Cosgrove, "Recollections and Reminiscences," *Cosgrove's Weekly*, August 26, 1911, in Melrose Scrapbook, 230, NSU.

Chapter VIII

GOING BACK
INTO THE UNION AT LAST

Despite the shock of Jackson's death and the army's heavy losses at Chancellorsville, the soldiers of the Army of Northern Virginia were soon in excellent mental and physical condition. Lee therefore decided to launch his second northern invasion that summer to relieve the enemy pressure on Virginia and to upset any offensive plans Hooker might have. With Ewell's corps leading the army, Lee planned to open an invasion route to Pennsylvania by clearing General Robert H. Milroy's Union forces out of the Valley. The Army of Northern Virginia rapidly marched over the towering Blue Ridge Mountains and by nightfall of June 13 had pushed Milroy's men back upon his headquarters at Winchester.[1]

After a night of drenching rain, Ewell continued his advance on Winchester by sending Early's division down the Valley Pike, while Johnson's men followed the parallel Front Royal Road. The federal defensive works at Winchester were formidable. A huge earthen fort blocked the direct route into town, and the six guns of a smaller bastion on a hill to the northwest covered the approaches to the main fort. After studying these works, Ewell decided the key to Winchester was the smaller bastion since its artillery commanded the main fortress. After leaving John B. Gordon's brigade and the Maryland Line to demonstrate against Winchester, Ewell sent Early's other three brigades toward the left to get into position to take the bastion.[2]

Local guides led Early's men on a quickly paced, winding, eight-mile hike so as to approach the bastion unseen. Utterly exhausted by the time they arrived, the men were allowed an hour's rest while

1. Edmond Stephens to parents, June 20, 1863, in Stephens Collection, NSU; *OR*, Vol. XXVII, Pt. II, 41–49, 313–15; Reed, *Private in Gray*, 35–36; Compiled Service Records, War Record Group 109, Microcopy 320, Roll 201, NA.
2. *OR*, Vol. XXVII, Pt. II, 459–64.

Early, Hays, and Captain William Seymour, Hays's newly appointed assistant adjutant general, crept forward to get a closer look at their target. Working their way to the edge of some woods, they were amazed to find that the Union sentinels "lazily paced their rounds" without once glancing in the hidden rebels' direction. Instead, they were watching Gordon's men skirmishing in front of town. Hurrying back to his waiting men, Early gave Hays orders to prepare his brigade for action while twenty pieces of artillery were rolled silently by hand into two fields flanking the woods. By 5:00 P.M. Hays had placed his Tigers in two lines—the 6th, 9th, and 7th regiments in front, with the 5th and 8th in support. When all was ready, Early gave the signal and the earth trembled with the roar of artillery.[3]

The small bastion was immediately enshrouded as the shells kicked up geysers of dust and smoke and tore huge craters in its earthen walls. Within minutes, Hays claimed, "scarcely a head was discovered above the ramparts." Taking advantage of the barrage, Hays inched his men through the forest to the base of the enemy's hill. Although the Tigers were scarcely two hundred yards from the bastion, the Yankees could not see them because of the dust and smoke. Convinced that the moment was right, Hays asked permission to storm the fort. But Early demurred and told the Louisianian to wait until the six federal guns were knocked out of action. By then, however, Hays was taking sporadic enemy fire and decided to launch the assault on his own before the Yankees could concentrate their guns on him.[4]

With their colors flapping in the breeze, Hays's two lines of Tigers silently emerged from the woods. Like the previous year, knots of civilians clambered onto rooftops to watch the Tigers tangle with the Yankees. When the Louisianians broke into a trot halfway up the slope, their "terrible, long shrill [rebel] yells" rent the air. The gray lines charged past a lone farmhouse perched on the grassy hill. There Lizzie and Alma Yonley stood watching from their doorway. Years later Lizzie wrote of the thrill she felt as Hays's Tigers rushed past her house "with banners flying and our own and the enemy's shells screaming over. . . . The storming of those

3. Seymour, "Journal," in Seymour Papers, UM.
4. *OR*, Vol. XXVII, Pt. II, 439–42, 459–64, 476–78; Compiled Service Records, War Record Group 109, Microcopy 320, Roll 201, NA; Seymour, "Journal," in Seymour Papers, UM.

breastworks was the grandest sight my eyes ever beheld." In 1900, the surviving Tigers presented Lizzie with a medal to honor her and Alma for caring for the Louisiana wounded after the battle.[5]

When Hays's yelping men reached the abatis protecting the fort, Early's artillery fell silent and the five hundred Union defenders sprang to the wall. In closing the gap to the fort, James Stewart, the 9th Louisiana's color-bearer, fell dead from a ball through his head. "Hoist those colors in the Ninth!" roared Hays, and the flag was grabbed up again. Stunned by the barrage and with only two guns still in operation, the Yankee defenders were barely able to fire a volley before the Confederates scaled the wall and jumped in on top of them.[6]

Lieutenant John Orr of the 6th Louisiana led the Tigers into the fort, hacking away with his saber at the Union color guards until he was finally run through with a bayonet. The federal gunners fought valiantly around their pieces, but the rest of the Yankees "were rather too nimble for us," remembered one Tiger. After shooting the artillery horses to prevent their crews from taking away the guns, the Tigers killed or captured the stubborn artillerymen. Working around the sixty-odd horse carcasses that littered the bastion, members of the 5th Louisiana's Orleans Cadets managed to turn the two working pieces around and fire several salvos at the fleeing enemy. In a small redoubt to the left, federal gunners tried to carry off two other guns but were foiled when a volley from the 7th Louisiana killed their horses. With the fort safely in hand, the Tigers began helping themselves to the ample supply of coffee, soup, and bread abandoned by the Yankees. As the men enjoyed their meal, the 9th Louisiana's huge colonel, William Raine Peck, collapsed on the wall after struggling up the hill. Wheezing and gasping for breath, he drew cheers and laughter when he yelled, "Bully! Bully! by God! Bully!! for the old Ninth, by God!!"[7]

5. Percy Gatling Hamlin, *"Old Bald Head" (General R. S. Ewell): The Portrait of a Soldier* (Strasburg, Va., 1940), 139; *Confederate Veteran,* XII (1900), 540.

6. Reed, *Private in Gray,* 36–37.

7. Lieutenant Joseph Warren Jackson to David F. Boyd, July 20, 1863, in Box 2, Folder 7, Boyd Civil War Papers, LSU; Reed, *Private in Gray,* 36–37; Seymour, "Journal," in Seymour Papers, UM; *OR,* Vol. XXVII, Pt. II, 451, 476–78; Bound Volume 5 in Association of the Army of Northern Virginia, LHAC.

The Louisiana Tigers were again showered with accolades for having taken the key to Winchester. Early wrote in his official report, "The charge of Hays' brigade upon the enemy's works was a most brilliant achievement." One Confederate artilleryman who provided cover fire for the Tigers claimed, "Our command witnessed many great and gallant charges during the operations of the Army of Northern Virginia (including Pickett's at Gettysburg and the Irish Brigade at Fredericksburg) yet we were generally agreed that for intrepidity, steadiness, and all other qualities which made up the veteran soldier we never saw this charge excelled, even in Lee's army." Hays's casualties in the close-quarters fight were moderate—twelve dead and sixty-seven wounded. Union losses were approximately fifty men, plus the eight cannons that were captured. Milroy and the fort's commander later claimed that ten thousand rebels stormed the fort and the Confederates lost four hundred men.[8]

Ewell was particularly impressed with the Louisianians. His view of the battle from a nearby hill was obscured by the dust and smoke that hung over the fort. After the Tigers rushed into the works, small groups of Union soldiers could be seen fleeing out of the smoke. But the struggle inside the bastion was hidden from view until a sudden breeze dramatically cleared the air. Ewell saw the pelican flags waving from the parapets and yelled, "Hurrah for the Louisiana boys!" A few days after the battle, Captain Seymour claimed that the general was still "very profuse in his praise of our Brigade." At a later meeting, Father Sheeran wrote that Ewell again acknowledged "the daring courage displayed by [the Tigers] in storming and capturing the enemy's breastworks. He said, next to God he was indebted to them for the almost bloodless victory." To show his appreciation, Ewell issued orders for this ridge of hills west of Winchester to be redesignated as "Louisiana Ridge" or "Louisiana Heights" on all military maps.[9]

With the small bastion now in Confederate hands, the Union

8. *OR*, Vol. XXVII, Pt. II, 46–47, 60–61, 464, 476–78; *Confederate Veteran*, IX (1901), 114.

9. Quoted in Hamlin, *"Old Bald Head,"* 139; Wilbur S. Nye, *Here Come the Rebels!* (Baton Rouge, 1965), 101; Seymour, "Journal," in Seymour Papers, UM; Durkin (ed.), *Confederate Chaplain*, 46–47; *Confederate Veteran*, VII (1900), 494–95; *ibid.*, IX (1901), 114.

forces found their main fort untenable. Ewell anticipated their evacuation of Winchester that night and dispatched Johnson's division to the Martinsburg Pike in the rear of town to cut off Milroy's retreat. Temporarily commanded by Colonel Jesse M. Williams, the 2d Louisiana Brigade led the division through the night, arriving at Stephenson's Depot as the eastern sky began to lighten.

Johnson had just finished deploying his men behind a stone fence alongside the road when Milroy launched a vigorous attack in an attempt to cut his way through the rebels. Clinging stubbornly to the wall, Johnson's men depleted nearly all of their ammunition while fighting off the Yankees. With only one round left apiece, the hard-pressed Confederates were subjected to thunderous cavalry charges on both flanks. Luckily, the Stonewall Brigade arrived in time to drive the cavalry back from Johnson's right flank, but Milroy and a thousand of his troopers were still maneuvering around the Louisiana regiments positioned on the left. Seeing the enemy cavalry snaking around their flank, Lieutenant-Colonel Ross Burke and Major Thomas N. Powell led the 2d and 10th Louisiana along a parallel route to try to head them off. For a short distance an intervening ridge separated the two columns, but then the ground leveled out, and "after a race of about 200 yards," wrote one Tiger, "we faced into line, jumped over a fence, fired into the enemy and charged." [10]

With supporting artillery fire, this deadly volley broke up Milroy's formation and sent it fleeing back down the road. The federal retreat became a rout when Johnson rode out and led the Tigers in pursuit. Soldiers with the 2d and 10th Louisiana ran down the color-bearers of two federal regiments and snatched away their flags, while other Louisianians accepted the surrender of hundreds of Yankees. After catching up with one Union lieutenant, a Tiger returned to his regiment with the officer's sword and pistol, plus nineteen of his men, who had surrendered. Losing only a handful of men, Williams' brigade had seized about six hundred of the approximately two thousand prisoners taken at Stephenson's Depot. [11]

The first phase of Lee's invasion was now completed. Losing only

10. Bartlett, *Military Record of Louisiana*, 46.
11. *Ibid.*, 45–46; *OR*, Vol. XXVII, Pt. II, 313–15, 336, 439–42, 499–503, 512–14; *Confederate Veteran*, VI (1898), 417; "Reminiscences of R. C. Murphy as Told to His Daughter," in Folder 1, Murphy Sandlin Collection, NSU.

269 men, Ewell's corps cleared Milroy's army from the Valley and opened the invasion route to Pennsylvania. In addition, twenty-eight cannons, three hundred wagons, four thousand prisoners, and a great number of small arms were seized. To prepare them for the long march ahead, Lee allowed his hungry men a free rein on much of the captured booty. "Such plundering of sutler wagons and all fancy notions of the Yankees'," Sergeant Stephens wrote his parents. "Our soldiers were just turned lose & told to go [to] it. I have as many nice clothing as I want, Sugar & coffee, rice & Everything else we wanted. I captured a fine lot of paper & Envelopes. I am writing to you on Yankee paper, pens, ink & envelopes." [12]

Within days after Milroy's rout, the confident Confederate army crossed the Potomac River into Maryland. In a jovial mood, Hays's men stripped down and tip-toed into the icy water with their clothes, muskets, and cartridge boxes held high. Watching from the bank, Seymour laughed when the Tigers screamed and shouted "most boisterously" as they entered the cold water. "It was amusing," he wrote, "to see the long lines of naked men fording it—their clothing and accoutrements slung to their guns and carried above their heads to keep them dry." [13]

When the Pennsylvania state line was finally reached, Hays's Tigers "shook M[arylan]d dust off of our feet and marched into the union to the tune of 'Dixie.'" Scores of civilians stood alongside the road to watch the invaders pass. Amused by their startled looks, the Louisianians told them with a smile "that we had Eat up the last mule we had and had come over to get some beef & bacon. Others said we were going back into the union at last." Southern Pennsylvania soon was swarming with haggard-looking graybacks, who destroyed bridges, railroad tracks, and government property. Although Lee's men dutifully obeyed his orders to respect private property, horses and needed supplies were seized in a polite but firm manner and were paid for with genuine, albeit worthless, Confederate money. [14]

The Louisiana officers seemed surprised at the lack of plundering by their men. One wrote that the Tigers "behave worse in Va.

12. Stephens to parents, June 20, 1863, in Stephens Collection, NSU.
13. Seymour, "Journal," in Seymour Papers, UM.
14. Jackson to Boyd, July 20, 1863, in Boyd Civil War Papers, LSU.

than they did in Penn.," an observation supported by Ewell when
he wrote home, "It is wonderful how well our hungry, foot sore,
ragged men behave in this land of plenty—better than at home."
Unlike past campaigns, some Tigers actually made good public re-
lations officers during the invasion. Father Sheeran wrote that the
Pennsylvanians told him the rebels' kind treatment of the civilians
had gained them new friends, and one Virginian recalled watching
a young boy rush breathlessly up to his mother crying, "Mother,
Mother! may I go to the camp with the rebels? They are the nicest
men I ever saw in my life. They are going to camp right out here
in the woods, and they are going to have a dance, too!" Standing
by the front gate was "a bowing, smiling, grimacing, shoulder-
shrugging Frenchman" from Hays's brigade. In broken English, he
promised the mother he would look after the boy. The mother had
already seen the Virginian befriend her younger son, so she reluctantly consented. The soldier wrote years later about watching the
young boy and his Tiger guardian disappear down the road: "If
the brigade did have the dance, then the lad saw what was really
worth seeing, for if there was anything Hays' Creoles did and loved
to do better than to fight, it was to dance, and their camp stag
dances, sandwiched in between a big march and a big battle were
said to be the most 'utterly utter' performance in the way of faun-
like pranks that grown and sane men ever engaged in."[15]

Some Tigers misinterpreted the Pennsylvanians' generosity in
sharing food and water with them as a sign of welcome. The 2d
Louisiana's Charles Batchelor, however, probably best described
the people's feelings toward the rebels when he wrote that they
readily gave food to passing soldiers, "only asking that their barns
and dwelling be spared." It was no secret that Early's division levied
a $28,600 tribute on York, Pennsylvania, and burned abolitionist
Thaddeus Stevens' ironworks near Greenwood. Although this act
was one of the few cases of destruction of private property by Lee's
army, most civilians were frightened of the invaders, nonetheless.[16]

The Pennsylvanians seemed particularly to dread the infamous
Louisiana Tigers. While passing through Gettysburg, one Tiger
was approached by a frightened woman, who begged, "Spare me

15. *Ibid.;* Richard S. Ewell to Lizzie Ewell, June 24, 1863, in Richard S. Ewell
Papers, LC; Stiles, *Four Years Under Marse Robert,* 200–201.
16. Charles Batchelor to father, October 18, 1863, in Batchelor Papers, LSU.

and my children, and you shall have everything we have got on the place!" She was, recalled Thomas Reed, "the worst scared woman I had ever seen." When told all he wanted was some food, the woman hustled Reed into her house to prepare it. Before she was finished, however, other famished Tigers wandered inside to partake of her hospitality. By the time they took their leave, Reed claimed, "the little woman was almost crazy." [17]

A member of the 7th Louisiana discovered one reason why the Tigers were so feared. When he walked into a home and politely asked if he could have some food, the mistress of the household told him to be seated and she would prepare a meal. While busying herself in the kitchen, she made light conversation and asked the soldier what regiment he belonged to. "Seventh Louisiana!" came the reply—and the woman swooned in a dead faint. Jumping up, the Tiger rushed to her side and knelt over the prostrate woman just as her husband walked in. When he angrily demanded an explanation, the shocked soldier told him of their short conversation. That explained it, the man replied. Confederate cavalry had galloped through town a short time before and informed everyone "that the La. Tigers would kill, burn & destroy everything & every body in the country." [18]

Although most Louisianians resented their bad reputation, some soldiers enjoyed perpetuating it. While Hays's and Robert Hoke's brigades marched through York, the Tigers and Tar Heels overheard a group of children near the street ask their father, "Why Papa I thought the Rebs had horns, where are they?" Turning toward them as they passed, the soldiers jabbed their bayonets at the children and scowled, "Here are our horns!" [19]

The Pennsylvanians, however, were not the only ones frightened of the Tigers. While crossing the Blue Ridge Mountains in Virginia several Louisianians stopped and received a meal at a nearby farm. The lady of the house revealed afterward that a number of rowdy soldiers had passed by earlier—probably Louisianians, she said. The Tigers said nothing until she asked where they hailed from. When the embarrassed men replied, "Louisiana," she "turned pale

17. Reed, *Private in Gray*, 39.
18. Jackson to Boyd, July 20, 1863, in Boyd Civil War Papers, LSU.
19. E. A. Patterson, "Story of the War," in Fredericksburg and Spotsylvania National Military Park, Fredericksburg, Va.

as death, then she flushed up as red as scarlet. Then she would turn pale again, then red again." Finding her voice at last, she exclaimed, "I tell you the very name of [a] Louisiana soldier is a horror to me, and I hope while you are under my roof you will behave yourselves." They did.[20]

The only serious trouble the Louisiana officers had with their men during the invasion was a four-day drunken spree by members of Hays's brigade. On June 26 Hays consented to give his soldiers a pint ration of whiskey before resuming the march. Several men who did not drink passed their rations on to friends, and soon numerous Tigers were roaring drunk. Most of the men enjoyed the occasion immensely, but some instances of fighting broke out. The brigade camped near Gettysburg that night, and several Tigers crept out of camp under the cover of darkness to procure more whiskey in town. "The whole brigade got drunk," wrote Seymour. "I never saw such a set in my life." A steady rain during the night turned the roads into quagmires, and the hungover men straggled badly the next day. As the brigade's number dwindled with every passing mile, Seymour hit upon a solution. As a soldier began to drop behind, Seymour pulled him out of line and threw him into the cook wagon atop "the sharp sides and projecting legs of pots & kettles, which sobered them speedily. These drunken fellows would not ride far before they begged most piteously to be taken out and allowed to walk." Although the brigade quickly sobered up on this dreadful march, one entire company in the 9th Louisiana became inebriated again two days later and engaged in "a general family fight" that left one officer badly injured and several men under arrest.[21]

Throughout most of the invasion, Stuart's cavalry had been cut off from Lee during a raid behind the Union lines, thus depriving the Confederate general of badly needed information on the Yankees' whereabouts. On the night of June 28 Lee learned for the first time that the Army of the Potomac had crossed the Potomac River and was closing in on his scattered army. To meet this threat, Lee ordered his far-flung divisions to begin concentrating at Cash-

20. Reed, *Private in Gray*, 68.
21. Seymour, "Journal," in Seymour Papers, UM; Jackson to Boyd, July 20, 1863, in Boyd Civil War Papers, LSU; Reed, *Private in Gray*, 41.

town or Gettysburg. Although slowed by the muddy roads, A. P. Hill was in Cashtown on June 30 and dispatched one of his brigades to Gettysburg to confiscate some badly needed shoes reportedly stored there. When these Confederates met resistance in Gettysburg from Union cavalry, they withdrew and returned on July 1 with Hill's division. Thus began the Battle of Gettysburg.

General George Meade had replaced the once-defeated Hooker as commander of the Army of the Potomac and hurried reinforcements to Gettysburg after skirmishing began there on June 30. Colliding in the rolling fields north of town, the two armies became engaged in a major battle as more and more units were sucked into the inferno. Elements of Ewell's corps were within fourteen miles of Gettysburg on the road from York when the battle began, and they rushed toward the sound of the rumbling guns. Shortly after noon Rodes's division arrived and was placed on the left of Hill's battling men, followed shortly by Early's division, which extended the line past Rodes's left. Early had Gordon's brigade hugging Rodes's left flank, with Hays on the left of Gordon and the brigades of Hoke and Smith extending further to the left. Placed atop a high plateau, the Tigers could see Rodes's men off to the right "driving the Yankees before [them] like sheep. It was," declared one Louisiana officer, "the prettiest sight I ever saw." [22]

In midafternoon Ewell advanced his eager line a mile and a half to the base of another plateau, where the right flank of General Oliver O. Howard's XI Corps was making a stand against Hill's divisions. While Confederate artillery pounded the struggling Yankee line, Early's men dressed their formation beside a stream that bordered the fifty-foot plateau. After a furious bombardment, the cannons fell silent, and Early's line rushed across the creek and scrambled up the plateau's slope toward the unsuspecting enemy. "Then came one of the most warlike & animated spectacles I ever looked on," recalled one of Ewell's aides. "Gordon & Hays charged across the plateau in their front, at double-quick, sweeping everything before them & scattering the extreme right of the enemy." [23]

The XI Corps disintegrated when its right flank was shattered by Early's charge and beat a hasty retreat back toward Gettysburg.

22. Jackson to Boyd, July 20, 1863, in Boyd Civil War Papers, LSU.
23. Brown, "Reminiscences of the Civil War," II, 57, in Brown Collection, SHC.

Hays's men were actually closer to town than many of the Union soldiers, and it became a foot race to see which side would enter it first. The Tigers met virtually no resistance from the beaten Yankees. "We shot them down, bayoneted them & captured more prisoners than we had men," claimed Lieutenant Joseph Jackson.[24]

When Hays won the race and cut off the retreat of at least 5,000 Union soldiers, the enemy began surrendering in droves. Captain Seymour brought in 250 alone when a federal colonel surrendered himself and his men. Hays reported that so many Yankees laid down their arms that he was uncertain what to do with them all. The general later wrote that he had no choice but to point the prisoners toward the rear and send them on their way unescorted. By the time Hays's Tigers finished combing the streets of Gettysburg, they had lost 7 men killed, 41 wounded and 15 missing but had taken an estimated 3,000 prisoners—approximately twice the brigade's strength.[25]

After securing Gettysburg, Hays deployed his men along its streets in preparation for an expected advance against the Yankees, who were now digging in on Cemetery Hill just beyond town. Within an hour of taking Gettysburg, Hays, Gordon, Early, and Rodes approached Ewell to argue for an immediate advance before Meade strongly fortified Cemetery Hill. There were still several hours of daylight left to accomplish this task, and it was obvious that the high ground of Cemetery Hill was the key to the battle. But Ewell was under orders from Lee to assault the hill only if he was certain of success, for Lee had no reserves to support him if the battle did not go well. In addition, Ewell had received reports, later proved erroneous, that a Union column was approaching his rear. After weighing all the factors, Ewell decided to postpone the attack until Johnson's division arrived from Carlisle. When Hays persisted in pushing for an advance, Ewell reportedly laughed and chided the Louisianian, asking if his Tigers never got a bellyful of fighting. Hays bristled and replied testily that his only concern was to prevent the unnecessary slaughter of his men in a later assault. It was later claimed that after the war Hays told Longstreet that the Loui-

24. Jackson to Boyd, July 20, 1863, in Boyd Civil War Papers, LSU.
25. *OR*, Vol. XXVII, Pt. II, 479–80; Seymour, "Journal," in Seymour Papers, UM.

siana Brigade could have taken Cemetery Hill that afternoon without losing ten men. Early, however, maintained that such a claim
was ludicrous because several thousand Union soldiers were in
position there by the time an assault could have been launched.[26]

Hays's men were angry over the lack of pursuit. As the afternoon
slowly passed, the Tigers watched more and more Union troops arrive on the hill to their front. Oaths and curses were muttered
along the line, and many openly exclaimed their wish "that Jackson
were here." The 15th Louisiana's Colonel David Zable remembered
that when Johnson's men finally arrived on the field late in the day
and still no advance was made, "the troops realized there was something wanting somewhere. There was an evident feeling of dissatis-
faction among our men [that] we were not doing [it] Stonewall Jackson's way."[27]

When darkness finally enveloped the field, the Yankees were left
undisturbed along the hills and ridges south of town. Ewell spent
that afternoon and evening deploying Johnson's division to the left
of Gettysburg to face the enemy on Culp's Hill, while Early's men
were positioned to the right along the base of Cemetery Hill. The
corps of Hill and Longstreet continued Lee's line further to the
right along Seminary Ridge. Lee made plans that night for Longstreet to open the attack next day from the right flank. Ewell's corps
would advance against Culp's and Cemetery hills on the left as soon
as Longstreet's guns were heard. Longstreet, however, dallied away
precious hours on July 2 and allowed Meade time to consolidate his
position on Cemetery Ridge. It was not until 4:00 P.M. that Ewell
finally heard Longstreet's attack and ordered his artillery to open
fire on the enemy positions.

Hays's men had moved out six hundred yards beyond the town
during the night and now lay between a roaring eighteen-gun bat-

26. Hamlin, *"Old Bald Head,"* 199; *Southern Historical Society Papers*, IV (1877),
296–97; Douglas Southall Freeman, *R. E. Lee: A Biography* (4 vols.; New York, 1935),
III, 76–78; Brown, "Reminiscences of the Civil War," II, 62–63, in Brown Collection, SHC; Early, *War Memoirs*, 266–71; *OR*, Vol. XXVII, Pt. II, 317–18, 444–46,
468–70.

27. Seymour, "Journal," in Seymour Papers, UM; untitled paper by David Zable,
December 12, 1903, in Reminiscences, Executive and Army of Northern Virginia,
LHAC; Glenn Tucker, *High Tide at Gettysburg: The Campaign in Pennsylvania* (Indian-
apolis, 1958), 173–78.

tery and Cemetery Hill. When the federal guns thundered back in defiance, the Louisianians had a spectacular view of the duel. It was, Seymour wrote, "a most exciting and thrilling spectacle. . . . The roar of the guns was continuous and deafening; the shot and shell could be seen tearing through the hostile batteries, dismounting guns, killing and wounding men and horses, while [occasionally] an ammunition chest would explode, sending a bright column of smoke up towards the heavens."[28]

To the left, Johnson's division was preparing to follow the bombardment with a strong push up Culp's Hill. Placed on the left of the division, Williams' Louisianians were tense and apprehensive. Since dawn, federal troops had been heard arriving on the hill, and all afternoon the Tigers listened to the Yankees felling trees and digging earthworks along its crest. Sikes Phillips, a member of the 2d Louisiana, felt an ominous foreboding when he found himself in the front line. He was relieved when his friend R. C. Murphy stepped up and offered to exchange places with him. At dusk the roaring guns finally fell silent, and orders were given to advance up the steep, rocky slope.

As the Tigers picked their way through the trees and rocks, the hilltop suddenly exploded in smoke and flame. From behind their barricades the Yankees unleashed a murderous fire upon the struggling rebels. Lieutenant-Colonel Michael Nolan, one of the first to fall, was killed leading the 1st Louisiana up the slope; Sikes Phillips was mortally wounded in the groin even though he stood behind R. C. Murphy. Williams' men became confused on the darkened hillside and soon lost all semblance of order. On the right the 1st Louisiana managed to force the Yankees out of part of their breastworks, but elsewhere the Tigers had to seek cover forty to one hundred yards from the enemy line. For four hours Johnson's Confederates clung to the rocky slope, banging away at the enemy. So many rounds were fired by the Tigers that muskets became fouled from excessive use and had to be replaced by weapons snatched up from the dead and wounded. It was past midnight when the firing slackened enough for the rebels to withdraw a short distance down the hill.[29]

28. Seymour, "Journal," in Seymour Paper, UM.
29. *OR*, Vol. XXVII, Pt. II, 503–505, 513, 532; *Confederate Veteran*, VI (1898), 417; Charles Batchelor to father, October 18, 1863, in Folder 6, Batchelor Papers,

A number of brave Tigers remained close to the Yankees and silently crept through the smoky woods in search of wounded comrades. Friends of Wolf Lichstenstein found him with a shattered arm lying within talking distance of the Yankees. Unable to move him without drawing the enemy's fire, the men could only strap a canteen to Lichstenstein's chest to alleviate his horrendous thirst and leave him where he was. Before daylight, the canteen was ripped apart by three Yankee bullets, and Lichstenstein had to suffer through an entire day without water. Charles Batchelor was shocked to find his younger brother, Albert, lying on the bloody slope. Albert, who had joined the company only three weeks earlier, now lay with a bullet-torn thigh and a ghastly head wound. Entering through his left cheek, the ball popped out the boy's right eye as it passed through his head and exited at his right temple. With the help of an officer who had found that he had lost his entire company in the fight, Batchelor carefully carried Albert to an ambulance in the rear. After a tearful embrace, Charles returned to Culp's Hill to seek out the other nineteen casualties among his twenty-six-man company. Although left in Gettysburg when Lee retreated on July 4, Albert miraculously recovered from his wounds.[30]

While Johnson's men fought among the rocks on Culp's Hill, Hays's Tigers launched an attack of their own against Cemetery Hill. The Louisianians had been in position for the assault since dawn, but like Johnson they were forced to wait until Longstreet opened his attack on the right. The waiting was made worse by federal sharpshooters, who were taking potshots at the Tigers with their scoped Whitworth rifles. Lieutenant Jackson wrote that "if any one showed themselves or a hat was seen above the fence a volley was poured into us." When Ewell and Early's engineer, Captain H. B. Richardson, rode past Hays's prone brigade, the two officers were warned of the sharpshooters. Ewell scoffed at the danger, however, because the federals were at least half a mile away. Within

---

LSU; Zable paper, December 12, 1903, in Reminiscences, Executive and Army of Northern Virginia, LHAC; Murphy, "Reminiscences," in Sandlin Collection, NSU.

30. Batchelor to James Batchelor, August 12, 1863, and n.d., in Folder 6, Batchelor Papers, LSU; Zable paper, December 12, 1903, in Reminiscences, Executive and Army of Northern Virginia, LHAC; Murphy, "Reminiscences," in Sandlin Collection, NSU.

moments, Ewell caught a ball in his wooden leg and Richardson was shot through the body.[31]

Hays was given temporary command of Hoke's North Carolina brigade for the assault on Cemetery Hill. Deployed behind a low ridge with Hoke on his left and Gordon in support, Hays anxiously listened for Johnson's advance on Culp's Hill. As they waited in line, every officer except the Tar Heels' Colonel Isaac Avery sent his horse to the rear, all preferring to go in on foot so as not to attract the enemy's fire. The Tigers were quiet and fearful, well aware of the reception awaiting them on Cemetery Hill. Forty-five men had already fallen to the deadly snipers, and throughout the previous night the federals were heard "chopping away and working like beavers" on the heights. As the sun descended in the west, the Louisianians finally heard the growing roar to their left that signaled Johnson's attack. At that moment, a solitary bugle wailed over the field, signaling Hays to advance. "I felt as if my doom was sealed," wrote Lieutenant Jackson, "and it was with great reluctance that I started my skirmishers forward."[32]

Rising up, the two Confederate brigades lunged forward and popped over the ridge into view. Seven hundred yards away, the federal batteries "vomit[ed] forth a perfect storm of grape, cannister, shrapnel, etc." wrote Seymour. "But 'Old Harry' shouted forward!" recalled Lieutenant Jackson, "and on we went over fences, ditches [and] thru marshy fields." The Tigers rushed down the ridge and into the shallow valley that lay between them and the cemetery. Federal infantry posted behind a stone fence at the base of the hill poured volleys of musketry toward the rebels. Fortunately, their aim was poor in the growing darkness, although Colonel Avery was shot from his horse and killed. The minié balls and shells shrieked overhead, but the rebels' momentum was maintained, and the first enemy line was finally reached. The Yankees put up a determined fight for the fence, Jackson claimed, "but with bayonets & clubbed guns we drove them back."[33]

31. Jackson to Boyd, July 20, 1863, in Boyd Civil War Papers, LSU; Brown, "Reminiscences of the Civil War," II, 77, in Brown Collection, SHC; Seymour, "Journal," in Seymour Papers, UM.

32. Jackson to Boyd, July 20, 1863, in Boyd Civil War Papers, LSU.

33. Seymour, "Journal," in Seymour Papers, UM; Jackson to Boyd, July 20, 1863, in Boyd Civil War Papers, LSU.

When this first federal line broke, two others lying behind it gave way with little resistance and fled back to Captain R. Bruce Ricketts' and Captain Michael Wiedrich's Union batteries on top of the hill. Scores of prisoners were scooped up in the pursuit, but Hays's men refused to slow down and simply ordered them back to the rear. Great gaps had been torn in Hays's line by the twenty federal cannons, but handfuls of Tigers and Tar Heels managed to fight their way into the federal batteries. The 9th Louisiana's Colonel Stafford sprinted ahead of his men so as to be the first to enter the battery, but he was passed by the fleet-footed Major John Hodges. The regiment's color-bearer followed close behind and defiantly jabbed his flag next to a smoking cannon. By then it was completely dark, and an eerie, savage fight raged around the guns between Hays's men and Adelbert Ames's Union brigade. A Louisiana officer grabbed for one battery's colors but was shot dead by its color-bearer, who in turn was killed by a bullet that splintered his flag-staff. Another Yankee felled a Tiger with a rock as he bent over to pick up Ames's fallen colors, and other federals overpowered the 8th Louisiana's color-bearer and took away his flag. General Hoke claimed that the Union artillerymen fought "with a tenacity never before displayed by them, but with bayonets, clubbed muskets, sword, and pistol, and rocks" the Confederates finally loosened their grip on the battery and forced them out.[34]

For the moment, Hays's Tigers had succeeded in penetrating the federal battle line, but the support needed to expand the breakthrough was not at hand. Rodes's division was to have joined in the attack on Hays's right, but there was no sign of his men. An ominous silence fell over Cemetery Hill as Hays's soldiers squirmed into position around the captured batteries, checked their cartridge boxes, and waited for the coming Union counterattack. Off in the blackness could be heard the muffled commands and shuffling feet of two Union brigades that were being rushed into the gap. The Yankees remained unseen, however, until they suddenly fired a terrible volley of musketry from only twenty feet away. Hays's men responded with a volley of their own, and the two lines collided again in a vicious hand-to-hand fight. This time the Yankees gained

34. Stafford, *General Leroy Augustus Stafford*, 40; Carl Schurz, *The Reminiscences of Carl Schurz* (3 vols.; New York, 1907, 1908), III, 25; *OR*, Vol. XXVII, Pt. II, 486.

the upper hand and beat the rebels back down the slope to the stone fence. At 10:00 P.M., Hays's bloodied brigades retired back to where Gordon was waiting for them at their starting point.[35]

For a brief moment, Lee's men had succeeded in breaking the strong defensive works along Cemetery Ridge and clearing a path to the rear of Meade's army. Most historians feel that if Hays had been properly supported, the Union army could have been wrecked that fateful night. Douglas Southall Freeman wrote, "The whole of the three days' battle produced no more tragic might-have-been than this twilight engagement on the Confederate left." And Union General Carl Schurz claimed, "The fate of the battle might [have hinged] on the repulse of this attack."[36]

The charge of Hays's brigades, however, was only one of many "ifs" at Gettysburg, and perhaps its potential in changing the course of the battle has been overstated. The Tigers and Tar Heels proved Meade's line was not invincible, but it is doubtful that Hays could have accomplished much more even if supported by Rodes or Gordon. With his large numbers of reserves close at hand, it is highly probable that Meade still could have contained Hays's limited breakthrough and held off Rodes at the same time in the confusing darkness. Of course, there are those who claim that if the Confederate attacks had been launched earlier in the day as planned, Hays's penetration could have been capitalized on before darkness enshrouded the hill. The truth is, however, that if Hays had launched his assault in better light, his men would have been annihilated before ever reaching the hostile batteries. Even Hays admitted that his men "escaped what in the full light of day could have been nothing less than horrible slaughter." About the only gain Hays's Tigers enjoyed on Cemetery Hill was the further embellishment of their fighting reputation; but this came at a cost of 21 dead, 119 wounded, and 41 missing. The 8th Louisiana's Colonel Trevanion Lewis was among the dead.[37]

35. *OR*, Vol. XXVII, Pt. I, 234, 457, 705–706, 715–16, 720, 722, 894; *ibid.*, Pt. II, 446–47, 556; Early, *War Memoirs*, 272–74; *Southern Historical Society Papers*, IV (1877), 279; Tucker, *High Tide at Gettysburg*, 292–97; Patterson, "Story of the War," in Patterson Collection, Fredericksburg and Spotsylvania National Military Park; Oliver Otis Howard, *Autobiography of Oliver Otis Howard, Major General, United States Army* (New York, 1907), 429.

36. Freeman, *R. E. Lee*, III, 102; Schurz, *Reminiscences of Carl Schurz*, III, 24.

37. *OR*, Vol. XXVII, Pt. II, 475, 480–85.

The Tigers returned to Gettysburg that night in a foul, disgusted mood. It was generally believed that Rodes had ruined an excellent opportunity to strike a staggering blow against the Yankees. The men ranted that once again the Louisiana Tigers had breached the Yankee line and others had failed to take advantage of it. "A madder set of men I never saw," wrote a federal prisoner who witnessed their return. "They cursed their officers in a way and manner that showed experience in the business. . . . It was simply fearful. . . . They said their officers didn't care how many were killed, and especially old Hays, who was receiving his share of the curses." A civilian who watched Hays's men rout the Germans of Howard's XI Corps the day before wrote, "There seemed now to be an entire absence of that elation and boastfulness which they manifested when they entered the town on the evening of the first of July." [38]

After spending a restless night in the streets of Gettysburg, Hays's brigade remained in reserve throughout July 3. Although not engaged during the day, the Tigers were still subjected to the frightfully accurate fire of the federal snipers. Thomas Reed remembered years later that "one of those globe-sighted guns" missed him by only four feet from a range of half a mile. [39]

To the left of town, the other Louisiana Tigers renewed their push up Culp's Hill at 4:00 A.M., July 3, and fought incessantly for seven hours. Tens of thousands of minié balls ripped through the trees, raining limbs on top of the Louisianians and killing an entire forest. It was, recalled Colonel Zable, "the most terrific [firing] we ever experienced." All that prevented the entire brigade from being killed was that in their haste the Yankees consistently fired too high. [40]

When General George Pickett's desperate charge on the afternoon of July 3 failed to crack Meade's tough defenses, Lee rested his weary men for one day and began the long, harrowing retreat to Virginia on the night of July 4. He had lost more than 20,000 men during the three-week invasion. Hays tallied up 36 dead, 201

38. Austin C. Stearns, *Three Years with Company K*, ed. Arthur A. Kent (London, 1976), 190–92; Earl Schenck Miers and Richard A. Brown (eds.), *Gettysburg* (New Brunswick, N.J., 1948), 182–84.

39. Reed, *Private in Gray*, 43; Handerson, *Yankee in Gray*, 63–64; *OR*, Vol. XXVII, Pt. II, 471–73.

40. Zable paper, December 12, 1903, in Reminiscences, Executive and Army of Northern Virginia, LHAC.

wounded, and 76 missing, and Williams counted 44 dead, 309 wounded, and 36 missing in the series of violent clashes. Casualty lists, however, are not consistent for the campaign. Another list puts Hays's losses at 194 and Williams' at 291. But even these staggering figures do not tell the entire story. On June 19, when the invasion was young, Hays had 1,626 officers and men on duty. On July 8, only 945 men answered roll call—the rest were casualties or straggling somewhere on the muddy roads.[41]

For the thousands of wounded, the nightmare that followed the battle was almost unbearable. R. G. Hancock wrote that he endured sheer torture when his shattered thigh swelled to twice its normal size as he bounced around in a rickety wagon for eighteen days during the retreat. Another twice-wounded Louisiana officer became delirious from his injuries and from grief over his brother's death and committed suicide in a Virginia hospital by slitting his own throat. Many of the Tigers who were too badly wounded to be moved had to be left behind in barns and houses. One group of Louisianians left unattended in a barn died at a fearful rate from lack of medical attention. Wolf Lichstenstein finally hired a farmer to bring water for the men, but the wounded continued to die, and the nauseating stench brought out legions of flies and rats. The wounded lay in agony for seven days before the farmer was paid to bring federal troops to save them.[42]

Despite the heavy losses, those Tigers who survived the clash unscathed retreated in good cheer—not at all like a defeated army. Slogging along in knee-deep mud, the Tigers "were as cheerful a body of men as I ever saw," reported Father Sheeran, "and to hear them, you would think they were going to a party of pleasure instead of retreating from a hard fought battle." Even when exhaustion engulfed them on the miserable retreat they did not lose their sense of humor. "Hello! John!" a member of the 9th Louisiana would cry out after an extended period of silence, "How would you

41. *OR*, Vol. XXVII, Pt. II, 330–31, 340, 506; Inspection report of Hays's brigade, June 19, July 8, 1863, in Early Papers, War Record Group 109, Entry 118, NA.
42. "A Leaf from Memory," *Cosgrove's Weekly*, January 4, 1911, in Melrose Scrapbook 230, NSU; Murphy, "Reminiscences," in Sandlin Collection, NSU; R. G. Hancock to Walter Stewart, April 19, 1908, in Folder 5, William and Walter Stewart Papers, Merritt M. Shilg Memorial Collection, LSU; John F. Gruber to David F. Boyd, August 25, 1863, in Boyd Civil War Papers, LSU.

like to be a soldier boy?" "Knock that fool in the head!" another would answer and a flush of laughter would perk them up for a while longer.[43]

The Louisianians were cheerful because they knew they had given their all against frightful odds and come away with their considerable pride intact. It was not the Tigers, they exclaimed, who lost the battle. Hays's men were particularly cocky. "Need I mention," wrote John F. Gruber to David F. Boyd, "that your gallant little Brigade won laurels upon laurels." In addition to briefly breaking the federal line on Cemetery Hill, he claimed, "At Winchester the[y] stormed a fortification with eight cannons scattering the rather bluish looking inmates in every direction. . . . Whatever stain the conduct and misdeeds of a few may have made upon its name, Hays' La. Brigade ranks second to none in bravery and daring, the —— Stonewall [Brigade] not excepted."[44]

Seymour claimed that the brigade received a great deal of recognition for its charge against the batteries on Cemetery Hill, and John Gruber wrote that Hays's reputation was greatly enhanced: "[Hays] is growing more popular in the army and disappointment is manifested, that he is not been ere this made a Major General. He has wonderfully improved, he handled his Brigade at Winchester & Gettysburg very skillfully, while the great requisite to keep cool, is more with him a matter of course; add to this his gallantry and the majical influence it has over his men, it is not to be wondered at, that [the Tigers] look for some appreciation of them and their leader's service."[45]

The gallantry of Hays and his men did not go unappreciated. In his official report, Ewell wrote that Hays's and Hoke's brigades' fighting on Cemetery Hill "was worthy of the highest praise. In this and at Winchester the Louisiana brigade and their gallant commander gave new honor to the name already acquired on the old fields of Winchester and Port Republic, and wherever engaged."[46]

Early also wrote highly of Hays's conduct, but he did not let it influence his stormy relationship with the brigade. He and the Tigers resumed their usual bickering shortly after Gettysburg. "Just

43. Durkin (ed.), *Confederate Chaplain*, 49–50; Reed, *Private in Gray*, 43.
44. Gruber to Boyd, August 25, 1863, in Boyd Civil War Papers, LSU.
45. *Ibid.*; Seymour, "Journal," in Seymour Papers, UM.
46. *OR*, Vol. XXVII, Pt. II, 450.

now a little feud is going on between old Jubal and our Brigade,"
declared John Gruber. "Using an insignificant incident as a protest,
he again denounced the Brigade in unmerciful terms and was impudent enough . . . to write a note embracing in substance his
charges." This note so enraged Hays's officers that they once again
pulled their trump card. "The officers unwilling to have their men
[labeled] as thieves very promptly took the matter in hand and by a
unanimous vote requested Gen. Hays to petition for a transfer to
some other division." As expected, this action brought Ewell into
the spat on the side of his Tigers. "Gen. Early is at present for once
on the stool of penitence," reported Gruber, "he having avowed his
willingness to retract anything said calculated to wound the feelings
of either officers or men."[47]

Lee succeeded in making his escape across the rain-swollen Potomac River and in early August began regrouping his army on the
Rapidan River. With only 713 officers and men left in Williams'
decimated brigade, the Louisiana officers petitioned Lee either to
apprehend the brigade's numerous deserters to refill the ranks,
consolidate it with another command, or send it someplace for garrison duty where the small command could perform a valuable service while its officers recruited replacements. Colonel Williams dis-
approved of garrison duty but did forward the petition through
channels in hope that his officers would be allowed to recruit.
Johnson, Ewell, and Lee all rejected the proposition, however, on
the grounds that the Army of Northern Virginia could ill afford to
lose, even temporarily, any one of its brigades.[48]

Colonel Williams' small brigade remained in line throughout the
summer of 1863. To rectify its command structure, Colonel Leroy
Stafford was promoted to brigadier-general that October and
transferred from the 9th Louisiana to assume command of the 2nd
Louisiana Brigade. The forty-one-year-old Stafford had earned a
reputation for being among the best of the Tiger officers. Born and
raised in Rapides Parish, Stafford was educated at the best schools
in Kentucky and Tennessee and became a prominent planter near
Cheneyville, Louisiana. Elected sheriff in 1846, he served in the
Mexican War and there as a private received the only military training he had before the Civil War. Stafford opposed secession in 1861

47. Gruber to Boyd, August 25, 1863, in Boyd Civil War Papers, LSU.
48. *OR*, Vol. XXVII, Pt. III, 1013–14.

but organized the Stafford Guards when some neighbors predicted that conservatives such as he was would not fight if war came. "Fond of a glass of liquor," and an avid card player, he was normally a pleasant man but could become "violent and somewhat tyrannical when aroused." Always in the forefront of battle, Stafford was once cited by General Johnson as the bravest man he ever met.[49]

Lee's choice of Stafford was not popular in the brigade. He and his staff were looked upon as "interlopers," who stole the command position from Williams, the brigade's senior colonel. It is not known why Lee chose an outsider to replace Williams. Stafford was an outstanding officer, but no bad marks can be found against Williams for the way he handled the brigade during the Pennsylvania campaign. Although Lee no doubt had good reasons for choosing Stafford, his appointment was greeted with anger and jealousy from the brigade's officers, and it took time for the new commander to be accepted. In justice to Williams, however, he never displayed any resentment at being passed over for the promotion.[50]

For several months following the Battle of Gettysburg, Lee's Tigers rested and licked their wounds. The campaign had left their ranks severely depleted but had not broken their fighting spirit. If anything, the Louisianians were more determined than ever to carry on the struggle, although it must have been apparent to most that the outlook was bleak. To his father, Charles Batchelor wrote:

> Like true patriots who are willing to loose life, property and all else they now hold [illegible] their rights, honor, and freedom. Unlike the weak kneed croakers of Mississippi and Louisiana (who are willing to abandon all their countrymen have so nobly struggled for just because Vicksburg or Port Hudson have fallen into the hands of the enemy) they still bare their noble breasts to the storm and with one voice shout we will never give over the struggle till Each one of us shall have been captured and borne away to dark and filthy dungeons to die— No, as long as there is one man left of Lee's noble army the enemy will never possess themselves of our soil.[51]

49. *Ibid.*, Vol. XXXVI, Pt. I, 1074; Stafford, *General Leroy Augustus Stafford*, 30– 34; Warner, *Generals in Gray*, 287–88; Handerson, *Yankee in Gray*, 29.
50. Handerson, *Yankee in Gray*, 65–66.
51. Batchelor to father, August 12, 1863, in Folder 6, Batchelor Papers, LSU.

Chapter IX

INTO THE WILDERNESS

The Army of Northern Virginia, less Longstreet's Corps, which was temporarily detached to the western theater, settled along the Rapidan River following the Pennsylvania campaign to guard its fords against a possible Union crossing. From September 14 to October 8, Hays's brigade picketed Raccoon Ford and listened to "the Yankee drums night & morning" across the river. Little fighting took place at the ford, but on September 16 Captain Frank Moore slipped two companies of the 5th and 9th Louisiana across the icy river and surprised the 5th New York Cavalry. Several federals were killed in the raid, including their commanding officer, and forty-two were captured. The Yankees accused Moore's men of murdering their major after he was captured, but the Tigers claimed he was killed when he fired on them after being told to surrender. Bolstered by this small success, Hays's confident Tigers wished daily that the Yankees would try to force a crossing; as William Oliver put it, "It is getting cold and we stand in need of [the] blankets and overcoats."[1]

The army slowly regained its strength during this quiet period as numerous sick and wounded men returned to their units. Surprisingly, even a number of Louisiana deserters, "some of whom we never expected to meet again," showed up in camp. Not all Tigers were so duty-conscious, however. A circular by the Bureau of Conscription dated September 14, 1863, claimed that many Loui-

1. William H. Oliver to Hiram Oliver, September 26, 1863, in Section 5, George Family Papers, VHS; Seymour, "Journal," in Seymour Papers, UM; Reed, *Private in Gray*, 49–50; Pas. R. Garcia to Marguerite E. Williams, October 1, 1863, in Folder 1, Marguerite E. Williams Collection, SHC; Compiled Service Records, War Record Group 109, Microcopy 320, Rolls 148 and 201, NA.

sianians were leaving the army by using fraudulent substitution papers.[2]

In early October, Lee took advantage of the improved condition of his men and lashed out at the enemy when he learned that Meade had weakened his army by sending two corps to Tennessee. The eager Confederates swung north of the Rappahannock River and clashed with their foe at Bristoe Station. A general battle failed to develop, however, and Lee contented himself with destroying Meade's railroad line before recrossing the river at Rappahannock Station. But after withdrawing across the Rappahannock, Lee left a brigade of infantry on the north bank to guard this single pontoon bridge in hopes that he would be able to resume the offense in the near future. Johnson's and Early's divisions encamped on the south bank and took turns sending brigades across the bridge to garrison a series of old federal earthworks on the opposite shore.[3]

On November 5 Meade beat Lee to the offensive by sending one column of infantry against Rappahannock Station and another against Kelly's Ford, a crossing on the Rappahannock downstream from the bridge. Seeing an opportunity to cripple part of this pincer movement, Lee ordered Early to hold the enemy in check at the pontoon bridge while Rodes and Johnson pounced on the Yankee column crossing at Kelly's Ford. At sunrise on November 6, Colonel Davidson Penn, acting commander while Hays was serving on a court-martial, jogged the Louisiana Brigade across the bridge to the earthworks. William Monaghan's 6th Louisiana and Captain A. L. Gusman's 8th Louisiana were sent four hundred yards beyond the right flank and center as skirmishers, while Peck's 9th Louisiana and Colonel T. M. Terry's 7th Louisiana occupied the trenches. Penn also had four guns of the Louisiana Guard Battery, which were placed in two redoubts within the line held by Peck's and Terry's men.

Occupying these works was a gamble because the position had

2. John Orr to J. M. Wilson, August 19, 1863, in Army of Northern Virginia Papers, Part I, LHAC; *OR*, Series IV, Vol. II, 808.

3. Freeman, *R. E. Lee*, III, 169–93; Seymour, "Journal," in Seymour Papers, UM; W. G. Ogden to father, October 21, 1863, in Ogden Papers, TU; Reed, *Private in Gray*, 50–51; Compiled Service Records, War Record Group 109, Microcopy 320, Rolls 148, 163, 187, NA.

several defects. Laid out in a semicircle with both flanks anchored
on the river above and below the bridge, the entire trench line was
commanded by a higher ridge several hundred yards out front. Attacking troops could mass unseen behind this ridge and advance
upon the Tigers from behind a railroad embankment that ran near
the rebels' right flank. There were several "dead points" along the
works that could not be reached by defensive fire, and, to compli-
cate matters, a dam below the bridge turned the river into an un-
fordable lake. If the Tigers ran into trouble on the north bank, the
narrow pontoon bridge was their only avenue of escape.[4]

November 6 passed uneventfully, but in the early morning of November 7 a large number of the enemy began massing in front of
the Louisianians. After watching the buildup for several hours,
Penn and Captain Seymour were convinced that Meade's entire V
and VI Corps were facing their brigade. Urgent messages were
sent across the river to Early, but it was not until 3:00 P.M. that Lee
and Early arrived at the bridge with reinforcements. By then Penn
had withdrawn all of his men into the trenches and Captain J. G.
Angell's 5th Louisiana had arrived from picket duty downstream.
At 4:00 P.M., Hays returned to resume command and received
three regiments of Hoke's brigade under Colonel A. C. Godwin as
reinforcements. Lee attempted to send another cannon over, as
well, but had to cancel the order when it appeared certain that federal sharpshooters would cut down the crew before they could get
into position. Lee finally decided not to send any more troops
across. He believed the Union activity was simply a demonstration
to mask the thrust at Kelly's Ford and that Hays and Godwin could
hold their position unaided because the Yankees had room to advance only on a two-brigade front. Even if his men did have to retreat, Lee thought, they could pull back across the bridge under the
protective fire of Early's men on the south bank.[5]

Unknown to Lee, this was not a demonstration but a full-scale
assault in the making. By dark the bridge was under a barrage
of fire from artillery and infantry that had virtually surrounded
Hays's position. Ferrying messages back and forth across the span,
Captain Seymour discovered just how dangerous the bridge had

4. *OR*, Vol. XXIX, Pt. I, 619–20, 626–27; Early, *War Memoirs*, 307–309, 316.
5. Early, *War Memoirs*, 309–13; *OR*, Vol. XXIX, Pt. I, 612–13, 618–29.

become—"the balls whistled around my head in a manner that was not musical in the least," he remembered. Seymour finally had to abandon his work and take cover in the trenches after his horse, "Dick Ewell," was hit in the leg.[6]

While darkness enveloped the river, Lee and Early watched as Hays's trench line suddenly erupted in jagged flashes of musket fire. A strong wind drowned out all noise of the firing, and when the flashes abruptly ceased, Lee dismissed it as a skirmish. He retired for the night, still convinced that the action was a feint. Early had no reason to believe otherwise until an aide sent to check on Hays's rations came galloping back saying that Tigers were streaming across the bridge in an apparent retreat. Early quickly alerted his men on the south bank and rode to the river to investigate.

Lee had been completely fooled by the Yankees. Masked by their artillery fire, a noisy wind, and the convenient railroad embankment, two brigades of the VI Corps had crept up to Hays's right, fixed bayonets, and swooped down on the Louisiana line. The muzzle flashes Lee and Early saw were the surprised Tigers fighting back. Scores of Yankees were cut down, and numerous others in the front lines tried to surrender, but the mass of federals behind them never slowed and soon swarmed over Hays's position without firing a shot. Their line pierced in two places, the 6th, 8th, and 9th Louisiana on the right were cut off from Godwin and the 5th and 7th Louisiana on the left.[7]

Fighting along the trench line was short but desperate, with bayonets frequently used. "Our men clubbed their muskets and used them freely over Yankees heads," wrote Charles Batchelor.[8] But it was a losing battle. Urged on by four unidentified officers on snow white horses, the Yankees skillfully surrounded the Confederates and began gathering hundreds of prisoners even after the anonymous officers were killed by the Tigers. When it became apparent that all was lost, the Confederates made their escape as best they could. Hays's courier, Charlie Stewart, was slapped on the back by a scowling federal and ordered off his horse. Stewart quickly

6. Seymour, "Journal," in Seymour Papers, UM.

7. *OR*, Vol. XXIX, Pt. I, 577, 585–90, 618–29; Early, *War Memoirs*, 313–15; Benedict, *Vermont in the Civil War*, 404–405.

8. Charles Batchelor to father, December 21, 1863, in Folder 6, Batchelor Papers, LSU.

complied, but the Yankee left after seeing that the animal was wounded and not likely to go anywhere. Stewart then remounted and managed to lash his wounded horse across the bullet-swept bridge, although the poor creature was shot five more times in the process. Surrounded by screaming Yankees, Hays was resigned to capture but could not sheath his saber in the crowd of fighting men. When his horse bolted on its own for the bridge, he reluctantly hung on and was able to escape across the span in a hail of gunfire. Peck and Seymour effected similar escapes, and Monaghan, Terry, and Major William Manning swam to safety.

Most of the Tigers were not so lucky. Scores of Louisianians and Tar Heels tried to swim the river but were shot in midstream or else retreated from the icy water to accept capture. When Lieutenant Charles Pierce's capture was imminent, he broke his sword over his knee and defiantly handed the hilt to the federals. Most of the Tigers' colors were seized, but color guard Leon Bertin saved the 7th Louisiana's flag by tearing it from the staff and hiding it under his shirt before surrendering.[9]

Within minutes after Hays's collapse on the right, Godwin and the other Tigers were overwhelmed on the left. Waiting at the south end of the bridge, Early was horrified as the flash of muskets and yells of the combatants marked the fight's progress. "I had the mortification," he wrote, "to hear the final struggle of these devoted men and to be made painfully aware of their capture, without the possibility of being able to go to their relief."[10]

The action at Rappahannock Station was unique in that it included one of the truly rare bayonet charges of the war. "Here the unusual sight of death by bayonet wounds was witnessed," remembered one Union veteran, "a dozen or more Confederate soldiers showing bayonet wounds, as well as some Union dead." Two tough, determined federal brigades had assaulted and captured the entrenched Confederates. The Tigers never accepted this defeat and made exaggerated claims about the battle's events. Following the

9. Patterson, "Story of the War," in Patterson Collection, Fredericksburg and Spotsylvania National Military Park; Peter W. Hairston Diary, November 7, 12, and 13, 1863, Vol. III, in Peter W. Hairston Collection, SHC; Seymour, "Journal," in Seymour Papers, UM; *Southern Historical Society Papers*, VIII (1880), 61–62; *OR*, Vol. XXIX, Pt. I, 591, 600.

10. *OR*, Vol. XXIX, Pt. I, 622.

fight, one Tiger wrote that they had "made many a Yankee bite the dust," and another rebel claimed, "The ground for 150 yards up to the very breastworks was literally covered with their dead and in some cases they were piled upon each other. . . . [Hays] certainly saw over one thousand *dead* upon the field."[11]

In truth, however, the Yankees had captured nearly 1,600 rebels at a loss of only 348 men. Muster rolls show that on November 10 fewer than 500 of Hays's men were left on duty—699 were listed as captured. Some regiments had literally disappeared. Of the 122 men in the 5th Louisiana, only one captain answered roll call following the clash.[12] It seemed as if Hays's famous command was lost forever. In a glowing editorial, the Richmond *Whig* wrote:

> We must be permitted . . . to express our sincere regret at the capture of a large portion of Hays' brigade. Decimated as it was, the nine hundred remaining Louisianians were worth their weight in gold to the army. . . . There is nothing to show that Hoke's brigade did not fight as bravely in the late affair as that of Hays's, but the imperishable record of the . . . [latter] in the great campaign in the Valley and in all the mighty battles in Virginia, Maryland and Pennsylvania, had endeared it to the whole country and particularly to the people of Virginia—Before they were trained, the Louisianians gave evidence of pluck and *elan* of the soldier by nature. . . . If now they are lost to Lee's army, we know not where the material will be found to replace them.[13]

There was, indeed, little left of "that skeleton Brigade of Louisianians," as J. S. Dea put it. "Her ranks cannot be swelled again. . . . [And] one or two more charges, I dare say, who will fill there ranks—there ghosts, I presume." The brigade was so reduced in numbers that there was even talk of consolidating Hays's brigade

11. Camille Baquet, *History of the First Brigade, New Jersey Volunteers from 1861 to 1865* (Trenton, 1910), 102; John McCormick to Williams, February 26, 1864, in Folder 1, Williams Collection, SHC; Hairston to wife, November 10, 1863, in Folder 33, Hairston Collection, SHC.

12. *OR*, Vol. XXIX, Pt. I, 590, 618–29; Monthly returns for Hays's brigade, October 30, November 10, 1863, in Early Papers, War Record Group 109, Entry 118, NA; Compiled Service Records, War Record Group 109, Microcopy 320, Roll 148, NA; Charles Cormier to unknown, November 15, 1863, in Army of Northern Virginia Papers, Part I, LHAC.

13. Richmond *Whig*, n.d., in Newsclippings and Miscellaneous Unidentified Material, LHAC.

with Stafford's. This idea never materialized although the remnants
of Hays's and Hoke's brigades were temporarily combined under
Hays's single command, a decision that so rankled the North Carolina officers that Early had to separate the Tigers' and Tar Heels'
camps to keep peace.[14]

Although Hays and Godwin had been crushed by only two Union
brigades, hardly anyone held the soldiers responsible for the loss.
One exception was the editor of the Richmond *Enquirer*, who apparently had doubts about the Tigers' defense. Colonel Peck was so
enraged by one editorial concerning the disaster that he wondered
aloud if the editor would foolishly challenge him to a duel if he
wrote the paper "a very insulting letter." Lee did not share the editor's views and told his staff that none of the officers directing the
defense should be blamed. He wrote in his report that "the courage
and good conduct of the troops engaged have been too often tried
to admit of question." The poor layout of the earthworks, darkness,
and the surprise of the assault were the most widely accepted reasons for the defeat, although Lee also felt that sharpshooters should
have been stationed far enough in advance to warn of the attack.[15]

The consensus of the army was that Lee himself was to blame for
not foreseeing what was developing and either sending Hays more
reinforcements or withdrawing the two brigades. One Tiger wrote
home, "You and everyone else will wonder why those brave men
were not reinforced in time to save them from destruction, nobody
knows but Genl. Lee, who I hope will account satisfactory for it."
The general admitted to Early that he had been surprised by the
attack and to his staff "rather intimated whatever blame there was
must attach to himself."[16]

In the final analysis, it did little good to second-guess reasons for
the defeat, although one Tiger held in prison on Johnson's Island
could not help but complain "at the fate, which through the stu-
pidity of some one, placed me here." Lee put the incident aside

14. Jno. S. Dea to Williams, January 29, March 5, 1864, in Folder 1, Williams Collection, SHC; Hairston Diary, November 9, 10, 12, 1863, in Hairston Collection,
SHC.
15. Hairston Diary, November 12, 1863, in Hairston Collection, SHC; *OR*, Vol.
XXIX, Pt. I, 613.
16. Cormier to unknown, November 15, 1863, in Army of Northern Virginia,
Part I, LHAC; Hairston Diary, November 12, 1863, in Hairston Collection, SHC.

and proceeded with the war. Meeting Hays the following day, he greeted the Louisianian, "General, this is a sad affair. How do you feel today?" "I feel, sir," the dejected Hays replied, "as well as a man can feel who has lost so many men." "That is all over now and cannot be helped," Lee assured him. "The only thing is to try to get even with them today." [17]

The Union victory at Rappahannock Station was matched by success in forcing a crossing at Kelly's Ford. To avoid being trapped along the Rappahannock, Lee burned his pontoon bridge and fell back across the Rapidan. But on November 26, Meade continued pressuring Lee by crossing the Rapidan on Lee's right and marching for his rear. In bitterly cold weather the army began shifting to the right to block Meade's advance. Since Ewell was on extended sick leave, Early temporarily took command of the II Corps, and Hays led Early's division on the march. On November 27, Hays found the federals in force around Locust Grove and began skirmishing while the rest of the army came into position.

Moving in on Lee's left, Johnson's division was shuffling down a narrow road not expecting any immediate enemy resistance when its wagon train in the rear came under heavy fire from a patch of woods to the left of the road. Taken by surprise with unloaded muskets, the division's infantry had to hurry back to the wagons and form a battle line in the thick woods. Suspecting the enemy to be merely cavalry raiders, the brigades charged through the narrow belt of timber with a cheer but were shocked by heavy volleys of musketry when they emerged onto a field surrounding Payne's Farm. Instead of cavalry, the outnumbered rebels were facing the entire federal VI Corps solidly emplaced behind a low rail fence 350 yards across the clearing. [18]

The Confederates were badly separated and disorganized from their jaunt through the woods and hastily took cover behind a rail fence bordering their side of the field. Stafford's men were lying low behind it when orders came down the line to charge. The protective fence came down, and the division rushed across the bullet-swept field toward the enemy. Stafford's brigade covered only 150

17. Thomas Gibbes Morgan, Jr., to mother, December 9, 1863, in Thomas Gibbes Morgan, Sr., and Jr., Papers, DU; Hairston Diary, November 12, 1863, in Hairston Collection, SHC.

18. *OR*, Vol. XXIX, Pt. I, 825–27, 830–36, 838, 843.

yards before finding itself unsupported by the other brigades and forced to fall back to the fence. The Louisianians tried three times to cross the field but were bloodily repulsed on each occasion. Fortunately, one Louisianian remembered, the federals "were about as bewildered as ourselves at the unexpected conflict" and failed to press their advantage. The Tigers lost heavily in the attacks, although most of the wounded were hit in the extremities and not seriously hurt. An exception was S. A. Johnson, who was shot through the back when the brigade retreated to the fence. After dragging the badly wounded soldier to safety, Johnson's comrades discovered his only concern was that people would think he was a coward when they learned where he had been hit. "He would not care for his wound," wrote J. M. Batchelor, "if it was only in front." Captain D. T. Merrick, brigade inspector-general, was one of the more fortunate wounded. He survived a bullet that unhorsed him when it hit the right side of his head above the mouth cavity, cutting off his left ear lobe as it exited on the other side.[19]

While the brigade sought shelter from the deadly missiles behind the jumble of fence rails, Stafford galloped constantly up and down the firing line on his horse, "Harry Hays." It was not until later that he disclosed to friends the reason for his recklessness. Stafford's horse was so badly frightened by the raging gunfire that the only way the general could control the poor creature was by keeping him in motion. Although some uninformed spectators marveled at this apparent bravery, Stafford found one who was not impressed. When he raced back to an artillery battery to redirect its firing, one of the crewmen remarked, "General, who was that crazy fellow on horse-back trying to get himself killed and at the same time show off by prancing his horse up and down the line of fire?" "Oh!" Stafford smiled as he rode off, "that was one of the officers in my brigade."[20]

When the heavy firing slackened at dark, a number of Tigers crept past their position to search for the wounded left between the lines. Unfortunately, federal skirmishers had slipped onto the contested ground before them and prevented the Tigers from collect-

19. Handerson, *Yankee in Gray*, 67; J. M. Batchelor to Albert Batchelor, n.d., in Batchelor Papers, LSU; *Confederate Veteran*, XV (1907), 325.
20. Quoted in Stafford, *General Leroy Augustus Stafford*, 42–43.

ing their men. When Stafford withdrew back to the road after dark, he was greatly dismayed at having to abandon most of his dead and wounded. Roll calls conducted around flickering camp-fires that night revealed that the brigade had suffered nearly half the division's fatalities with thirty dead, ninety-six wounded, and two missing.[21]

Finding the enemy too strongly entrenched to assault, Lee re-tired behind Mine Run, dug in, and dared Meade to attack him. Meade, however, refused to take the bait and settled in on the op-posite side of the stream. For several days the two armies shivered in the cold, damp ditches and exchanged volleys of musketry across Mine Run. During the standoff, Stafford's and Hays's men had the additional displeasure of watching several of their comrades dragged beyond the lines to be shot. Stafford's scheduled execution had a bizarre ending when the two condemned men escaped their fate by suddenly bolting for the Union line across Mine Run.[22]

Hays's shooting had a more predictable ending. Twenty-year-old Cain Comfort, an Irish member of the 6th Louisiana, had deserted his company several months earlier. Comfort, "a sullen, cross, ugly fellow, who seemed to be entirely devoid of pride and sensibility," then hired out as a substitute for three hundred dollars and joined the Union army. He had the misfortune of being captured by his old company during the Bristoe Station campaign and was sen-tenced to be shot for desertion.[23]

On November 30 the Tigers stood along the earthworks as a shackled Comfort was led to the head of a grave dug fifty yards away. When the chains were removed, Comfort's hands were tied behind him, and twelve of his former comrades stepped forward with muskets. While a priest stood by whispering prayers and offer-ing Comfort a crucifix to kiss, Captain Seymour read the charge and sentence and asked Comfort if he had any last words. The doomed man quietly replied that he had never "pulled a trigger against his old comrades" and had resolved never to do so when he joined the enemy. He added that he harbored no ill-will against

21. *OR*, Vol. XXIX, Pt. I, 846–49, 870–75; Bartlett, *Military Record of Louisiana*, 48; Charles Batchelor to father, December 12, 1863, in Folder 6, Batchelor Papers, LSU.

22. Casler, *Four Years in the Stonewall Brigade*, 198.

23. Seymour, "Journal," in Seymour Papers, UM.

Seymour or the firing squad, for he knew they were only doing
their duty. Seymour then turned to the executioners and told them
it would be an act of mercy if they aimed well. Within seconds Comfort was killed by nine balls through his head. "I hope," Seymour
wrote, "that I may never witness a like scene again." Although
Seymour's account of this incident seems clear, there is some confusion about the identity of the man executed. Seymour claimed he
was John Connolly, but a 6th Louisiana muster roll gives his name
as Cain Comfort. Official muster rolls are usually more reliable
than an individual's memory, but Andrew B. Booth's records of
Louisiana Confederate soldiers show that both of these men survived the war.[24]

When Meade finally tired of the stalemate and withdrew from
Mine Run, the Louisianians returned to picket duty along the
Rapidan. Although the men were in good physical condition that
winter and early spring of 1863–1864, they were sorely lacking in
food and clothing. At times, a daily ration in Stafford's brigade consisted of a quarter pound of meat and one pound of cornmeal, with
an occasional small amount of coffee and sugar. As early as October, a number of soldiers in the 6th Louisiana claimed they were
"totally barefoot & nearly naked," and in December, 250 of Hays's
men reportedly had no blankets. Some regiments were reduced to
burning corn shucks for fuel during this time of need, when the
weather was often so cold that ink froze in the men's pens as they
wrote home. "It is a great wonder," wrote Seymour, "that these
men do not freeze to death these terribly cold nights. Many of them
use pine leaves and boughs wherewith to shield them from the
cold, while others sit up by the fires all night, and, borrowing the
blankets of their more fortunate comrades, sleep during the day."[25]

Some relief for the clothing shortage was found by seeking out-

24. *Ibid.*; Reed, *Private in Gray*, 59–60; Bound Volume 6 in Association of the
Army of Northern Virginia, LHAC; Booth (comp.), *Louisiana Confederate Soldiers*, II,
401, 414.

25. Dea to Williams, March 5, 1864, and Garcia to Williams, January 5, 1864, in
Folder 1, Williams Collection, SHC; Seymour, "Journal," in Seymour Papers, UM;
Compiled Service Records, War Record Group 109, Microcopy 320, Roll 163, NA;
7th Louisiana Volunteers Quartermaster document, March, 1864, in *ibid.*, Chap. V,
Vol. 205; Oliver to Oliver, September 26, 1863, in George Family Papers, VHS;
Handerson, *Yankee in Gray*, 53; H. Evans to unknown, January 10, 1864, in H. Evans
Letter, LSU; Batchelor to sister, April 3, 1864, in Batchelor Papers, LSU.

side help. General Stafford appealed to Louisiana's civilians to send his men whatever clothing they could spare, but whether he succeeded is unknown. Hays had better luck in dealing with the Virginians, whom Sergeant Stephens claimed "seem to regard this Brigade as a big muscle in Lee's Army." The people of Richmond made some donations to the tattered brigade, and Stephens wrote that the citizens of Lynchburg raised $20,000 "on behalf of the band of Exiles, as we call ourselves." Apparently, however, Stephens was in error concerning the generosity of the latter. Records of the 6th Louisiana indicate that supplies from Lynchburg came only after a "levy" was placed on the city to supply each of Hays's men with a coat and blanket. Stephens and the other Tigers mistakenly believed that this precious clothing came freely from the Virginians and was in gratitude for the brigade's service to the Old Dominion.[26]

The cold, miserable winter had a depressing effect on the Tigers. Reflecting on his long military career, one soldier complained, "I am almost wild. I do not think that I will ever be fit again to associate with respectable people. I have not spoken to a lady for two years [for] I have been in the woods since I left home." Father Sheeran found that Stafford's war-weary men were very susceptible to "the enemy of peace and charity" that winter and that so many men chose desertion as a means of escape that it "even threatened to break up the organization of our brigade." On February 18, 1864, Lee wrote Secretary of War James Seddon to express his deep concern at the Louisiana desertions. He claimed that no one could account for the high desertion rate in Stafford's command since "every attention is given to the wants of the men and every effort [is] made to supply them with food and clothing." Stafford was on leave in Richmond at the time for an unexplained operation, but Lee hoped he would return soon, as "it may produce some change in the disposition of his men." But there is no evidence that Stafford's return improved the situation. Although most of the Tigers who deserted went over to the enemy lines, not all of the Louisianians looked so kindly upon the federals. H. Evans wrote a friend, "I do not care about knowing the doings of the Yanks in your part of

26. Stephens to Mr. and Mrs. T. E. Paxton, January 14, 1864, in Stephens Collection, NSU; Compiled Service Records, War Record Group 109, Microcopy 320, Roll 163, NA.

the world. You can't learn me anything about them—I know the beasts too well. I know their nature as well as I do my door. I know that in the whole catalogue of crimes they have left nothing undone to change their well deserved reputation of cowardly dogs."[27]

Despite the numerous desertions, there remained a solid core of Tigers who were undaunted by the hardships and found various ways to combat the loneliness and battle fatigue. Both Hays's and Stafford's brigades built wooden theaters that winter and organized minstrel shows. One Tiger claimed that Hays's troupe "perform Every night, and it is crowded. Some times all the Generals in the Corps is in with their wife to see the performances." A minstrel troupe established by Stafford's and Walker's brigades charged a dollar admission to its show to raise money for the widows and orphans of Confederate dead. Writing their own material, the soldiers put on several musicals and satirical plays, with the most popular performance being a skit depicting army surgeons drinking and playing cards while nearby wounded suffered.[28]

One of the most popular forms of entertainment in the rebel camps was snowball fighting. Each dusting of snow brought out squads of men from the Deep South, who laughed and chased one another until exhausted. On March 23, after a particularly heavy snowstorm, this sport became a massive event when the Stonewall Brigade and Stafford's men challenged Generals George Doles's and Stephen Ramseur's brigades to a fight. The Georgians and Tar Heels surprised Walker's and Stafford's brigades by taking up the gauntlet and chasing them for over a mile before breaking off the engagement. One of the Louisiana officers, however, refused to accept the defeat and sent out "conscript officers" to round up reinforcements while he hunted for General James Walker to come take command of a new offensive. Battle flags began to unfurl, drummers beat the long roll, and staff officers galloped through camp shouting orders as eight thousand men gathered to take part in the mock battle. Stafford arrived to lead the Louisiana Brigade, while more of Rodes's division assembled on a nearby hill with

27. Evans to unknown, January 10, 1864, in Evans Letter, LSU; Durkin (ed.), *Confederate Chaplain,* 73, 78; *OR,* XXXIII, 1187.

28. Garcia to Williams, March 22, 1864, in Folder 1, Williams Collection, SHC; Robertson, *Stonewall Brigade,* 216–17; Casler, *Four Years in the Stonewall Brigade,* 204.

Doles and Ramseur to make snowballs and scream threats of anni-
hilation at Johnson's division forming below.

Walker accepted the Louisianians' request to lead a new charge
and devised an elaborate battle plan. While Stafford hid his brigade
in a patch of woods on the right, Walker would lead the rest of
the division against Rodes's line, briefly engage it, and then retreat
to draw them from their hilltop. When the "enemy" passed the
woods, Stafford would strike their flank and Walker would turn to
counterattack.

When Walker began his advance, Father Sheeran wrote, "The
lines were so regularly formed, the movements so systematic, the
officers displaying so much activity at the head of their commands,
their men fighting so stubbornly, now advancing on the opposite
column, now giving way before superior numbers that one would
forget for a moment that it was merely a sham." Walker rode directly into Rodes's division and was pelted by hundreds of snowballs. Within seconds, he and his horse were covered with snow.
"Retreat! Retreat!" he yelled, and the men stumbled back down
the slope with Rodes's men chasing them, "almost exhausted with
laughter." At the critical moment, Stafford rushed from the woods,
and "once more there was a vast cloud of snow from breaking balls
that filled the whole air." [29] Johnson's division turned, routed Rodes's
stunned men, and chased them for over a mile back through their
own camps. "Many prisoners were captured and sent to the rear,"
remembered one onlooker. Another claimed, "The Louisianians
. . . stole some cooking utensils from Rodes's men and kept them."
After five hours of fighting, the exhausted soldiers finally called it
quits, and the victorious Tigers "came home as proud as if they had
gained a victory over the Yankees." [30]

Spring arrived soon after the epic snowball battle and instilled a
new fighting spirit into the Tigers. Morale was further lifted when
approximately five hundred of the men captured at Rappahannock Station were exchanged and returned to Hays's brigade by

29. Durkin (ed.), *Confederate Chaplain*, 78–79; Ben LaBree (ed.), *Camp Fires of the Confederacy* (Louisville, 1899), 58.

30. La Bree, *Camp Fires of the Confederacy*, 58; Casler, *Four Years in the Stonewall Brigade*, 202; Robert Harris, Jr., to W. Crawford Harris, March 25, 1864, in MSCA; Durkin (ed.), *Confederate Chaplain*, 79.

early March. "I am very glad to see," wrote J. R. Garcia, "that we will
have a good Brigade once more to make the Yankees Skedaddle
from the Valley." Most of the Tigers shared Garcia's desire to get
back at the Yankees. J. S. Dea wrote, "I hope with the blessings of
God if nothing happens to me I will witness another Yankee run in
that sweet Valley of Virginia." The Louisianians especially wanted
to test the mettle of the highly touted Ulysses S. Grant, who had
just taken over the Union armies. The Army of Northern Virginia,
wrote Charles Batchelor, was "anxious to meet the Yankees' greatest general under the immortal Robert E. Lee." Although Batchelor firmly believed peace would come if the South could only win a
few more battles, he was under no delusion. "Pray continually and
fervently for us my dear sister," he added.[31]

The Tigers soon got their chance to strike the enemy, for on May
4 Grant began crossing the Rapidan on Lee's right to draw the rebel
general into battle. Hoping to intercept the federal column while it
passed through the tangle of thickets known as the Wilderness, Lee
ordered Longstreet to join the army from his camps near Richmond, while Ewell's and Hill's corps hurried eastward along the
parallel Orange Turnpike and Plank Road, respectively. The Confederates were enthusiastic on May 5 as they closed in on the Chancellorsville area, where Jackson had been victorious a year earlier.
"I never saw our men so cheerful," wrote Father Sheeran. "The
poor fellows had little idea of the terrible conflict in which they
were about to engage."[32]

After deploying Johnson's division astride the Orange Turnpike,
with Rodes and Early in support, Ewell began inching his way into
the dark Wilderness on the morning of May 5. Ewell moved cautiously because he was under orders not to bring on a general engagement until Longstreet arrived and to regulate his advance to
Hill's progress on the Plank Road to his right. At 11:00 A.M. the column suddenly halted when word was passed quietly down the line
that the Yankees had been spotted ahead. As the ambulances and

31. Garcia to Williams, March 22, 1864, in Williams Collection, SHC; also see
Reuben Allen Pierson to sister, March 28, 1864, in Folder 17, Carver Collection,
NSU; Charles S. Hollier, Company F, 8th Louisiana Volunteers, pension file, in
LSA; Dea to Williams, January 29, 1864, in Williams Collection, SHC; Batchelor to
sister, April 3, 1864, in Folder 7, Batchelor Papers, LSU.
32. Durkin (ed.), *Confederate Chaplain*, 86.

wagons began pulling off the road to make room for the infantry to
deploy, Stafford took his men into the woods on the left, sent out
sharpshooters, and waited.

Shortly after the federals were seen, the right center of Johnson's
division was viciously attacked by the Yankees. Smoke boiled above
the green foliage as Johnson's entire line began firing blindly toward the sound of the cheering Yankees. The federals killed General J. M. Jones when they smashed his brigade and sent it reeling
backward. Ewell desperately threw Rodes's division and Gordon's
brigade into the melee and after a bitter fight managed to close the
gap. When the Union brigades withdrew three hundred yards,
both sides hurriedly dug in and tried to retrieve some of the
wounded from the path of several brush fires begun by the intense
firing.[33]

Taking advantage of this temporary lull, Ewell straightened out
his confused line by placing Rodes on the right of the road, Johnson astride it, and sending Early through the woods to extend
Johnson's left. Impatient for orders, Stafford rode back to get his
instructions while his men scratched out makeshift earthworks,
cooked dinner, and quietly smoked in the lush jungle. The woods
around the Louisianians seemed to come alive with wild game
flushed out by the noise and fires. Colonel Zebulon York brought
peals of laughter from the Tigers when he chased a frightened fox
down the trench line, and a turkey that bolted from the underbrush was greeted by rebel yells and a volley of musketry. Even a
skittish rabbit was run down and caught by some of the more nimble
soldiers. This entertainment was cut short, however, when several
men who had ventured beyond the line came rushing back through
the brush crying breathlessly that federal skirmishers were only
a short distance away. The soldiers grabbed their muskets and
scrambled to their feet just as Stafford rode back into camp. When
told of the situation, he ordered the brigade to fall back one hundred yards and reform. After the men got into position, hundreds of ramroads rattled down muskets as officers gave the order,
"Load!" When all was ready, Stafford rode out in front of his men

33. *Ibid.*, 86–87; Freeman, *R. E. Lee*, III, 269–76; Edward Steere, *The Wilderness Campaign* (New York, 1960), 144–83; E. M. Law, "From the Wilderness to Cold Harbor," in Johnson and Buel (eds.), *Battles and Leaders*, IV, 121–28.

and cautiously picked his way through the bushes to meet the expected Union assault.[34]

The brigade had covered a quarter mile of timber, remembered
Assistant Adjutant General Henry Handerson, when off to the
right erupted "the most tremendous roll of musketry it was ever
my fortune to hear." The noise in that direction was almost deafening, yet the "dusky woods" to Stafford's front remained eerily quiet.
It was 3:00 P.M., and the terrific firing was Grant's VI Corps crashing through the thickets toward Ewell's line. Stafford's own front
soon was crawling with Yankees, who stopped short along a low
ridge and pumped volleys of heavy musket fire into the Louisianians. With hat in hand, Stafford spurred his horse across a gully
fronting the brigade and waved his men forward. The federals
quickly retreated across a narrow field and drew up in a new position along the opposite tree line. Stafford was preparing to push
across this field when a courier came galloping out of the thickets,
pointing frantically to the left and screaming, "They are coming!"
Stafford at first did not believe this excited aide because Walker's
brigade was supposedly on the Tigers' left flank. But it quickly became apparent that the Virginians had not kept up and Colonel
Henry Brown's New Jersey brigade had pushed into the gap.[35]

Stafford hurriedly ordered the fifty men of the 1st Louisiana
holding the left to bend back perpendicular to the main line and
hold off the charging Yankees. The commanding officer there,
however, either misunderstood his instructions or panicked and
simply waved his sword overhead and yelled for his men to rally
around him. The resultant mob offered no resistance to the ag-
gressive Yankees and succeeded only in making themselves an easy
target. Realizing he could not hold off this flank attack, Stafford
yelled over the uproar for Handerson to make his way to the right,
find Steuart's left flank, and guide the brigade to it. Handerson had
barely ridden out of sight when he blundered into another Yankee
line sweeping through the woods and was captured.

By then, resistance was hopeless. Cut off from both Confederate
brigades on his flanks, surrounded by nearly impassable thickets,
and blinded by smoke from the woods fires, Stafford could only

34. Durkin (ed.), *Confederate Chaplain*, 86–87.
35. Handerson, *Yankee in Gray*, 70.

order his men to withdraw to the right and make their way back to the original line. Calmly sitting astride his horse, Stafford waited until the last man of the 1st Louisiana filed past before turning to close up the rear. Suddenly, the general was knocked from his horse by a bullet that severed his spine when it cut through his body from armpit to shoulderblade. The paralyzed Stafford was scooped up by several men and carried back to the trenches, where the others were busily reinforcing their works. It is not known how many men Stafford lost in the thirty-minute clash, except that the 10th Louisiana had six killed, nineteen wounded, and eight missing.[36]

While the brigade dug in along an old woods road, Hays's men came trotting by on their way to extend Johnson's left. These Tigers, especially the 9th Louisiana, were shocked to see "poor Stafford" laid out under a shady tree beside the road, suffering from the agonizing wound. Although in a hurry to reach their assigned position, the men slowed as they passed, and each one spoke a few soft words of encouragement and sympathy to the stricken officer. Stafford, in turn, told them he was ready to die if need be and urged them to fight to the last man. Many of the soldiers left the general believing he might recover from the ghastly wound, but Stafford died in Richmond on May 8. Stafford's death was said to have "cast a gloom over the city." President and Mrs. Davis attended his funeral and watched as the Louisiana general was laid to rest in a grave beside that of Major Roberdeau Wheat.[37]

Hays's brigade soon arrived on Walker's left and began preparing to advance through the woods. Captain Seymour was dispatched to inform Walker of the impending assault, but his 25th Virginia was the only regiment that actually joined in the attack. When all was ready, Hays pushed the men into the thickets and almost immediately engaged the enemy. Firing as they slowly advanced, the Tigers drove the Yankees through the woods with ease, although the dense timber and smoke broke up the brigade's alignment and dis-

36. Bartlett, *Military Record of Louisiana*, 12, 49; Handerson, *Yankee in Gray*, 69–71; Stafford, *General Leroy Augustus Stafford*, 44–51; Richmond *Enquirer*, May 10, 1864; Robertson, *Stonewall Brigade*, 218–20; McHenry, *Recollections of a Maryland Confederate*, 274–75.

37. Stafford, *General Leroy Augustus Stafford*, 44–48; Seymour, "Journal," in Seymour Papers, UM.

organized the men. Sergeant E. L. Stephens, whose letters chronicle so much of the Tigers' activity, fell victim to this confusion. A
little advanced of the main line, Stephens was kneeling down shooting under the brush when he was mortally wounded by a comrade's
bullet that struck him in the buttocks and destroyed his intestines as
it passed through his body.[38]

After advancing half a mile, the Tigers suddenly emerged onto a
field and spotted a long line of federals partially hidden in the pine
woods on the other side. These two Union brigades of Generals
David Russell and Thomas Neill heavily outnumbered Hays's small
band, but the Louisianians were caught up in the excitement of the
chase and recklessly pushed on through the field. The Yankees patiently waited, leveled their muskets, and cut down the advancing
gray line. Russell and Neill then sent their men swarming around
Hays's flanks, completely cutting off the 25th Virginia and capturing 300 of its members. Hays frantically extracted his command
from the slaughter and withdrew back across the field "under a
murderous fire." The retreat continued through the thickets, finally halting at the original line. There the shattered brigade used
tin cups and bayonets to throw up some hasty earthworks and nervously scanned the underbrush in front for any sign of the enemy.
The weary Tigers were not at all certain whether they could repel a
concerted attack, for the brief charge had cost them 250 men—
over one-third of Hays's command.[39]

John Pegram's brigade slid in on Hays's left and came under a
heavy attack late in the day but managed to beat it off with the help
of the 6th Louisiana. With darkness rapidly approaching in the
smoky woods, the opposing lines dug in a few hundred yards apart
along parallel ridges. Isolated sorties and constant skirmish fire
were kept up well into the night as brave soldiers on both sides
ventured into the smoldering no-man's land to drag the helpless
wounded to safety.

38. Ezra Denson to John F. Stephens, May 24, 1864, in Stephens Collection,
NSU; Seymour, "Journal," in Seymour Collection, UM.

39. Seymour, "Journal," in Seymour Collection, UM; *OR*, Vol. XXXVI, Pt. I,
1071, 1077–78; Jubal A. Early, *A Memoir of the Last Year of the War for Independence . . .
in the Year 1864 and 1865* (Lynchburg, 1867), 16–20; W. S. Dunlop, *Lee's Sharpshooters; or, the Forefront of Battle* (Little Rock, 1899), 390; G. P. Ring to wife, May 6,
1864, typescript copy, in Army of Northern Virginia, Part I, LHAC.

The day's fighting had been unlike any experienced before. The dense woods prevented the use of artillery, and the battle degenerated into a series of scattered fire fights. On Ewell's right, Hill's corps became heavily engaged along the Plank Road and was almost crushed until Longstreet's timely arrival saved the day. Longstreet fell to the curse of the Wilderness later in the day when he was mistakenly shot by his own men. When darkness finally ended the vicious assaults, the Wilderness glowed for miles as hundreds of fires spread among the dead and wounded trapped between the lines.

Hill and Longstreet resumed their heavy fighting on May 6, but Ewell's line was comparatively quiet. Deadly sniper fire and occasional probes kept the men alert, but the bloody assaults of the previous day were lacking. Captain G. P. Ring of the 6th Louisiana found time to jot a note to his wife during this interlude. In closing, he wrote: "With a trust in Providence for his continued favors, and the Hope abiding that this will be the last fight and that I may escape safely, with all my love—I had got this far when the enemy made a severe attack on us, which was for a half hour, when they fled to the shadows of obscurity. I am now out with my company skirmishing and the bullets are whistling all around me. I have just had another man killed, but this is nothing when you get used to it."[40]

The only major development on Ewell's front came late in the day, when Gordon found Grant's right flank unprotected and positioned his brigade to strike it. The surprise blow came just at dark, and the Yankee flank was thrown back nearly a mile when darkness ended the pursuit. Hays was supposed to join the attack once the federal flank was dislodged, but Neill's Union brigade in his front refused to abandon its works, and the Tigers' participation was limited to heavy skirmishing.[41]

After a second hellish night of fires and screaming wounded, May 7 dawned strangely quiet. It was soon apparent that Grant had abandoned his Wilderness line and was moving southeastward

40. G. P. Ring to wife, May 6, 1864, typescript copy, in Army of Northern Virginia, Part I, LHAC.

41. Seymour, "Journal," in Seymour Papers, UM; *OR,* Vol. XXXVI, Pt. I, 1071, 1077–78; Early, *Memoir of the Last Year of the War,* 16–20; Steere, *Wilderness Campaign,* 431–53; Freeman, *R. E. Lee,* III, 285–97.

toward Spotsylvania to turn Lee's right flank. While other units moved out to intercept him, the Tigers were left behind to help collect the dead and wounded. "Never was there a more grim and ghastly spectacle of the horror and terrible destructiveness of War," wrote Seymour. Father Egidius Smulders, a Louisiana chaplain, later discovered packs of wild dogs devouring the dead and visited a field hospital, where some of the wounded told of being "horrified as they . . . heard the shrieks of hundreds of the wounded enemies who were burned in their field hospitals."[42]

After fanning out into the scorched woods, Hays's men soon had a large number of badly wounded federals laid out along the trenches. "A ghastly exhibition of torn and mutilated humanity it was," recalled Seymour. Those who could withstand it were moved to field hospitals, but the mortally wounded "were left to die on the ground where they laid." By nightfall, all were dead—the last to succumb being a frightened German who spoke no English. As he gasped for breath, the Tigers crowded around him out of morbid curiosity. When tears began to roll down the doomed man's face, one Tiger blandly remarked that he must be thinking "of his vrow and little ones." Shortly, the man appeared to be dead, and another Louisianian knelt down and began rummaging through his pockets. A bystander appeared horrified at such callousness and warned the soldier that the Yankee's ghost would haunt him if robbed before he was actually dead. When the Tiger recoiled, the concerned Louisianian bent over, felt the pulse, and declared that the German was indeed "dead as a door nail." The second Tiger then removed all the valuables from the body, much to the chagrin of the other but "to the amusement of the bystanders."[43]

While racing toward Spotsylvania on May 8, Lee was forced to make command changes to fill the positions of the five generals who were killed or wounded. The disabled Longstreet was replaced by General Richard Anderson, and Early was given temporary command of the III Corps because Hill was too ill to continue. Lee then had to decide who would command Early's division. The logical choice was Hays because of his seniority, his temporary command of it at Mine Run, and his outstanding war record. But Lee

42. Seymour, "Journal," in Seymour Papers, UM; Egidius Smulders to Henry B. Kelly, March, 187[?], in Smulders Papers, Confederate Personnel, LHAC.
43. Seymour, "Journal," in Seymour Papers, UM.

chose Gordon instead. Although most historians feel that Gordon won the promotion because of his initiative in launching the flank attack on Grant's Wilderness line, this alone cannot explain Lee's decision. Gordon was without question an excellent officer, but he was nearly one year Hays's junior in rank, and his combat record could not be considered better than the Louisianian's. Perhaps Lee blamed Hays for the debacle at Rappahannock Station or, more probably, acted out of sheer intuition. Whatever the reason, the promotion created a difficult situation.

Not wanting to offend Hays, Lee had to find a graceful way to pass him over. In a confidential note to Ewell, Lee ordered Hays's brigade transferred to Johnson's division and consolidated with Stafford's. Lee justified this move by saying the two brigades were so small they could no longer function well separately and it would place all the Louisianians in one command. Moving Hays out of the division also conveniently opened the way for Gordon's promotion and supposedly soothed Hays's feelings by putting all the Tigers under his command.[44]

While Hays was in overall command, the terms of the order called for both brigades to keep their separate organization, with Colonel York commanding Stafford's men and Colonel Peck over Hays's. Although there had been talk of such a consolidation before, the change was not well received by the Louisianians. There is no record of Hays's thoughts on the subject, but the rest of the Tigers vocally opposed the new brigade. In August, Major Edwin L. Moore wrote, "The discipline in this command is lax. . . . [It] is composed of the discontented fragments of Hays' and Stafford's brigades. . . . Both officers and men bitterly object to their consolidation into one brigade. Strange officers command strange troops, and the difficulties of fusing this incongruous mass are enhanced by constant marching and frequent engagements." Assistant Adjutant General H. E. Paxton best summed up the Tigers' feelings when he wrote, "The troops of the old organizations feel that they have lost their identity, and are without the chance of perpetuating the distinct and separate history of which they were once so

44. Clifford Dowdey, *Lee's Last Campaign: The Story of Lee and His Men Against Grant—1864* (Boston, 1960), 194; Freeman, *R. E. Lee*, III, 304–305; Allen P. Tankersley, *John B. Gordon: A Study in Gallantry* (Atlanta, 1955), 146–47; Moore, *Louisiana Tigers*, 176; *OR*, Vol. XXXVI, Pt. II, 974; *ibid.*, Vol. LI, Pt. II, 902.

proud. This loss of prestige must excite to some extent a feeling of discontent."[45]

Discontented or not, the Louisianians had to live with the order and spend the last year of the war together as a unit. With a total strength of scarcely a thousand men, the new "Hays Brigade" was a pitiful remnant of the twelve thousand eager Tigers who came to Virginia three years earlier.

45. *OR*, Vol. XLIII, Pt. I, 610.

Chapter   X

ALL PLAYED OUT

Lee's fleet-footed Confederates arrived at Spotsylvania just minutes ahead of the Yankees. By sundown of May 9 the weary rebels had thrown up three miles of trenches and had settled confidently behind their earthworks to await the federal assault. Although formidable, this chain of works had a weak link in its left center, where the line jutted out in a great angle as it followed a low ridge. Holding the angle, or "Mule Shoe" as the rebels dubbed it, was Johnson's division, with Jones's brigade holding the apex, Steuart on the eastern side, and Hays and Walker on the western side. Sporadic skirmish fire throughout May 9 hampered the Louisianians' attempts to strengthen their position. While supervising his men, Hays was struck by a stray ball or a sharpshooter's bullet and collapsed in the ditch seriously wounded.

There is a great deal of confusion over who took command of the Tigers after Hays was wounded. Captain Seymour claimed that Colonel Monaghan assumed control of the consolidated brigade and kept the Tigers at their work. If this is true, both Peck and York must have been absent during the battles around Spotsylvania because neither of these senior colonels took command when Hays was shot. Further evidence of their absence is that Colonel Jesse M. Williams supposedly led York's brigade during the Spotsylvania fight, and in late May when Monaghan fell ill, Colonel Alcibiades DeBlanc took over the Tigers.

Lee soon recognized the danger posed by the isolated Mule Shoe and began constructing a new line across its base to eliminate it. Until the new works were finished, Johnson's men would have to remain alert against any Union attacks against them. On May 10 Grant hit the western side of the angle to the left of Walker and punched a hole through the Confederate defenses. Although the penetration was contained and then sealed by the rebels, Lee wor-

ried even more over the jutting angle. But on May 11, after inspecting the Mule Shoe, Lee was convinced that Johnson could hold the
angle with the support of twelve cannons placed behind him. In the
early afternoon, Ewell took a further precaution when he ordered
Monaghan to split his command in two and to send the 1st Louisiana Brigade to replace George Doles's brigade on Walker's left. In a
steady rain, Monaghan slid his men to the left and occupied Doles's
muddy works amid much grumbling from the Tigers over having
to rely on strangers' defenses. Their outlook changed, however,
when they were told this was the weakest part of the line, having
been penetrated on May 10, and that Ewell had personally requested that the most dependable brigade of the corps hold it. The
danger of the position was emphasized when the 8th Louisiana's
color guard thoughtlessly stood to plant the regiment's flag on the
works and was immediately killed. All heads remained low afterward when the brigade went about the gruesome task of removing
the federal dead that still lay in and about the trenches. Every man
was able to collect at least three muskets from among the dead, but
attempts to bury the men ended when the Tigers were fired upon
by the Yankees.[1]

When night fell, an ominous feeling pervaded the Confederates
holding the treacherous angle. A gloomy fog and drizzle that enveloped the trenches could not muffle the low rumble of a massive troop movement somewhere in the blackness ahead. Officers
strained in the night to decipher the meaning of the noise, and couriers rushed news of the mysterious movement to Lee. Lee believed
Grant was again pulling out to make a run for the Confederate
right flank and ordered Johnson's artillery to withdraw from the
angle so he could move quickly if that proved to be true. Monaghan, however, was convinced that the rumbling was the Yankees
preparing to attack and dispatched Seymour at midnight to impress his feelings upon Johnson. Johnson agreed with the Louisianian's assessment of the situation and urgently requested that Ewell
send the artillery back.[2]

In an atmosphere charged with foreboding, the Tigers peered

1. Seymour, "Journal," in Seymour Papers, UM.
2. *Ibid.*; Freeman, *R. E. Lee*, III, 306–26; *OR*, Vol. XXXVI, Pt. I, 1071, 1073,
1080; Dunlop, *Lee's Sharpshooters*, 456–66; Howard, *Recollections of a Maryland Confederate*, 292–94.

anxiously into the darkness and double-checked their muskets by pulling the loads to replace the damp powder. The 2d Louisiana Brigade received some assistance after midnight, when a Virginia regiment was brought up in support. "What's the matter here?" yelled one irritated Virginian. "You've had us waked up before day and brought out of our shelter into the rain?" "We will have the Yankees over here directly to take breakfast with us!" an unsympathetic Tiger shot back.[3]

Daylight on May 12 came slowly through the mist and fog. For the past few hours, the rumbling out front had ceased, and a tense quiet had settled over the trenches. As objects slowly became visible the Tigers nervously listened for the expected gunfire from their skirmishers posted beyond the breastworks. It was still barely light when the scattered popping of skirmish fire broke the silence. The shooting rose in tempo, signaling to Johnson's men that the Yankees were, indeed, on the move. Suddenly, off to the right "burst upon our startled ears a sound like the roaring of a tempestuous sea," wrote Seymour. All eyes turned toward the angle's apex, and one of Monaghan's men jumped up, pointed to the right, and yelled, "Look out, boys! We will have blood for supper!" Through a break in the fog in front of Jones's brigade could be seen wave after wave of madly cheering federal troops bearing down on the angle. In the rear of Jones's men came Johnson's missing artillerymen galloping back to their position just in time to be overwhelmed by the Yankee flood.[4]

Jones's brigade was smothered by the blue tide with hardly a shot fired. Grant's screaming Yankees then fanned out to both sides of the angle and came tearing down the trench line with a vengeance. The steady rain resumed as the Union assault washed upon York's and Steuart's brigades. The Louisianians managed only a few shots before being swallowed by the federals. Colonel Jesse M. Williams, temporarily commanding the 2d Louisiana Brigade, was killed in the brief struggle, but most of the brigade was disarmed and sent through the enemy lines as prisoners.[5]

3. *Confederate Veteran*, II (1894), 36.
4. Seymour, "Journal," in Seymour Papers, UM; Reed, *Private in Gray*, 75.
5. R. G. Cobb to Albert Batchelor, June 4, 1864, in Batchelor Papers, LSU; T. J. Stoern to J. A. Chalaron, June 9, 1864, in Flags, LHAC; Howard, *Recollections of a Maryland Confederate*, 295–98; Bartlett, *Military Record of Louisiana*, 49; Moore, *Louisiana Tigers*, 176; Worsham, *One of Jackson's Foot Cavalry*, 139–40.

Further to the left Monaghan watched as the brutal onslaught swept relentlessly toward him over the 2d Louisiana Brigade, then Walker's brigade. Monaghan ordered his men to slide 150 yards to the left and to realign perpendicular to the breastworks. The Tigers moved quickly but not before thirty-eight men on the right flank were seized by the federals. The brigade had barely gotten into position along a small hill when the federals swept upon them "yelling like devils." Monaghan roared, "Fire!" and the Tigers obliterated the first blue line. But others took their place, and the Yankees continued pushing forward. Time after time, the federals rushed upon Monaghan, but "those houseless, landless warriors of Louisiana . . . presented a front as firm as a ledge of rock," remembered one soldier, and managed to contain the Union penetration to the angle itself.[6]

The fighting along Monaghan's line was among the fiercest of the war, with the two armies often embraced in deadly hand-to-hand combat. "I have been in a good many hard fights," wrote Captain Ring, "but I never saw anything like the contest of the 12th. We lay all day and night in the Breastworks in mud five inches deep, with every kind of shot and shell whistling over us, amongst us, *in us*, about us, so that it was as much as your life was worth to raise your head above the works."[7]

Fourteen officers in Monaghan's brigade were shot that day, with Colonel Bruce Menger, "one of the best field officers in our Brigade," among the dead. Despite the heavy losses, the line held, and soon Gordon rushed in reinforcements that pushed the federals across the breastworks. Both armies clung to opposite sides of the works and blasted each other from point-blank range. In a driving rainstorm, the trenches filled with water, drowning some of the wounded, and the incessant firing shredded scattered postoak trees behind Monaghan's line. Some men fired as many as four hundred rounds during the fight and had to pick up weapons from among the dead and wounded when their muskets fouled from excessive use. For hours the battle raged, neither side able to dislodge the other. While the Confederates tenaciously clung to their position, Lee hurriedly finished the line along the angle's base. Finally, long

6. Dunlop, *Lee's Sharpshooters*, 41; Seymour, "Journal," in Seymour Papers, UM.
7. G. P. Ring to wife, May 15, 1864, typescript copy, in Army of Northern Virginia Papers, Part I, LHAC.

after dark—sixteen hours after the fight began—the new works were finished, and the exhausted gray defenders were able to disengage and fall back.[8]

When Monaghan reassembled his shattered brigades in the morning, he found the 2d Louisiana Brigade almost annihilated. Most of the brigade was captured, with the 10th Louisiana alone losing four dead, seven wounded, and fifty-seven missing. The 1st Louisiana Brigade lost fewer men captured but had a staggering number of killed and wounded. One small company of the 9th Louisiana had twelve men killed, and only sixty members of the 6th Louisiana were left to answer roll call on the morning of May 13. Many of the Louisiana dead, having been horribly mutilated by the concentrated musket fire, were buried without being identified. The scene along Monaghan's position defied description with mangled bodies lying in heaps among the works. "May God grant that I may never again experience such sensations or witness such scenes," wrote Father Sheeran. "The sights are shocking. The smell is still more offensive."[9]

The Louisiana Tigers were able to contain Grant's breakthrough on the angle's western side but have never been given credit for it. Standard histories of the fighting at Spotsylvania treat the Louisiana brigades as if both were positioned with the 2d Louisiana Brigade and were captured in the first moments of the battle. Virtually all accounts of the battle cite Gordon as saving Lee's army by rushing in reinforcements to seal the breach and ignore the critical role Monaghan's men played. If not for Monaghan's quickness in laying out a defensive position perpendicular to the trenches, the Yankees would have continued flanking the rebel brigades all the way down the western side. "Genl. Ewell says our Brigade saved his left, by the determined stand we made which checked the enemy's advance," wrote Ring. "I hope he will mention it in his report." He did not.[10]

8. Seymour, "Journal," in Seymour Papers, UM; *OR*, Vol. XXXVI, Pt. I, 1072–73; unidentified newspaper clipping in Newsclippings and Miscellaneous Unidentified Material, LHAC; G. Norton Galloway, "Hand-to-Hand Fighting at Spotsylvania," in Johnson and Buel (eds.), *Battles and Leaders*, IV (1898), 177.

9. Durkin (ed.), *Confederate Chaplain*, 88–89; Ring to wife, May 15, 1864, and Casualty list of Company I, 9th Louisiana Volunteers, in Army of Northern Virginia Papers, Part I, LHAC; Bartlett, *Military Record of Louisiana*, 12.

10. Ring to wife, May 15, 1864, in Army of Northern Virginia Papers, Part I, LHAC.

Lee's army was so shot up from the two weeks of slaughter that changes in the command structure were again necessary. Hill was well enough to return to his corps at this time, so Early resumed command of his division. This displaced Gordon, but since Johnson was among those captured on May 12, the Georgian inherited his wrecked division. All the Virginians remaining in the division were consolidated under William Terry's command, and the few surviving Louisianians were put under Colonel Zebulon York, who must have rejoined the command shortly after the battle. There was little for York to command, however, for the Tigers had lost a staggering 808 men captured, besides several hundred killed and wounded, since the beginning of the campaign.[11]

York's promotion over the two brigades proved to be permanent, for Hays never rejoined his Tigers in Virginia after being wounded at Spotsylvania. Upon recovering from his wound, Hays was sent to Louisiana to recruit for the Tiger brigades. Despite his absence, the Louisianians remained in good hands. Colonel York was a forty-four-year-old native of Maine and an original member of Tochman's Polish Brigade. As lieutenant-colonel of the rowdy 14th Louisiana, he earned a reputation for bravery "that amounted to rashness" and for profanity that put to shame even some Tigers.[12]

The Tigers' activities are difficult to chronicle following the fight at the "Bloody Angle." Most of the Louisianians were dead or captured by the end of May, and few letters were mailed during this time because it was nearly impossible to forward mail to occupied Louisiana. In addition, few official records were kept for the remainder of the war because Lee's army was almost constantly in contact with the enemy and officers had little time for paperwork.

After a short rest, York's brigade was brought back to the line on May 14. When the federals attacked its position that day, a number

11. *OR*, Vol. XXXVI, Pt. I, 1073; unidentified newspaper clipping in Newsclippings and Miscellaneous Unidentified Material, LHAC.

12. Compiled Service Records of Confederate General and Staff Officers, War Record Group 109, Microcopy 331, Roll 122, NA; Warner, *Generals in Gray*, 347–48; Conner (ed.), "Letters of Lieutenant Robert H. Miller," 88; *OR*, Vol. XXXVI, Pt. II, 974; *ibid.*, III, 873–74; *ibid.*, Vol. XLI, Pt. II, 1000; *ibid.*, IV, 1073; Henry J. Egan to brother, June 21, 1864, in J. S. Egan Family Papers, LSU; Durkin (ed.), *Confederate Chaplain*, 65, 93; Sigmund H. Uminski, "Poles and the Confederacy," *Polish American Studies*, XXII (1965), 102.

of Yankees threw down their weapons and surrendered without a fight. Captain Ring reported that these federals believed the war would end that summer and being sent to a prison camp was "the safest way to escape the danger of the campaign." Four days later, the Yankees launched another assault against York's men, but this time they had no opportunity to surrender. Charging in four lines, they were repulsed by the Tigers' accurate fire while still three hundred yards away. When the Yankees broke and fled, Henry Egan claimed, the Tigers mounted their works in jubilation and "called to them to come back, but they had no notion of coming again." Grant's persistent attacks and his staggering losses convinced the Louisianians that he would bleed the federal army white by summer's end. "We have met a man this time," wrote Captain Ring, "who either does not know when he is whipped, or who cares not if he loses his whole Army, so that he may accomplish an end. . . . He seems determined to die game if he has to die at all." Striking a similar note, Egan told his brother: "I thank God they have at last got a leader (or rather I should say a master) who will drive them on to the slaughter and if he can only goad them on for a short time longer at the rate he has been doing it since the 5th of May; there will be but few of them left by the time this campaign closes. I think Gen. Grant's appointment to the command of the 'Grand Army of the Potomac' is a perfect God send to the Confederacy. . . . Grant is the only Yankee general who has ever given us the advantage of fighting on our own chosen ground. . . . Our cause never looked brighter." [13]

Egan was overly optimistic about the South's strategic position, but his comments on Grant's heavy losses were accurate. Because his costly frontal assaults had netted no gains, Grant withdrew from Lee's front on May 19 and slid further to the rebels' right, first to the North Anna River and on May 27 toward Cold Harbor. York's Tigers were exhausted as Lee rapidly shifted his army to parry these new thrusts. The Louisianians had been under fire nearly every day for the past three weeks and had covered a vast distance over muddy roads. Upon arriving at Cold Harbor, they again came under a heavy fire from the Union trenches across the way. On

13. Ring to wife, May 15, 1864, in Army of Northern Virginia Papers, Part I, LHAC; Egan to brother, June 21, 1864, in Egan Papers, LSU.

June 1 the Yankee sharpshooters claimed three Tigers. One bullet killed an officer and wounded another man in the 15th Louisiana, and Lieutenant-Colonel Germain Lester of the 8th Louisiana was killed later in the day when the brigade joined in an attack on Grant's right flank.[14]

June 2 was another wet, dreary day, but it was also a proud day for York because he received notice of his promotion to brigadier-general and permanent command of the two Louisiana brigades. Both armies skirmished and positioned battle lines throughout June 2 in preparation for a major assault the next day. Grant's infamous attack on Lee's entrenched Confederates on June 3 gained no advantage for himself and resulted only in massive casualties. It is not known what role York's consolidated brigade played in the repulse, but the Tigers were apparently one of the few commands that had a difficult time in repelling the Yankees since the 10th Louisiana's flag was captured by the 11th Connecticut Volunteers during the fight.[15]

After several more days of skirmishing, the federals disappeared on June 9, only to resurface later near Petersburg. While Lee prepared to counter this move, he received ominous news on June 11 that the Union army of General David Hunter had defeated the Confederate forces in the Valley and was seriously threatening Lee's rear and supply line by moving against Lynchburg. To stop Hunter's raiders, Lee had no choice but to dispatch the II Corps to the Valley. On June 13 the corps was led toward Lynchburg by Jubal Early, who had replaced an ill Ewell as corps commander. On the same day, eight Louisiana congressmen petitioned Davis to allow the men of York's brigade a ninety-day furlough to return to Louisiana to gather new recruits. Even though the Louisiana Brigade's comple-

14. Egan to brother, June 21, 1864, in Egan Papers; D. T. Merrick to E. D. Willett, December 9, 1863, in Reminiscences, Executive and Army of Northern Virginia, LHAC; *Confederate Veteran*, VI (1898), 506; Freeman, *R. E. Lee*, III, 334–71; Seymour, "Journal," in Seymour Papers, UM; Bartlett, *Military Record of Louisiana*, 49–50; *OR*, Vol. XXXVI, Pt. I, 1073–74.

15. Seymour, "Journal," in Seymour Papers, UM; Reed, *Private in Gray*, 80–81; Compiled Service Records of Confederate General and Staff Officers, War Record Group 109, Microcopy 331, Roll 275, NA; Freeman, *R. E. Lee*, III, 373–89; Bartlett, *Military Record of Louisiana*, 18; Bound Volume 8 in Association of the Army of Northern Virginia, LHAC; unidentified newspaper clipping in Box 1, Grace King Collection, SHC; unidentified newspaper clipping in Flags, LHAC.

ment was now less than half that of an infantry regiment, the army could not afford to lose the Tigers. Davis rejected the petition, and the brigade accompanied Early to the Valley.[16]

Early's orders were to destroy Hunter's army and threaten Washington and Baltimore by moving down the Valley toward the Potomac River. Lee hoped the federals would be forced to strip the Army of the Potomac in order to meet Early's thrust and therefore relieve some of the pressure against Petersburg. In a brutal march, Early's exhausted corps won the race to Lynchburg, where Francis T. Nicholls, the Louisianians' former commander, had a small garrison. Hunter then withdrew from the area, and in less than a month Early maneuvered the Yankees from the Valley with hardly a shot fired.[17]

Having saved Lee's supply line, Early then crossed the Potomac River to threaten Washington. But on July 9, he found General Lew Wallace drawn up behind Monocacy Creek to meet him. Early knew a frontal attack across the Monocacy bridge would be suicidal. He therefore ordered Rodes's and Ramseur's divisions to demonstrate near the bridge while Gordon slipped his division across the creek a mile downstream to hit the federal left flank. So as not to be detected, all of Gordon's men were told to discard anything that might make noise. Canteens, knapsacks, and all the luxuries accumulated on the march were piled up and left behind— much to the dismay of the Louisianians, who knew they would never see their precious belongings again.

Gordon discovered a ford below the bridge and managed to wade his men across the stream while the Yankees' attention was diverted to Ramseur and Rodes. Gordon could see the Yankees drawn up behind a low rail fence that snaked across a hill in his front. After studying the federal position, he sent Clement Evans' brigade through a patch of woods on the right and had York deploy a battle line near the creek. When all was ready, Evans burst out of the woods and hit the Yankees' flank with volleys of musketry. York's

16. Freeman, *R. E. Lee*, III, 392–402; *OR*, Vol. LI, Pt. II, 1008.

17. *OR*, Vol. XXXVI, Pt. II, 971, 1071; *ibid.*, Vol. XXXVII, Pt. I, 156, 346, 727, 756–60, 768; Frank E. Vandiver, *Jubal's Raid: General Early's Famous Attack on Washington in 1864* (New York, 1960), 6–7, 19, 35–37, 64; William W. Old Diary, June 13–July 9, 1864, in Miscellaneous Manuscripts Collection, LC; Bound Volumes 5, 6, and 7 in Association of the Army of Northern Virginia, LHAC.

line then surged forward with Terry's brigade following on the left. Scores of Tigers and Virginians were cut down when the federals opened fire from 125 yards, but the two brigades managed to reach the fence and send the Yankees scattering with a point-blank volley. After regrouping, the rebels chased after the enemy but were hit hard by a second Yankee line when they reached a small branch at the bottom of the hill's back slope. Early later recalled that so many of his men were shot down along the creek that the water was red with blood for 100 yards. But the Confederates kept up the pressure, and soon the Yankees "ran like sheep without a Shepard," according to General York. Falling back to a sunken road, the federals made a stand and this time checked York's and Terry's advance. Under a murderous fire, members of the 9th Louisiana madly waved their regimental flag at the Yankees, losing four color-bearers in rapid succession before Wallace finally withdrew his men.[18]

Gordon's division lost heavily in the attacks on Wallace's line, but the Confederates emerged the victors when the federals withdrew and left hundreds of prisoners behind. The clash was "one of the sharpest & most bloody fights of the war," wrote Seymour. York claimed that, having cost the Louisiana Brigade from 25 to 50 percent of its force, it was the bloodiest and fiercest encounter he had ever participated in. At a cost of approximately seven hundred men, Early had inflicted two thousand casualties on Wallace, with most of the Yankee losses occurring in front of the Tigers. Looking over the field the next day, Father Sheeran wrote: "On the crest of the hill where our men first attacked the enemy, we saw a regular line of dead Yankee bodies. A little in the rear they were to be seen lying in every direction and position, some on their sides, some on their faces, some on their backs with their eyes and mouths open, the burning sun beating upon them and their faces swarmed with disgusting flies."[19]

18. Zebulon York to B. B. Wellford, July 18, 1864, in Reel 1, White, Wellford, Talia-ferro, and Marshall Collection, SHC; L. H. Stewart to J. F. Stephens, November 27, 1864, and Henry M. King to J. F. Stephens, August 15, 1864, in Stephens Collection, NSU; Old Diary, July 9, 1864, in Miscellaneous Manuscripts Collection, LC; Van-diver, *Jubal's Raid*, 110–18; Robertson, *Stonewall Brigade*, 231; *OR*, Vol. XXXVII, Pt. I, 193, 200; John B. Gordon, *Reminiscences of the Civil War* (New York, 1903), 310–13.

19. Seymour, "Journal," in Seymour Papers, UM; Durkin (ed.), *Confederate Chaplain*, 94.

Following the battle, Early acknowledged York's role in the victory when he rode up to the Louisianians and said simply, "General, you have handled your command well and it has done its duty nobly." "This I shall ever consider a complament of note," wrote York, "coming from one of the most cross grained & faultfinding Gens. in the C. S. Army."[20]

With the path to Washington opened, Early's column quickly reached the capital's outskirts and threw the city into a panic when it skirmished with the Yankee defenders. Timely federal reinforcements, however, made a full assault impractical, and on July 12 the Confederates withdrew back toward Virginia. After several sharp rear-guard actions, Early encamped in the Valley near Strasburg, where he would be able to keep the pressure on Washington. Although successful in drawing away some of Grant's army from Petersburg, Early's raid also nearly ruined the Louisiana Brigade with its forced marches and constant skirmishing. Disenchanted by the forced consolidation of the brigades, Richard Colbert wrote from the Valley on July 24: "I am tired of being pulled & hauled about as we are, no officers, no Brigade. [It is] not [right] taken all the flags out of our brig. but one, all out [of the] 2nd La. but one, only four line officers in our Regt., all played out, and the men are playing out fast too. Nearly ever man is his own Gen. in our Brig. . . . Seventy-nine men in our regt. and some thirty or forty in the other Regt. . . . I tell you we have no discipline at all now. I am getting very tired of it. . . . I fear our brig. will lose all the glory it has won in Va."[21]

Instead of losing their laurels as Colbert feared, the Tigers actually enhanced their reputation the very day he wrote his letter. Early firmly believed that one more Confederate victory in the Valley might clear the federals out of the region. Therefore, when he learned that the Yankees were converging on Winchester, a few miles north of his camps, he did not hesitate to attack. On July 24, Early smashed the Union forces at Kernstown, just south of Win-

20. York to Wellford, July 18, 1864, in White, Wellford, Taliaferro, and Marshall Collection, SHC.

21. *OR*, Vol. XXXVII, Pt. I, 348–49; Old Diary, July 11, 1865, in Miscellaneous Manuscripts Collection, LC; Bartlett, *Military Record of Louisiana*, 51–52; Richard Colbert to Mrs. E. M. Potts, July 24, 1864, in Folder 57, North Louisiana Historical Association's Archives, CC.

chester. The Yankees put up a stiff fight at first but then slowly retired toward Winchester. When the town was reached, the duty of
dislodging the federals from its streets again fell to the Tigers. Captain G. P. Ring accomplished this task with only a thin skirmish
line—the main Confederate force barely firing a shot. Ring recalled how his men shot down dozens of federals as they fled across
a stubble field. On through town the Yankees ran, finally halting
behind a stone fence. Ring's skirmishers drew a deep breath as they
prepared to hit this line, for the federal position was a strong one
and taking it would likely cost considerable casualties. To the Tigers' delight and surprise, however, the Yankees jumped up and
fled as soon as Ring's men began the assault. The Tigers lost only
thirteen men, and the battle then became a lark as they laughed
"about the race we were running." "The enemy just double quicked
to Williamsport and I don't know but what they are going yet,"
wrote Colbert. "They were perfectly demoralized, though we captured but few as they were Hunter's men & they think we will kill
the last one of them as they treated our citizens so outragious down
about Lynchburg." [22]

With only light losses, Early had inflicted more than 1,500 casualties on George Crook and pushed him back to the Potomac. Early
remained in the Valley for the rest of the summer to keep the federal forces in the area occupied and unable to reinforce Grant.
Through the end of August, Early's command marched constantly
but always stayed one step ahead of the Yankees. York's brigade,
numbering only 614 men, was exhausted, ragged, poorly clothed,
even more poorly disciplined, and still seething with anger over the
consolidation of the two brigades. By the end of August, the Tigers
had marched more than eight hundred miles since leaving Lee and
had been engaged in seventeen battles and major skirmishes—one
of which was with federal cavalry near Shepherdstown on August
25 that claimed the life of Colonel Monaghan. [23]

On September 19 General Philip Sheridan, who had taken command of the Union forces in the Valley after the debacle at Kerns-

22. Ring to wife, July 24, 1864, typescript copy, in Army of Northern Virginia
Papers, Part I, LHAC; Colbert to Potts, July 24, 1864, in North Louisiana Historical
Association's Archives, CC.

23. *OR*, Vol. LXIII, Pt. I, 609–10, 1002; Bartlett, *Military Record of Louisiana*, 52;
Early, *Memoir of the Last Year of the War*, 74–75.

town, attacked Early outside Winchester. Sheridan had learned that Early had weakened his army by sending part of his force to Lee and decided the time was right to finish off this annoying rebel army. The hard-driving Yankees were forcing Ramseur's division back when Gordon arrived and threw his men into the faltering line. As York deployed his brigade along the edge of a large field, Captain Ring could clearly see Sheridan's men advancing toward them. They came "in beautiful order with their bright gun barrels reflecting back the rays of the sun in a way to make your eyes water." Soon the long gray line stepped out to meet its foe and swept over the clearing toward the Yankees. It was, wrote Seymour, "the beautiful and rare sight of two opposing lines charging at the same time."[24]

Both sides proudly advanced without firing a shot. Then at two hundred yards they halted, drew aim, and cut one another down with minié balls. "I had the pleasure," wrote Ring, "of seeing and participating in the prettiest stand up, fair open fight that I have ever seen." For ten minutes blue and gray traded volleys across the field, but as Ring boasted, "Southern pluck was too much for our Yankee friends," and the federals retreated to the shelter of some timber. "We of course raised a Louisiana yell," Ring claimed, "and [went] after them pouring a fire into their backs that soon made the ground black with their hateful bodies." Gordon's entire division took up the chase, but the Louisianians outran their sister brigades when they heard rumors that a Union regiment from Louisiana faced them. Finding himself in advance of the rest of the division, York fell back a hundred yards and then turned to beat off two determined Union counterattacks. "I never saw our brigade fight better," wrote Ring. "The fact of these renegades being opposite to us seemed to nerve each man's arm and make [his] aim certain. . . . I think and firmly believe that every man in Hays' and Stafford's Brigades killed his man that day."[25]

Following these attacks, the battle slacked off to a prolonged skirmish until midafternoon, when Sheridan's cavalry rode through Early's horsemen on the left flank. The Confederate cavalry screen

24. Ring to wife, September 21, 1864, typescript copy, in Army of Northern Virginia Papers, Part I, LHAC; Seymour, "Journal," in Seymour Papers, UM.
25. Ring to wife, September 21, 1864, in Army of Northern Virginia Papers, Part I, LHAC.

folded and galloped for the rear, uncovering the flank of Early's infantry. "It soon became a rout on our part," admitted Ring, who stood seventy-five yards behind York's firing line watching the Confederate line come unhinged regiment by regiment. Seeing the enemy's line breaking up, the Union infantry charged across the field. Instead of fleeing, the Tigers dug in their heels and cut down line after line of the advancing bluecoats. For crucial minutes, York's men stood alone covering the panicked retreat of their comrades. The field became littered with bodies as the Louisianians maintained a rapid fire against the enemy. One federal flag was seen to fall five times in five minutes, but the Yankees kept coming and soon overwhelmed the Tigers. Every mounted officer in the brigade was wounded by the hail of bullets and shrapnel, including General York, who had to leave the field when a ball shattered his left wrist.[26]

Unable to withstand such a barrage, the Louisiana Brigade finally yielded its ground and fell back through some woods. The Tigers emerged onto another field and were startled to see "that the gig was over with us unless some extriordinary dispensation of Providence [intervened]. . . . All over the plain," wrote Ring, "men could be seen flying to the rear, officers riding to and fro trying to rally and reform the men. It was a mortifying, but a very exciting scene." General Gordon was seen riding over the field carrying the Stars and Bars. Galloping up to Ring, he shouted, "Form your men, Captain, I know they will stand by me!" But it was useless. Small groups of soldiers would halt and draw up a line, but then the excited Yankees would send them scattering. With the Louisianians bringing up the rear, Early's demoralized men fled through the streets of Winchester and finally halted miles away at Fisher's Hill.[27]

The army was humiliated at the Third Battle of Winchester (or Opequon Creek), although the Tigers' conscience was eased by the knowledge that they had covered the retreat and enabled most of the men to escape. The price for their heroism was high, however, for 154 of the brigade were casualties. As they dug in on Fisher's

26. *Ibid.;* Bartlett, *Military Record of Louisiana,* 37–38; Seymour, "Journal," in Seymour Papers, UM; unidentified article on the 2d Louisiana's flag in Flags, LHAC.

27. Ring to wife, September 12, 1864, in Army of Northern Virginia Papers, Part I, LHAC.

Hill, the men discussed the turn of events and speculated as to what caused the defeat. Some Louisianians believed the lack of shoes hampered the army's fighting ability, but the general consensus was that Sheridan's cavalry precipitated the rout with its brutal charge on Early's left flank. "If the Yankee Infantry had fought half as well as their Cavalry," wrote Ring, "we would not have any army here this morning."[28]

Early had lost approximately one-fourth of his men at the Third Battle of Winchester, including Generals Rodes and Godwin killed. Demoralized over the defeat, the Confederates on Fisher's Hill were apprehensive as they watched a huge dust cloud slowly wind toward them on September 21. That morning Sheridan's victorious army began drawing up in Early's front, and skirmish fire erupted along the line. The Louisiana sharpshooters posted beyond Early's works were heavily engaged with their Yankee counterparts throughout the morning. When it came time to relieve them, Seymour had one of the brigade's officers put on a private's coat before going out so as to be less conspicuous. But this precaution proved of no value, for the officer had not been on the firing line ten minutes when he was killed by a federal sharpshooter.[29]

Not expecting Sheridan to launch an attack on his entrenched line, Early was surprised on the afternoon of September 22 when a heavy Union column emerged on his left flank. Caught off guard, the army repeated its Winchester performance. Regiment after regiment came loose from left to right and fled to the rear. Again the Louisiana Brigade stood its ground alone, covering the retreat of its sister brigades. Not until they were almost surrounded did the Tigers abandon their line. All organization was lost, Seymour recalled, for escape "required the greatest fleetness of foot." Within minutes, Early lost another twelve hundred men to Sheridan's Yankees, but by holding the federals at bay for crucial minutes the Louisianians prevented the loss from being higher. After withdrawing safely up the Valley, Early reportedly told the Tigers, "I saw you at Fisher's Hill and pointed to you as an example for others

    28. *Ibid.*
    29. Seymour, "Journal," in Seymour Papers, UM; Bartlett, *Military Record of Louisiana,* 87, 90.

to take pattern by. If all had stood as you did, the issue would have been different than from what it was."[30]

Luckily for Early's shattered army, Sheridan abandoned his pursuit of the defeated rebels. By stopping to lay waste to the Valley to ensure that it would never again serve as the breadbasket of the Confederacy, the Yankee general gave Early precious time to regroup. Within a month, Early was back at Fisher's Hill and ready to do battle. On October 18 a weakened but determined Early was preparing again to attack the enemy bivouacked north of Cedar Creek between Strasburg and Winchester. Learning that Sheridan was absent from the Yankee camp, Early believed it was the proper time to hit the enemy while they were leaderless. The Confederate plan called for the divisions of Joseph Brevard Kershaw and Gabriel Colvin Wharton to pin down the enemy at the main crossing on Cedar Creek while Gordon's division eased into position on the far right, where it could strike the federal flank at daylight.

As at the Monocacy, surprise was of the upmost importance, and all canteens, knapsacks, and equipment that might clank or rattle were piled up and left behind when the division started down a narrow mountain trail to the Yankees' left. Daylight was rapidly approaching by the time Gordon was in position and began deploying his men in a thick fog. As the men stumbled into line, several officers called for two volunteers from each company. When the needed men stepped forward, they were solemnly told to follow behind the attacking column and to shoot any soldier who tried to retreat. Every attempt was being made to prevent another rout.

The Battle of Cedar Creek followed a now familiar pattern. When the divisions of Kershaw and Wharton began a diversion on the Yankees' front, Gordon swept out of the fog upon the federal flank. Gordon's men were overpowering as they slammed into the Union line and sent it reeling back through the federal camps. Victory was achieved all along the rebel line, with thirteen hundred prisoners and eighteen cannons seized in the attack. But then Early's pursuit fizzled. As much as one-third of his famished army fell out of ranks to plunder the captured camps, thus giving the

---

30. Seymour, "Journal," in Seymour Papers, UM; unidentified newspaper clipping in Newsclippings and Miscellaneous Unidentified Material, LHAC; Compiled Service Records, War Record Group 109, Microcopy 320, Rolls 148 and 163, NA; OR, Vol. XLIII, Pt. I, 556; Bartlett, *Military Record of Louisiana*, 52–53.

Yankees time to regroup and make a stand. When Sheridan was able to rejoin his beaten men that afternoon, the federals put together a formidable counterattack that netted several hundred prisoners and pushed Early's disorganized mob back to Fisher's Hill. Losses in the Louisiana Brigade are unknown in this disaster except that the 10th Louisiana had one man killed, three wounded, and nine missing. A company in the 6th Louisiana could lay claim to the most discouraging losses—it entered the fight with two men, and both were shot.[31]

Early's defeat at Cedar Creek ended the fighting in the Valley. This was fortunate for the Louisiana Brigade because it was in poor shape to participate in any more campaigns. With a little over five hundred men left on the rolls, the command was reorganized into a battalion for easier handling, although it officially remained on the books as two separate units constituting a consolidated brigade. The ten regiments were combined to make six companies—such as Company D being made up of the 5th, 6th, and 7th Louisiana Volunteers under Major William Manning. An additional change was the selection of a new commander for the Tigers. When York failed to return to the brigade after his mangled arm was amputated, Colonel William Raine Peck of the 9th Louisiana was chosen to lead the Tigers. Known in the army as "Big Peck" because of his huge, six-foot, six-inch, three-hundred-pound frame, the Madison Parish native had risen swiftly through the ranks from a private in the Milliken Bend Guards to colonel of the 9th Louisiana. He was well liked by the men and proved to be a capable leader.[32]

Efforts were made to secure new recruits for Peck's brigade that winter, but none was successful. One bizarre scheme was a plan to send General York to Salisbury, North Carolina, to try to get recruits from among the German and Irish Catholics who were held in the prisoner of war camps there. Taking with him Fathers James Sheeran and Egidius Smulders, York did go to Salisbury after re-

31. *OR*, Vol. XLIII, Pt. I, 561–64, 581; Bound Volume 6 in Association of the Army of Northern Virginia, LHAC; Bartlett, *Military Record of Louisiana*, 19, 53–54; *Confederate Veteran*, X (1902), 165; *ibid.*, II (1894), 75–76; Seymour, "Journal," in Seymour Papers, UM.

32. *OR*, Vol. XLII, Pt. III, 912, 1195, 1365; Bartlett, *Military Record of Louisiana*, 54; Monthly return for York's brigade, November 28, 1864, in Bound Volume 42, Association of the Army of Northern Virginia, LHAC; Warner, *Generals in Gray*, 231; Brown, "Reminiscences of the Civil War," I, 27, in Brown Collection, SHC.

covering from his amputation and seemed at first to enjoy some
success. The Yankees were dying at a rate of twenty to thirty a day,
had no hope of being exchanged, and seemed grateful to have
Catholic priests to administer to their religious needs. At one time,
York had approximately eight hundred prisoners set aside as potential recruits, but apparently every one of them balked at actually
joining the rebel army.[33]

Since there were so few Tigers left, the men hoped they would be
furloughed and allowed to visit home that winter, but this was not
to be. On December 7 the brigade joined the rest of Gordon's division in leaving the Valley and heading for Petersburg to reinforce
Lee's beleaguered army. Upon their arrival, remembered J. H. Cosgrove, "the men were cheerless, and though disheartened, determined to 'stay to the finish.'"[34]

The Tigers were placed near Hatcher's Run on Lee's extreme
right, but little is known of their activities there. A sharp clash at
Hatcher's Run on February 6 cost the Tigers six dead and seventeen wounded and is the only known battle the Tigers engaged in
that winter. The hunger, atrocious weather, and deadly Yankee fire
made the months spent on the Petersburg line among the worst of
the war. The Louisianians often lay exposed to sleet and rain for
days at a time, and food was nearly nonexistent. Gordon's men
sometimes fed themselves by picking corn feed out of horses' tracks,
but on one occasion a starving Tiger in the 9th Louisiana found the
Yankees to be generous providers of rations. When a federal picket
shouted over the trenches and asked what the Louisianians were
having for supper, the Tiger replied that they would not be fed until late the next day. The sympathetic Yankee then held up a large
chunk of meat and told the Louisianian if he wanted it he could
come over safely. The Tiger's companions were convinced it was a
trick, but the hungry soldier slipped out of his trench that night

33. Egidius Smulders to Henry B. Kelly, March, 187[?], in Smulders Papers, Confederate Personnel, LHAC; Buckley, *A Frenchman, a Chaplain, a Rebel,* 227; Compiled Service Records of Confederate General and Staff Officers, War Record
Group 109, Microcopy 331, Roll 275, NA; *OR,* Vol. XLVI, Pt. II, 1089–90; *ibid.,* Series II, Vol. VII, 178; *ibid.,* Series IV, Vol. III, 824–25, 1029.

34. J. H. Cosgrove, "Recollections and Reminiscences," *Cosgrove's Weekly,* August
26, 1911, in Melrose Scrapbook 230, NSU; Stewart to Stephens, November 27, 1864,
in Stephens Collection, NSU.

and yelled, "Yank, don't shoot! I came after that piece of meat!" The kind federals guided him into their line and loaded him down with meat, hardtack, bread, and coffee before sending him on his way.[35]

The dreadful conditions took a heavy toll on Peck's brigade. Of his army, Lee wrote, "The physical strength of the men, if their courage survives, must fail under this treatment." Apparently both physical strength and courage failed many Tigers, for desertions again racked the command. Nine Tigers deserted on February 19 alone, and at least nineteen others abandoned their comrades that winter. Sickness and desertions were rampant and began to deplete the strength of the brigade at a frightful rate. By the end of February, only 401 men were left on duty, with several companies having only two members and some having completely vanished. The brigade also lost Peck when he was promoted to brigadier-general that February and transferred to the western theater. The 10th Louisiana's Colonel Eugene Waggaman, who now was leading York's old brigade, replaced Peck as brigade commander.[36]

Soon after assuming command, Waggaman shifted the men to a new position near the famous "Crater." For a month the Tigers lay in their cold, muddy trenches under constant artillery and sharpshooters' fire. Morale sagged as it became apparent that victory was almost impossible. Desertions increased, but that solid core of determined soldiers who had seen the brigade through other trying times remained undaunted. Everyone, including Lee, knew the fight was at its end unless a miracle saved them from the Petersburg siege. In mid-March Lee concluded that a breakout was the only hope for his tattered army and ordered Gordon to investigate the possibility of cutting through Grant's encirclement. After examining the lines, Gordon found a weak link in the Union position. The opposing works were a mere 150 yards apart at the federal position called Fort Stedman, and the winter rains had greatly deteriorated the fort's walls. If the federal pickets and the *chevaux-de-frise* protecting the approaches could be removed without alarm, Gordon believed, the fort could be captured and a hole punched into

35. *OR*, Vol. LXVI, Pt. I, 390–92; *Confederate Veteran*, XVII (1909), 532.

36. *OR*, Vol. LXVI, Pt. I, 382; *ibid.*, Vol. XLII, Pt. II, 956; *ibid.*, Pt. III, 936; *ibid.*, Vol. XLVI, Pt. I, 389; *ibid.*, Pt. II, 280, 287, 603; *ibid.*, Pt. III, 204, 373; Bound Volume 2 in Association of the Army of Northern Virginia, LHAC.

Grant's line. Lee concurred with his lieutenant and gave Gordon
half the army to accomplish the breakout in the predawn hours of
March 25.[37]

By this time, Gordon was in command of the II Corps and Clement Evans led the division that included Waggaman's brigade. During a strategy meeting with his officers, Evans suddenly turned to
Waggaman and declared, "On account of the valor of your troops,
you will be allowed the honor of leading off in the attack. This you
will make with unloaded arms."[38] Although Waggaman probably
questioned the honor of leading such a suicidal attack, plans were
finalized for him to send as the first wave three companies—one
hundred men—to silence the pickets and clear away all obstructions. To accomplish this, the first few Louisianians would pretend
to be deserters and then nab the pickets once they were within the
federal lines. The three Tiger officers leading these companies
would then assume the names of known Yankee officers and disori-
ent the federals by issuing confusing orders in the dark. Once the
fort was taken, the rest of Gordon's men would fan out to either
side, enlarge the breakthrough, and cut a path to Grant's rear,
where Lee could either wreck the Army of the Potomac or make a
break for safety.

Gordon's line began preparing for the attack at 3:00 A.M. With
axes in hand to clear the obstructions, the three Tiger companies
were finally ready. Suddenly one of the Yankee pickets shouted,
"What are you doing over there, Johnny? What is that noise? Answer quick or I'll shoot!" Hearts raced as it appeared the movement
had been detected. But then a rebel hollered back, "Never mind,
Yank! Lie down and go to sleep. We are just gathering a little corn.
You know rations are mighty short over here." This response apparently satisfied the inquisitive Yankee for the works again fell silent. Shortly afterward, Gordon turned to the same soldier and
ordered him to give the signal for the assault. The rebel hesitated,
then yelled, "Hello, Yank! Wake up; we are going to shell the woods.
Look out; we are coming!"[39]

After this chivalrous warning, Lieutenant R. B. Smith led the

37. Freeman, R. E. Lee, IV, 12–19.
38. Quoted in Bartlett, Military Record of Louisiana, 39.
39. Gordon, Reminiscences of the Civil War, 408–409.

Louisiana sappers forward. Silently picking their way toward the enemy, the Tigers quickly captured the Yankee pickets and cleared the obstructions without a shot being fired. With the rest of Gordon's force following close behind, Lieutenant Smith scaled the walls of Fort Stedman and leaped among the garrison. The two hundred Yankee defenders were caught completely by surprise, but the federals quickly rallied and fought back against the gray mass tumbling in on top of them. Blue and gray battled "as if they had drank two quarts of brandy," claimed one Tiger. Scratching, clawing, and rolling in the muddy trenches, the two sides grappled hand to hand, but the Tigers finally prevailed. At a slight loss the Louisianians captured most of the feisty Yankees, plus three mortars and four cannons, which were swung around and fired at the retreating federals.[40]

As daylight crept upon the contested trenches, five hundred yards of Yankee works were in Confederate hands, along with several hundred prisoners and seventeen cannons and mortars. Despite this success, however, the attack quickly fizzled. Guides failed in the confusion, and several Confederate units got lost in the maze of earthworks or wandered into other commands and disorganized the attack. The Yankees then mounted a counterattack, managed to contain the breakthrough, and began lobbing shells into the captured works. Waggaman's brigade had lost over half its complement by daylight and then came under a vicious Yankee attack. The Tigers took refuge in Fort Stedman and shot down a number of federals before the Yankees swept over them. Another frantic hand-to-hand fight raged in the trenches before the Tigers spiked the captured artillery and made a dash for their own lines "under a terrible fire of artillery and musketry." The survivors of Waggaman's decimated command finally returned to their original line. Encountering Evans, Waggaman remembered his remarks about the "honor" of leading the attack. Glancing over his wrecked brigade, the Louisianian asked if they had done their duty. "They did," was Evans' simple reply.[41]

The unsuccessful breakout at Fort Stedman sealed Lee's fate. Knowing that the Confederates were beaten, Grant swung around

40. Bartlett, *Military Record of Louisiana*, 40.
41. *Ibid.*

on April 1 to strike the rebels' right flank. The Yankees badly defeated Lee's men at Five Forks and tightened the noose around the
Army of Northern Virginia. At 10:30 A.M., Sunday, April 2, Waggaman and Major Thomas Powell passed several Tigers as they
were walking to church. Jokingly, Waggaman asked if they would
get to church on time. Major Powell glanced at his watch and remarked, "Hardly, unless we leave quickly." His words were cut short
by the dull thud of a minié ball striking his head. The major collapsed dead, and a thunderous roar swelled all around Petersburg
as Grant launched his final assault on Lee's line.[42]

   This part of Lee's right center was so weak that the Louisiana soldiers were spaced fifteen feet apart. The Yankees managed to break
through one part of the line near the Crater but were contained
when Waggaman hurled his tiny brigade into the breach and recaptured two hundred yards of works. Just as the gap was plugged,
Gordon received word from Lee apprising him of the Five Forks
disaster and instructing him to hold the federals back while the rest
of the army evacuated the Petersburg line. Orders went out to Gordon's brigades not to waste men on retaking lost positions but
simply to hold the Yankees at bay. For twenty-two hours the Louisiana Tigers hugged their breastworks under a raging storm of lead
from the federals, who still held the Confederate trenches on either side of them. Numerous Tigers were killed during the day—
all reportedly shot through the head when they carelessly rose up
out of the trenches. Some soldiers passed the time by placing their
hats on a pole and seeing how many bullets perforated them in a
given time. Finally, at 1:30 A.M., April 4, Waggaman was told to pull
the men out and catch up with the rest of the army as it headed for
Amelia Courthouse forty miles to the west. There Lee planned to
receive badly needed supplies by rail and then join Joe Johnston's
army in North Carolina.[43]

   42. *Ibid.*, 19, 39–41, 55; unidentified newspaper clipping in Newsclippings and
Miscellaneous Unidentified Material, LHAC; *OR*, Vol. XLVI, Pt. I, 173, 382–83;
George L. Kilmer, "Gordon's Attack at Fort Stedman," in Johnson and Buel (eds.),
Battles and Leaders, IV, 580; Burke Davis, *Gray Fox: Robert E. Lee and the Civil War*
(New York, 1956), 363–66.
   43. Bartlett, *Military Record of Louisiana*, 41–42, 55; Gordon, *Reminiscences of the
Civil War*, 420–23; Freeman, *R. E. Lee*, IV, 229–40.

For a week the Louisiana Brigade fought in the mud and rain as part of the army's rear guard. Waggaman's men often held their ground against repeated federal attacks and then ran for safety only when nearly surrounded, sometimes running past Yankees scarcely twenty yards away. Ammunition ran low, and food was in short supply—a daily ration for each Tiger consisted of only one biscuit and one ounce of bacon. Lee made it safely to Amelia Courthouse but found no supplies and was forced to continue his flight toward Farmville and Appomattox Courthouse.

On April 6, Colonel Edmund Pendleton, commanding the 15th Louisiana, hastily scrawled a message to his wife on the back of an envelope. Despite Ewell's and Anderson's corps having been nearly destroyed that day at Sailor's Creek, Pendleton remained confident as he wrote:

> The whole army of Gen'l Lee is now within ten miles of Farmville. After a severe battle at Petersburg on Sunday 2nd April in which our lines were broken & our communications cut, we have been compelled to fall back to a more defensible line. I am sorry to think that this implies the abandonment of the greater part of Va. & it is not unlikely you & my dear children will be left in the Enemy's hands, tho' I hope not. I shall use my utmost exertions to come to see you. Our Army is not whipped—indeed it is strong & ready to fight to-day. . . . I write this hasty note on the march & will endeavor to write you more fully in two or three days. Love to all.[44]

On April 7 Lee halted his ragged army at Appomattox Courthouse and fought fiercely against the Union corps that now had him surrounded. On the morning of April 9 Lee asked Gordon if he could smash through the blue encirclement and open an escape route to the mountains of western Virginia. Gordon issued orders for Evans' division to make the assault against the Union line posted half a mile away across a freshly plowed field. With only 178 men present for duty, Waggaman deployed his Tigers and joined in this last charge of the Army of Northern Virginia. Moving out under heavy artillery fire, the Louisianians raised the rebel yell for the last time and stumbled dog-tired across the furrowed field. One federal line was dislodged from behind a fence and its flag seized after a

44. Edmund Pendleton to wife, April 6, 1865, in Coles Collection, SHC.

Tiger bayoneted the color guard. Then as the screaming Tigers closed in on the Yankee artillery, orders suddenly arrived for Waggaman to disengage and return to the main line. The bewildered Tigers returned as ordered and lay exhausted on the ground, confused over the reasons for breaking off a successful attack. Then word was murmured quietly through the ranks—Lee had surrendered.[45]

45. Gordon, *Reminiscences of the Civil War*, 423–24, 430, 436–38; Freeman, *R. E. Lee*, IV, 107–20; Bartlett, *Military Record of Louisiana*, 42, 55–56; *Southern Historical Society Papers*, XV (1887), 184; *Confederate Veteran*, IV (1896), 90; *ibid.*, VI (1898), 524; *ibid.*, VII (1899), 357; *OR*, Vol. XLVI, Pt. I, 1303; New Orleans *Times-Picayune*, February 15, 1931, in Melrose Scrapbook 228, NSU.

CONCLUSION

Unbelievable at first, the rumor of Lee's surrender was all too true. For weeks, the men knew the war's gloomy end was near, but the actual surrender shook the Louisiana Brigade to its core. Thinking the rebels' side arms would be taken, Colonel Waggaman threw away his old family sword for a second time in the war rather than surrender it. He then put the brigade into line and had a piece of the colors cut off and given to him before the flag was taken away. Waggaman later presented a piece of the Tigers' flag to Lee's daughter as a memento. Apparently not all of the battle flags were surrendered. Colonel Pendleton hid the 15th Louisiana's flag on his person and carried it home with him. Regiments resembled squads as the worn-out Tigers crowded around their tattered banners on the hills outside Appomattox. The 10th Louisiana had a mere 16 men present, and Waggaman's largest command, the 9th Louisiana, had only 68. When the Tigers stacked their arms and were paroled by Grant's army, only 373 men were left on duty in the two Louisiana brigades.[1]

Losses among the Louisiana soldiers in Virginia had been appalling. Casualty figures are not complete and vary with different sources, but of some thirteen thousand men who served with the Tigers, more than three thousand died during the war—approximately two thousand being killed or mortally wounded in combat and thirteen hundred dying from other causes—giving the Tigers a mortality rate of 23 percent. All of the units suffered extensive casualties, but some distinctions are the thirteen lieutenants killed or mortally wounded in the 2d Louisiana during an eighty-day period in the summer of 1862 and the thirty-two color-bearers killed

1. John Fitzpatrick to W. H. Lee, September 7, 1877, in John Fitzpatrick Letterbook, LSU; *Southern Historical Society Papers*, XV (1887), 184; R. A. Brock, *The Appomattox Roster* (1887; rpr. New York, n.d.), 4, 6, 230–37, 456.

or wounded in the 10th Louisiana—six dying in the Battle of Chancellorsville. The position of commanding officer in the 2d Louisiana Brigade seems to have been jinxed. Within months after assuming command, all five executives—Starke, Nicholls, Stafford,
Williams, and York—were killed or seriously wounded. The 9th
Louisiana is a good example of regimental losses because it has
some of the best records available. The DeSoto Blues suffered a
mortality rate of 40 percent, and Company I had nearly a 100
percent casualty rate with sixty-eight fatalities and ninety men
wounded. The records of Company G illustrate how volunteer
companies dwindled to only a handful of men by war's end. By
January 16, 1865, the fates of the 154 men who served in this unit
were as follows: died, 50; deserted, 31; discharged, 25; killed or
mortally wounded, 13; disabled and retired, 13; present for duty, 8;
transferred, 5; missing, 4; on sick or wounded furlough, 3; promoted, 1; and prisoner of war, 1.[2]

The Tigers' division and corps commanders recognized the great
sacrifices the Louisianians made over four years of war. On April 11,
1865, General Evans issued his farewell address to Waggaman's
brigade:

> The sad hour has arrived when we who served in the Confederate
> Army so long together must part, at least for a time. But the saddest
> circumstances connected with the separation are that it occurs under
> heavy disaster to our beloved cause. But to you, Colonel, and to our
> brother officers and brother soldiers of Hays' and Stafford's Brigades,
> I claim to say that you can carry with you the proud conscience that in
> the estimation of your commanders you have done your duty. Tell
> Louisiana, when you reach her shores, that her sons in the Army of
> Northern Virginia have made her illustrious upon every battle ground,
> from first Manassas to the last desparate blow struck by your com-
> mand on the hills of Appomattox, and tell her, too, that as in the first,
> so in the last, the enemy fled before the valor of your charging lines.
> To the sad decree of an inscrutable Providence let us bow in humble
> resignation awaiting *His will* for the pillar of cloud to be lifted. For

2. *Southern Historical Society Papers*, XXVI (1898), 378–79; "Louisiana Troops in
Virginia," n.p., in Melrose Scrapbook 228, NSU; "The DeSoto Blues," n.p., *ibid.*,
#235; John Dimitry, *Louisiana*, 322–25, Vol. X of Clement Evans (ed.), *Confederate
Military History* (10 vols.; Atlanta, 1899); Consolidated report, Company G, 9th Loui-
siana Volunteers, January 16, 1865, in Bound Volume 42, Association of the Army of
Northern Virginia, LHAC.

you, and for your gallant officers and devoted men, I shall always cherish the most pleasing memories, and when I say farewell, it is with a full heart, which beats an earnest prayer to Almighty God for your future happiness.[3]

The next day Gordon followed suit:

In parting with the Louisiana Brigade of this Army I cannot omit to offer the tribute which is due to as heroic a devotion, as ever illustrated the arms of any people.

Coming with glorious ardour into the support of a cause, which sacred in itself, is doubly consecrated to-day by its dead; you have carried your enthusiasm into a hundred battles, filling your comrades and Countrymen with pride and your enemy with fear.

Steadily and unshaken have you passed throughout the struggle, with untarnished record. Your name is without the shadow of a stain. Your conduct in the closing hours is as lofty as when with full ranks you struck and exulted in victory.

Take with you soldiers in parting the unfeigned admiration of my heart.[4]

The Louisiana Tigers were the Dr. Jekyll and Mr. Hyde of the Confederacy. They were drunken, lawless renegades who often posed a greater threat to the South's civilians than did the Yankees. Montgomery, Alabama; Grand Junction, Tennessee; and Lynchburg and Petersburg, Virginia, felt the Tigers' wrath—as did countless farmers, who suffered wholesale losses of livestock to the pilfering soldiers. Yet when it came to fighting, the Tigers were rated among Lee's most dependable soldiers. Such battlefield exploits as Starke's brigade holding with rocks the line at Second Manassas were seen as the epitome of southern bravado and became an integral part of the mystique that came to surround the Confederate soldier. Jackson owed much of his fame to the actions of Taylor's brigade in the Shenandoah Valley, and the Confederate army was saved from disaster by the little-known stand the 1st Louisiana Brigade made at Spotsylvania's Bloody Angle and the rear-guard action of York's brigade at Winchester and Fisher's Hill.

The same men who pillaged towns and delighted in drinking

3. C. A. Evans to Colonel Eugene Waggaman, April 11, 1865, in Box 1, Folder 3, Jastremski Papers, LSU.

4. John B. Gordon to Colonel Eugene Waggaman, April 12, 1865, *ibid.*

and fighting also knelt in knee-deep snow at Fredericksburg to celebrate Easter, held frequent revivals and prayer meetings, and astonished everyone on the dreary Petersburg line by building an elaborate chapel for religious services. During the bitter winter of 1862–1863, when Early desired to be rid of his Tigers because of their pillaging, Hays's brigade donated $3,000 for the relief of the destitute citizens of shelled-out Fredericksburg; and in the same month the hell-raising 14th Louisiana raised $1,200 for the orphans in Richmond.[5]

The Tigers were a paradox. Despite their exalted military record and reputation for devotion to duty, the Louisiana commands were racked by desertions throughout the war. No exact figures are available for this malady, but the 1st, 2d, 5th, 6th, 7th, 8th, 9th, and 15th Louisiana Volunteers had at least 900 deserters out of a total strength of 9,250. Those commands with large numbers of foreign members or farmers from the piney hills of North Louisiana suffered the most desertions because these two segments of the population harbored a strong sense of Unionism and sometimes abandoned the rebel cause. The Irish-dominated 6th Louisiana led the regiments in deserters with 232 of 1,146 members (20 percent). The 15th Louisiana (14 percent) and 5th Louisiana (11 percent) ranked second and third, respectively, and the North Louisiana farmers of the 9th Louisiana ranked fourth with a desertion rate of 8 percent. Entire companies were sometimes wrecked by these desertions. From May 1 to August 31, 1862, the 15th Louisiana had 98 men desert, with 27 of 55 members of one company abandoning the cause. Men taking leaves without permission were almost as prevalent as deserters. The 2d Louisiana's Company G had 15 of 33 men absent without leave at one time.[6]

A large number of the Louisiana deserters and prisoners of war took the oath of allegiance to the United States. Throughout the Civil War and after Appomattox, members of the Confederate ar-

5. Contributions for the Relief of the Fredericksburg Sufferers, Harry T. Hays Brigade, in Slaughter Papers, Part I, Fredericksburg and Spotsylvania National Military Park. For details of the Tigers' religious side, see Rev. John William Jones, *Christ in the Camp or Religion in Lee's Army* (Richmond, 1887), Durkin (ed.), *Confederate Chaplain*, and Buckley, *A Frenchman, a Chaplain, a Rebel.*

6. Muster roll, 15th Louisiana Volunteers, May 1–August 31, 1862, in Gertrude B. Saucier Papers, LSU.

mies were required to swear allegiance to the United States Constitution to win their freedom or regain their civil rights. At least 275 Tigers are known to have taken the oath, with the Irishmen of the 6th Louisiana again leading the regiments with 76. Although some men deserted and then took the oath of allegiance, most oaths were given after the Louisianians were captured. A surprising number of men joined the Union army after swearing their allegiance, as did the member of the 6th Louisiana who was executed at Mine Run for his transgression. Of 25 members of Company B, 7th Louisiana Volunteers, captured at Rappahannock Station, 6 took the oath of allegiance and 4 of these joined the Union army—becoming contemptibly labeled "Galvanized Yankees" by their old comrades. Inside both flaps of a diary belonging to the 5th Louisiana's Sergeant T. W. Reynolds is scrawled a message that most Tigers adhered to when it came to such things: "Daniel W. Linder, Co. F, 5th La. Regt. Took the Oath of Allegiance to the U.S. government Dec. 23, '63. The C[onfederate] S[tates] are willing to get rid of all such as he was. *Branded* in the Regt. as a *damned coward*." [7]

Such incidents caused anyone with the slightest Union sentiments to be looked upon with suspicion. A memorandum by Colonel Henry B. Kelly marked "strictly secret" claimed, rightfully or not, that a member of his 8th Louisiana was a spy. Isaac D. Marx, it read, was "a good looking fellow, dark complected, about 5½ feet high, black Eyes and moustache—he is a rascal, and is lurking around a[s] a great Southern man [illegible]—he is in the pay of the Washington Government." [8]

Deserters, criminals, cowards—and perhaps spies—were a part of the legacy left by the Louisianians in Virginia. They were a rough-and-tumble lot—eager to fight, even more eager to drink and play. Cursed and branded as devils by civilians, welcomed as a godsend by cornered generals, the Louisiana Tigers contributed a colorful chapter to that era of American history known as the Civil War.

7. T. W. Reynolds Diary, in Army of Northern Virginia Papers, Part II, LHAC; Muster roll, Company B, 7th Louisiana Volunteers, n.d., in Saucier Papers, LSU.

8. Memorandum by Col. Henry B. Kelly, March 23, 1862, in Folder 9, Polk, Ewell, Brown Collection, SHC.

APPENDIX

Most of the statistical data on the number of desertions, oaths, places of birth, and deaths in individual companies were obtained from original muster rolls.[1] These muster rolls do not contain complete information for each soldier. Therefore, the statistics are not without error. They are simply a summation of the information that is available. Such data should be used for comparison purposes and not viewed as precise.

1st Louisiana Volunteers

The 1st Louisiana Volunteers were mustered into service for twelve months on April 28, 1861. The regiment's total enrollment during the war was 960. Of these, 162 were killed or mortally wounded, 74 died of disease, 1 was accidentally killed, at least 88 deserted, 12 took the oath of allegiance to the United States, and 8 were discharged under foreign protection. Almost all of the regiment's members were from the New Orleans area; most were clerks, farmers, and laborers. Of the 843 members who gave a place of birth on the muster rolls, 292 were born in states outside of Louisiana, 226 in Louisiana, 202 in Ireland, 59 in the Germanic states, 34 in England, 10 in France, 9 in Canada, 6 in Scotland, 2 in Poland, and 1 each in Belgium, Brazil, and Switzerland.

Albert G. Blanchard, an 1829 West Point graduate, was elected

1. Unless otherwise stated, the sources used for the Appendix are Bound Volumes 1–10 and 12, in Association of the Army of Northern Virginia, LHAC; *Adjutant General's Report, State of Louisiana* (New Orleans, 1890), 246–53; *Biennial Report of the Secretary of State of the State of Louisiana to His Excellancy Samuel D. McEnery, Governor of Louisiana, 1886–1887* (Baton Rouge, 1888), 114–26; "Louisiana Troops, Infantry, Local Designations of Companies by Regiments and Battalions," in Bibliographical Material, LHAC.

colonel of the regiment and served until he was promoted to brigadier-general on September 21, 1861. Lieutenant-Colonel William G. Vincent succeeded him until the regiment was reorganized in April, 1862. At that time, Major Samuel R. Harrison was elected colonel. Harrison resigned in June, 1862, and was replaced by Lieutenant-Colonel W. R. Shivers, who served until he was forced to resign in 1864 because of wounds. He was succeeded by Lieutenant-Colonel James Nelligan.

During the war, 19 officers of the regiment were killed or mortally wounded. One officer died of disease, 2 deserted to the enemy, and 2 were cashiered from the service.

All of the regiment's companies, except the Caddo Rifles (Caddo Parish) and Davis Guards (Lexington, Kentucky), were from the New Orleans area.[2] The original officers and companies of the regiment were as follows: Colonel Albert G. Blanchard, Lieutenant-Colonel W. G. Vincent, and Major W. R. Shivers.

> *Montgomery Guards,* Captain Michael Nolan commanding. Men of Irish extraction composed 77 percent of this company, but surprisingly only 10 percent deserted during the war, an extremely low figure for a foreign-dominated company.
> *Louisiana Guards, Co. B,* Captain C. E. Girardey commanding. This company was transferred to an artillery unit around February, 1862.[3]
> *Davis Guards,* Captain Ben W. Anderson commanding. This company was from Lexington, Kentucky, and was attached to the regiment in New Orleans. It was ordered transferred to a Kentucky brigade on August 2, 1861.[4]
> *Louisiana Guards, Co. C,* Captain Frank Rawle commanding.
> *Caddo Rifles,* Captain C. Dailee commanding. This company lost 29 percent of its men to death during the war.
> *Orleans Light Guards, Co. A,* Captain Charles E. Cormier commanding.
> *Orleans Light Guards, Co. B,* Captain T. M. Dean commanding.
> *Orleans Light Guards, Co. C,* Captain Charles N. Frost commanding.
> *Orleans Light Guards, Co. D,* Captain P. O'Rourke commanding.
> *Emmet Guards,* Captain James Nelligan commanding.

2. Powell A. Casey, "Confederate Units from North Louisiana," *North Louisiana Historical Association's Journal,* VI (Spring, 1975), SU-A; *OR,* Vol. LI, Pt. II, 209.

3. Albert G. Blanchard, article on the Louisiana Guards in Reminiscences, Executive and Army of Northern Virginia, LHAC.

4. *OR,* Vol. LI, Pt. II, 209.

Records indicate that during the course of the war the following companies were also attached to the regiment: Slocomb Rifles (Rapides Parish), Red River Rebels, Rapides Rangers (Rapides Parish), Shreveport Rifles (Shreveport), Lecompte Rifles (Lecompte), Shreveport Greys (this company transferred to the regiment from the 1st Louisiana Battalion on June 27, 1862), Tiger Bayou Rifles (from Carroll Parish, this company transferred to the regiment from the 14th Louisiana Volunteers on August 5, 1861), Catahoula Guerrillas (from Catahoula Parish, this company apparently transferred to the regiment from the 15th Louisiana Volunteers after the summer of 1862), Crescent Blues (a New Orleans company, this unit also transferred to the 1st Louisiana from the 15th Louisiana after the summer of 1862), and St. Paul's Chasseurs a Pied (also known as St. Paul's Foot Rifles, this company apparently transferred to the regiment from the 1st Battalion, Louisiana Zouaves).[5]

2d Louisiana Volunteers

The 2d Louisiana Volunteers were mustered into service for twelve months on May 11, 1861. The regiment's total enrollment during the war was 1,297. Of these, 218 were killed or mortally wounded, 181 died of disease, 4 were killed accidentally, at least 88 deserted, and 4 took the oath of allegiance. The regiment consisted mainly of farmers but also had a large number of clerks. Of the 1,020 members who gave a place of birth on the muster rolls, 655 were born in states outside of Louisiana, 263 in Louisiana, 41 in the Germanic states, 37 in Ireland, 7 in Canada, 5 each in England and Scotland, 2 each in Poland, France, and Italy, and 1 in Denmark.

Louis G. DeRussy was elected colonel of the regiment but resigned in July, 1861. Captain William M. Levy was elected colonel at that time and served until Major J. T. Norwood was elected colonel when the regiment was reorganized in May, 1862. When Norwood was mortally wounded at Malvern Hill, Lieutenant-Colonel Jesse M. Williams took command of the regiment. Colonel Williams was killed on May 12, 1864, at Spotsylvania, and was succeeded by Lieutenant-Colonel Ross E. Burke.

The original officers and companies of the regiment were as fol-

5. *Ibid.*, 214; *ibid.*, LIII, 815–16.

lows: Colonel Louis G. DeRussy, Lieutenant-Colonel John Young, and Major J. T. Norwood.

Pelican Greys, from Monroe, Captain A. H. Martin commanding.
Vienna Rifles, from Vienna, Captain H. W. Perrin commanding. This company suffered a 37 percent death rate during the war.
Moore Guards, from Alexandria, Captain John Kelso commanding.
Vernon Guards, from Jackson Parish, Captain Oscar M. Watkins commanding.
Claiborne Guards, from Homer, Captain John W. Andrews commanding. This company suffered a 31 percent death rate during the war.
Floyd Guards, from Carroll Parish, Captain John W. Dunn commanding.
Greenwood Guards, from Caddo Parish, Captain William Flournoy commanding.
Lecompte Guards, from Lecompte, Captain William M. Levy commanding.
Atchafalaya Guards, from Point Coupee and Avoyelles Parishes, Captain R. M. Boone commanding.
Pelican Rifles, from DeSoto and Natchitoches parishes, Captain Jesse Williams commanding. Of the 109 original members of this company, 33 were students or teachers. In all, 151 men served in the company. Only 32 survived the war, and 31 of these suffered wounds.[6]

Records indicate that the Moorehouse Fencibles were also attached to the regiment at times during the war.

5th Louisiana Volunteers

The 5th Louisiana Volunteers were mustered into service for the duration of the war on June 4, 1861. The regiment's total enrollment during the war was 1,074. Of these, 161 were killed or mortally wounded, 66 died of disease, 2 were killed accidentally, 1 was murdered, 1 was executed, at least 118 deserted, and 32 took the oath of allegiance. The vast majority of the regiment's members were common laborers and clerks. One member complained that the regiment was mostly "uneducated Irishmen," but this was an

6. Natchitoches *Times,* April 12, 1929, in Melrose Scrapbook 1, NSU.

exaggeration.[7] Of the 528 members who gave a place of birth on the muster rolls, 200 were born in Louisiana, 121 in other states, 94 in Ireland, 59 in the Germanic states, 25 in England, 12 in France, 7 in Switzerland, 3 each in Canada and Scotland, 2 in Cuba, and 1 each in Mexico and Poland.

Theodore G. Hunt was elected colonel of the regiment and served until his resignation in August, 1862. Hunt was described by General Lafayette McLaws as "an old gentleman of independent manner, and an open talker, was [a] member of Congress from Louisiana and has a considerable opinion of his influence and of his ability both as a soldier and a member of Society."[8] Lieutenant-Colonel Henry Forno took command of the regiment upon Hunt's resignation. During the war, 13 of the regiment's officers were killed or mortally wounded, 4 died of disease, 1 was killed in a duel, 2 deserted to the enemy, and 1 was dismissed from the service for cowardice.

All of the companies, except the Louisiana Swamp Rangers (from St. Helena Parish), were from New Orleans.[9] The original officers and companies of the regiment were as follows: Colonel Theodore G. Hunt, Lieutenant-Colonel Henry Forno, Major W. T. Bean, and Adjutant J. B. Norris.

Bienville Guards, Captain Mark L. Moore commanding. This company suffered a 24 percent desertion rate during the war.

Orleans Cadets, Co. B, Captain Charles Hobday commanding. In this company, 46 percent were foreign-born, and it suffered a 20 percent desertion rate.

Louisiana Swamp Rangers, Captain E. J. Jones commanding. This company had 72 percent foreign-born, and 39 percent of the members deserted or took the oath of allegiance.

Orleans Southrons, Captain O. F. Peck commanding. This company had a very high (34 percent) desertion/oath rate, but surprisingly only 22 percent were foreign-born.

Crescent City Guards, Captain John A. Hall commanding.

Perret Guards, Captain Arthur Connor commanding. It was claimed

7. Theodore Mandeville to Rebecca Mandeville, August 27, 1861, in Box 2, Folder 12, Mandeville Papers, LSU.

8. Lafayette McLaws to wife, July 30, 1861, in Folder 4, McLaws Collection, SHC.

9. Casey, "Confederate Units from North Louisiana," SU-B.

that this company consisted mostly of gamblers. One soldier wrote that "to be admitted one must be able to cut, shuffle, and deal on the point of a bayonet." [10]

Chalmette (Rifle) Guards, Captain A. E. Shaw commanding. This company had 59 percent foreign-born. It suffered a 28 percent desertion/oath rate and a 28 percent death rate.

Carondelet Invincibles, Captain Bruce Menger commanding.

DeSoto Rifles, Captain W. B. Koontz commanding.

Monroe Guards (Rifles), Captain Thomas Dolan commanding.

Records also show the Louisiana Greys as being a company in the regiment. [11]

6th Louisiana Volunteers

The 6th Louisiana Volunteers, also known as the Irish Brigade, were mustered into service on June 4, 1861, with eight companies for the duration of the war and two for twelve months. The regiment's total enrollment during the war was 1,146. Of these, 219 were killed or mortally wounded, 104 died of disease, 5 were killed accidentally, 1 was executed for desertion, 1 drowned, at least 232 deserted, and 76 took the oath of allegiance. The regiment was composed mainly of New Orleans Irish laborers, who were said to be "turbulent in camp and requiring a strong hand, but responding to kindness and justice, and ready to follow their officers to the death." [12] Of the 893 members who gave a place of birth on the muster rolls, more than half were foreign-born. There were 455 born in Ireland, 139 in Louisiana, 130 in other states, 110 in the Germanic states, 29 in England, 9 in Canada, 7 in France, 6 in Scotland, 5 in Nassau, 2 in Sweden, and 1 in Holland. Of all the Louisiana Tiger regiments, the 6th Louisiana had the highest known percentage of foreign-born members (54 percent) and desertions and oaths (27 percent).

The 6th Louisiana had three successive colonels killed in action. Isaac G. Seymour was first elected colonel of the regiment but was

10. Quoted in Dufour, *Gentle Tiger,* 120.

11. Compiled Service Records, War Record Group 109, Microcopy 320, Roll 148, NA.

12. Taylor, *Destruction and Reconstruction,* 39.

killed on June 27, 1862, at Gaines' Mill. Lieutenant-Colonel Henry B. Strong then took command and served until he was killed at Antietam on September 17, 1862. Lieutenant-Colonel William Monaghan succeeded Colonel Strong and led the regiment until he, too, was killed in a skirmish near Shepherdstown, Virginia, on August 25, 1864. Lieutenant-Colonel Joseph Hanlon succeeded Monaghan and served until the end of the war. Besides these commanders, 15 other officers were killed or mortally wounded, 1 was killed accidentally, 2 died of disease, and 3 deserted to the enemy.

All of the regiment's companies were from New Orleans, except the St. Landry Light Guards, Tensas Rifles, and Union and Sabine Rifles. These companies were named after their native parishes. The original officers and companies of the regiment were as follows: Colonel Isaac G. Seymour, Lieutenant-Colonel Louis Lay, and Major S. L. James.

Irish Brigade, Co. A, Captain James Hanlon commanding. This company had no native-born Louisianians as members. It was 95 percent foreign-born and suffered a 34 percent desertion/oath rate.

Irish Brigade, Co. B, Captain William Monaghan commanding. Ireland was the birthplace of 71 percent of this company.[13]

Mercer (Rifle) Guards, Captain Thomas F. Walker commanding.

Violet Guards, Captain William H. Manning commanding.

St. Landry Light Guards, Captain Nat Offut commanding.

Orleans Rifles (Guards), Captain Thomas F. Fisher commanding.

Tensas Rifles, Captain Charles B. Tenney commanding.

Pemberton Rangers, Captain Isaac A. Smith commanding. This company had no native-born Louisianians as members; 98 percent were foreign-born, with 78 percent of these being Germans. The company suffered an astonishing 41 percent desertion/oath rate.[14]

Union and Sabine Rifles, Captain Arthur McArthur commanding.

Calhoun Guards, Captain Henry B. Strong commanding. In this company 93 percent were foreign-born, with 90 percent of these being Irish; 31 percent deserted or took the oath of allegiance.

Records indicate that the Southron Guards also served in the regiment.[15]

13. Lonn, *Foreigners in the Confederacy,* 108.

14. *Ibid.*

15. Compiled Service Records, War Record Group 109, Microcopy 320, Roll 163, NA.

7th Louisiana Volunteers

The 7th Louisiana Volunteers, sometimes called the Pelican Regiment, were mustered into service for the duration of the war on June 5, 1861. The regiment's total enrollment during the war was 1,077. Of these, 190 were killed or mortally wounded, 68 died of disease, 2 were killed accidentally, 1 was murdered, 1 was executed, at least 53 deserted, and 57 took the oath of allegiance. The regiment was composed mostly of clerks, laborers, and farmers and was described by Richard Taylor as a "crack regiment."[16] Many of its members belonged to the prestigious Pickwick Club of New Orleans, which presented a flag to the regiment before it left for Virginia.[17] Of the 974 members who gave a place of birth on the muster rolls, 373 were born in Louisiana, 331 in Ireland, 179 in states outside of Louisiana, 42 in the Germanic states, 24 in England, 9 in Canada, 5 in France, 3 in Switzerland, 2 each in Scotland and Sweden, and 1 each in Hungary, Spain, Italy, and the West Indies.

Harry T. Hays was elected colonel of the regiment and served until he was promoted to brigadier-general on July 25, 1862. Lieutenant-Colonel Davidson B. Penn succeeded him and commanded the regiment for the remainder of the war. During the war, 13 officers were killed or mortally wounded and 1 died of disease.

All of the companies were from New Orleans except the Livingston Rifles (Livingston Parish), Baton Rouge Fencibles (East Baton Rouge Parish), and Irish Volunteers (Donaldsonville). The 7th Louisiana was an exception to the rule of foreign-dominated regiments having high desertion rates. The Virginia Guards had a 63 percent foreign makeup yet only a 10 percent desertion rate. The Sarsfield Rangers were 75 percent foreign but lost only 10 percent to desertion, and the Irish Volunteers were 92 percent Irish yet had only a 17 percent desertion/oath rate.

The original officers and companies of the regiment were as follows: Colonel Harry T. Hays, Lieutenant-Colonel Charles de-Choiseul, and Major Davidson B. Penn.

American Rifles, Captain W. D. Ricarby commanding.
Livingston Rifles, Captain T. M. Terry commanding.

16. Taylor, *Destruction and Reconstruction,* 39.
17. William Harper Forman, Jr., "William P. Harper in War and Reconstruction," *Louisiana History,* XIII (1972), 57.

Virginia Guards, Captain Robert Scott commanding.
Virginia Blues, Captain D. A. Wilson, Jr., commanding. This company
  was 80 percent Irish and suffered a 23 percent desertion/oath rate
  and a 27 percent death rate.
Sarsfield Rangers, Captain J. Marc Wilson commanding.
Crescent Rifles, Co. B, Captain G. T. Jett commanding.
Crescent Rifles, Co. C, Captain S. H. Gilman commanding.
Continental Guards, Co. A, Captain George Clark commanding.
Baton Rouge Fencibles, Captain Andrew S. Herron commanding.
Irish Volunteers, Captain W. R. Ratliff commanding.

8th Louisiana Volunteers

The 8th Louisiana Volunteers were mustered into service on June
15, 1861, with seven companies for the duration of the war and
three for twelve months. The regiment's total enrollment during
the war was 1,321. Of these, 252 were killed or mortally wounded,
171 died of disease, 2 were murdered, 1 was killed accidentally, at
least 8 deserted, and 56 took the oath of allegiance. The regiment
mainly was composed of farmers and laborers and represented at
least eighteen foreign countries. Of the 1,114 members who gave a
place of birth on the muster rolls, 542 were born in Louisiana, 299
in other states, 141 in Ireland, 44 in the Germanic states, 26 in
France, 21 in England, 8 in Canada, 5 in Mexico, 4 each in Belgium
and Holland, 3 each in Denmark, Norway, Scotland, and Sweden,
2 each in Brazil and Switzerland, and 1 each in Cuba, Italy, Mar-
tinique, and Russia. In his memoirs, Richard Taylor inaccurately
claimed that the regiment was raised from the Bayou Teche region
of Louisiana and was composed of Creoles. This was incorrect,
however, for few of its companies were from the Teche country.
Judging from Taylor's description of the regiment, however, the
Creoles were the most conspicuous element of the command because of their language, lively music, and dancing.[18]

Henry B. Kelly was elected colonel of the regiment and served
until his resignation in April, 1863. He was succeeded by Lieutenant-Colonel Trevanion D. Lewis, who was killed on July 2, 1863, at
Gettysburg. Lieutenant-Colonel Alcibiades DeBlanc then took
command of the regiment. During the war 19 of the regiment's offi-

18. Taylor, *Destruction and Reconstruction,* 40; W. R. Lyman, "Cross Keys and Port
Republic," in Reminiscences, Executive and Army of Northern Virginia, LHAC.

cers were killed or mortally wounded, 1 died of disease, and 1 deserted to the enemy.

The original officers and companies of the regiment were as follows: [19] Colonel Henry B. Kelly, Lieutenant-Colonel Francis T. Nicholls, and Major John B. Prados.

> *Rapides Invincibles,* from Alexandria, Captain Lee Crandell commanding. This company had a 26 percent death rate during the war.
>
> *Phoenix Guards,* from Ascension and Assumption parishes, Captain L. D. Nicholls commanding. This company had a 29 percent death rate during the war.
>
> *Bienville Rifles,* from New Orleans, Captain Aug. Larose commanding. This company had men from twelve foreign countries. Of its 142 members, 20 percent deserted or took the oath.
>
> *Creole Guards,* from Baton Rouge, Captain J. L. Fremaux commanding. Only 34 percent of this company was foreign-born, yet it suffered a 28 percent desertion/oath rate, and 29 percent of its members died during the war.
>
> *Franklin Sharpshooters,* from Winsboro, Captain G. A. Lester commanding. This company lost 33 percent of its members to death during the war.
>
> *Sumter Guards,* Captain F. Newman commanding. This company was 67 percent foreign-born, and it had a 27 percent desertion/oath rate.
>
> *Attakapas Guards,* from St. Martin Parish, Captain Alex. DeBlanc commanding.
>
> *Cheneyville Rifles (Blues),* from Cheneyville, Captain P. F. Keary commanding.
>
> *Opelousas Guards,* from St. Landry Parish, Captain James C. Pratt commanding.
>
> *Minden Blues,* from Minden, Captain John L. Lewis commanding. This company had a 24 percent death rate during the war.

9th Louisiana Volunteers

The 9th Louisiana Volunteers were mustered into service on July 6, 1861, with six companies for the duration of the war and four for twelve months. The regiment's total enrollment during the war was 1,474. Of these, 233 were killed or mortally wounded, 349 died of

19. Compiled Service Records, War Record Group 109, Microcopy 320, Roll 187, NA.

disease, 4 were killed accidentally, at least 115 deserted, and 25 took the oath of allegiance. The regiment was composed almost exclusively of North Louisiana farmers. Of the 1,168 members who gave a place of birth on the muster rolls, 652 were born in states outside of Louisiana, 399 in Louisiana, 85 in Ireland, 21 in the Germanic states, 5 in England, 2 in Canada, 1 each in France, Norway, and Poland, and 1 listed as "Indian."

Richard Taylor was elected colonel of the regiment and served until he was promoted to brigadier-general on October 21, 1861. He was succeeded by Lieutenant-Colonel E. G. Randolph, who led the regiment until Captain Leroy A. Stafford was elected colonel when the regiment was reorganized in May, 1862. Stafford served until he was promoted to brigadier-general on October 8, 1863, at which time he was succeeded by Lieutenant-Colonel William R. Peck. Peck, too, was promoted to brigadier-general on February 18, 1865, but it is uncertain who succeeded him as commander of the regiment.

The 9th Louisiana Volunteers claimed several honors during the war. The regiment was the largest of Lee's Tigers, and three brigadier-generals were promoted from its ranks. It also had the highest death rate among the Louisiana regiments in Virginia and was the only regiment that had more men die of disease than in battle. During the war, 19 officers were killed or mortally wounded and 5 died of disease.

The original officers and companies of the regiment were as follows:[20] Colonel Richard Taylor, Lieutenant-Colonel E. G. Randolph, and Major W. J. Walker.

> *Bossier Volunteers,* from Bossier Parish, Captain John H. Hodges commanding. Of the members of this company, 88 percent were born in states outside of Louisiana. The death rate during the war was 38 percent.
> *Bienville Blues,* from Bienville Parish, Captain W. B. Pearce commanding. Of the members of this company, 64 percent were born in states outside of Louisiana. The death rate during the war was 38 percent.
> *Brush Valley Guards,* from Bienville Parish, Captain W. F. Gray commanding. Of the members of this company, 82 percent were born

20. *Ibid.,* Roll 201.

in states outside of Louisiana. The death rate during the war was 47 percent.

DeSoto Blues, from DeSoto Parish, Captain H. L. Williams commanding. This company lost 39 percent of its members to death during the war.

Colyell Guards, from Livingston Parish, Captain J. S. Gardner commanding. The death rate of this company was 39 percent during the war.

Jackson Greys, from Jackson Parish, Captain J. R. Cavanaugh commanding.

Washington Rifles, from Washington Parish, Captain Hardy Richardson commanding. The death rate of this company during the war was 61 percent.

Moore Fencibles, from Homer, Captain R. L. Capers commanding. The death rate of this company during the war was 30 percent, and 20 percent deserted, mostly to the Trans-Mississippi Department to join other military units. Records indicate that this was done frequently by men who wished to continue to fight but wanted to be closer to home.

Stafford Guards, from Rapides Parish, Captain Leroy A. Stafford commanding. The death rate of this company during the war was 38 percent.

Milliken Bend Guards, from Madison Parish, Captain William R. Peck commanding. The death rate of this company during the war was 42 percent. This was the only company in the 9th Louisiana with a large number (55 percent) of foreign-born. Only 1 man deserted, however, and 15 took the oath of allegiance.

10th Louisiana Volunteers

The 10th Louisiana Volunteers' muster rolls do not appear in the Bound Volumes at Tulane University. Therefore, some information is lacking. This regiment was mustered into service for the duration of the war on July 22, 1861. Its total enrollment during the war was 845, of which 142 were killed or mortally wounded, 58 died of disease, 3 were murdered, and 2 were killed accidentally. The regiment was composed mainly of foreigners, one company having men from fifteen nationalities and another made up primarily of Greeks and Italians.[21]

21. Wiley, *Johnny Reb*, 323; New Orleans *Times-Picayune*, May 16, 1926.

Mandeville Marigny was elected colonel of the regiment and served until his resignation in July, 1862. Marigny was a former French army officer, who patterned the 10th Louisiana after the French regiments with which he had previous experience. The French language was used in giving commands during drill.[22] Marigny was succeeded by Lieutenant-Colonel Eugene Waggaman, who commanded the regiment until the end of the war.

During the war, 13 officers were killed or mortally wounded and 2 died of disease. The original officers and companies of the regiment were as follows: Colonel Mandeville Marigny, Lieutenant-Colonel J. C. Denis, and Major Felix DuMonteil.

Shepherd Guards, Captain Alex. Phillips commanding.
Hewitt Guards, from Bayou Lafourche, Captain R. M. Hewitt commanding.
Confederate States Rangers, Captain W. H. Spencer commanding.
Louisiana Rebels, Captain John M. Legett commanding.
Orleans Blues, Captain W. B. Barnett commanding.
Derbigny Guards, Captain L. T. Bakewell commanding.
Louisiana Swamp Rifles, Captain D. W. Dickey commanding.
Tirailleur's D'Orleans, Captain Eugene Waggaman commanding.
Orleans Rangers, Captain Edward Crevon commanding.
Hawkins Guards, Captain Charles F. White commanding.

Records also indicate that the Stars of Equality and Atchafalaya Rifles were companies of the regiment.[23]

14th Louisiana Volunteers

The 14th Louisiana Volunteers' muster rolls do not appear in the Bound Volumes at Tulane University. Therefore, some information is lacking. This regiment was mustered into service for the duration of the war on June 16, 1861. The regiment had its origin in the Confederate government's efforts to gather support for the war from all segments of the southern populace. To help win over the foreign-born element, the government authorized the raising of a

22. New Orleans *Daily Picayune*, April 19, 1861.
23. Compiled Service Records, War Record Group 109, Microcopy 320, Roll 217, NA.

Polish Brigade in New Orleans. The regiment was initially known as the 1st Regiment Polish Brigade, although hardly any Poles were members. The regiment was said to have had only nine companies originally and was not officially recognized as the 14th Louisiana Volunteers until a tenth was added in September, 1861.

The regiment's total enrollment during the war was 1,026. Of these, 184 were killed or mortally wounded, 85 died of disease, 5 were killed or mortally wounded during the riot at Grand Junction, Tennessee, and 1 each was killed accidentally, executed, and drowned. The members were predominantly German, French, and Irish, with the majority being Mississippi River boatmen. The regiment was extremely hard to discipline because of the variety of nationalities and languages and the malicious nature of many of its members.[24]

Valery Sulakowski, a Polish immigrant, was elected colonel of the regiment and served until his resignation in January, 1862. He was succeeded by Lieutenant-Colonel R. W. Jones, who also resigned in August, 1862. Lieutenant-Colonel Zebulon York then took command and served until his promotion to brigadier-general on June 2, 1864. He was succeeded by Lieutenant-Colonel David Zable. Although no field officers died during the war, 10 line officers were killed or mortally wounded, 1 died of disease, and 5 deserted to the enemy.

The original officers and companies of the regiment were as follows: Colonel Valery Sulakowski, Lieutenant-Colonel R. W. Jones, and Major Zebulon York.

Armstrong Guards
Jefferson Cadets (Guards) Records show that this company also served with the 15th Louisiana Volunteers.
Askew Guards This company also appears to have served with the 15th Louisiana Volunteers.
McClure Guards
Concordia Infantry (Rifles)
Avegno Rifles
Nixon Rifles
Lafayette Rifle Cadets
Franco (Rifle) Guards

24. Bartlett, *Military Record of Louisiana*, 44.

Empire (Parish) Rangers This company exchanged places with the
Quitman Rangers of the 3d Louisiana Battalion in December, 1861.

Six of these companies were from New Orleans and one each
from Plaquemines, Point Coupee, Tensas, and Concordia parishes.
Available records indicate that these ten companies made up the
1st Regiment Polish Brigade, but as mentioned above, one official
source states that the regiment originally had only nine companies.
The explanation for the discrepancy is that the Franco (Rifle)
Guards were disbanded for their role in the Grand Junction riot.
Records show that a tenth company was added in September, 1861,
allowing the regiment to be designated officially as the 14th Louisiana Volunteers. One source identifies this company as the Catahoula Guerrillas of Wheat's Battalion, but this is not substantiated
by other sources. The Tiger Bayou Rifles of Carroll Parish were
added in the summer of 1861 but ordered transferred to the 1st
Louisiana Volunteers on August 5, 1861. Either the Catahoula
Guerrillas were added to the regiment in September, 1861, or the
records are in error on the date, and the unit became the 14th Louisiana Volunteers when the Tiger Bayou Rifles were added.[25]

15th Louisiana Volunteers

The 15th Louisiana Volunteers were originally designated the 2d
Regiment Polish Brigade, although no known Poles were members
(see the 14th Louisiana Volunteers for details on the Polish Brigade). The regiment was mustered into service with eight companies for the duration of the war on June 16, 1861. Upon entering
Confederate service, it was renamed the 3d Louisiana Battalion
with a promise to become the 15th Louisiana Volunteers once two
more companies were added to it. This occurred when two companies of Henry St. Paul's battalion were added on August 2, 1862.
   The regiment's total enrollment for the war was 901. Of these,
143 were killed or mortally wounded, 98 died of disease, 1 was executed, at least 130 deserted, and 13 took the oath of allegiance. The

25. *Ibid.*, 46; *OR*, Vol. LI, Pt. II, 214; Compiled Service Records, War Record
Group 109, Microcopy 320, Roll 253, NA; Casey, "Confederate Units from North
Louisiana," SU-D.

regiment was composed mainly of farmers, laborers, and clerks. Of the 520 members who gave a place of birth on the muster rolls, 161 were born in Louisiana, 157 in other states, 118 in Ireland, 36 in the Germanic states, 17 in England, 11 in France, 10 "Indians," 6 in Scotland, 3 in Canada, and 1 in Russia.

Charles M. Bradford was elected lieutenant-colonel of the 3d Louisiana Battalion and served until his resignation in December, 1861. Major Edmund Pendleton then took command and served until the battalion was designated the 15th Louisiana Volunteers. At that time Lieutenant-Colonel Francis T. Nicholls of the 8th Louisiana Volunteers was made colonel of the newly created regiment. When Colonel Nicholls was promoted to brigadier-general on October 14, 1862, Lieutenant-Colonel Edmund Pendleton succeeded him as commander. Nine of the regiment's officers were killed or mortally wounded during the war.

All of the regiment's companies were from New Orleans, except the Grosse Tete Creoles of Iberville and West Baton Rouge parishes and the Davenport Rebels (Rifles) from Morehouse Parish. The original officers and companies of the regiment were as follows:[26] Lieutenant-Colonel Charles M. Bradford and Major Edmund Pendleton.

Askew Guards This company also appears to have served with the 14th Louisiana Volunteers.

Quitman Rangers In December, 1861, this company exchanged places with the Empire (Parish) Rangers of the 14th Louisiana.

St. Ceran Rifles This company was 74 percent foreign-born, and it suffered a 25 percent desertion rate.

Grivot (Guards) Rifles

St. James Rifles (Rebels) This company lost 45 percent by desertion to the enemy, but it is unknown whether the company had a large number of foreign-born members.

Bogart Guards

Grosse Tete Creoles The death rate of this company was 31 percent during the war.

Davenport Rebels (Rifles) The death rate of this company was 42 percent during the war.

26. D. T. Merrick to E. D. Willett, December 9, 1893, in Reminiscences, Executive and Army of Northern Virginia, LHAC; Compiled Service Records, War Record Group 109, Microcopy 320, Roll 266, NA.

In the summer of 1862 the Catahoula Guerrillas of Wheat's Battalion and the Crescent (City or Rifles) Blues of St. Paul's Battalion joined the 3d Louisiana Battalion. Both of these companies were ordered to join the battalion on June 21, 1862, but because of heavy fighting on the Peninsula they waited until after the Seven Days' campaign before doing so. Records also show the Jefferson Cadets (Guards) of the 14th Louisiana Volunteers and the Louisiana Turcos as being members of the regiment. The former company was 58 percent foreign-born, and it suffered a 32 percent desertion rate during the war. Many of these deserters left the company to join cavalry units.

1st Special Battalion, Louisiana Infantry

The muster rolls for Wheat's Battalion do not appear in the Bound Volumes at Tulane University. Therefore, some information is lacking. The 1st Special Battalion, Louisiana Infantry, commonly known as Wheat's Battalion, was mustered into service with five companies for the duration of the war on June 9, 1861. The total enrollment of the battalion during the war was 416, of which 39 were killed or mortally wounded, 15 died of disease, 2 were executed, and 1 was killed accidentally.

Few Civil War commands consisted of companies as diverse as those of Wheat's Battalion. The Catahoula Guerrillas were largely made up of planters' sons, the Walker Guards was a company of soldiers of fortune, and the Tiger Rifles had numerous criminals within its ranks. Wheat's Battalion was so rowdy and "so villainous . . . that every commander desired to be rid of it."[27] The entire battalion was quickly dubbed the "Tigers" because of its unruly behavior, and the term soon became synonymous for all of the Louisiana infantry in the Army of Northern Virginia.

Roberdeau Wheat was elected major of the battalion and served until he was killed on June 27, 1862, at Gaines' Mill. Apparently no one was selected to replace Wheat as commander of the battalion. Because of heavy casualties during the Valley campaign and the Seven Days, the battalion was disbanded on August 21, 1862.[28]

27. Taylor, *Destruction and Reconstruction*, 17.
28. New Orleans *Daily Item*, August 25, 1896, in Scrapbook, Boyd Papers, LSU.

All of the battalion's companies were from New Orleans, except the Catahoula Guerrillas of Catahoula Parish. The companies of Wheat's Battalion were as follows:[29]

> *Walker Guards,* Captain Robert A. Harris commanding. It was claimed that every member of this company had served under William Walker during his filibuster expedition to Nicaragua in the 1850s.[30]
> *Old Dominion Guards,* Captain O. P. Miller commanding.
> *Tiger Rifles,* Captain Alex White commanding.
> *Delta Rangers,* Captain H. C. Gardner commanding.
> *Catahoula Guerrillas,* Captain J. W. Buhoup commanding. Sometime before the Seven Days' campaign, Captain Buhoup was granted a request to have his company transferred to Henry St. Paul's battalion. Later it joined Coppens' Battalion, and after the Seven Days, the company was transferred again to the 3d Louisiana Battalion. The company also appears to have served with the 1st Louisiana Volunteers and possibly with the 14th Louisiana.[31]

Records also show the Orleans Claiborne Guards and Wheat's Life Guards as being part of the battalion. The Orleans Claiborne Guards were assigned to the battalion in June, 1861, and could have been a replacement company for the departing Catahoula Guerrillas, although the Guerrillas did not leave until months later.[32]

1st Battalion, Louisiana Volunteers

The muster rolls of Dreux's Battalion do not appear in the Bound Volumes at Tulane University. Therefore, some information is lacking. The 1st Battalion, Louisiana Volunteers, commonly known as Dreux's Battalion, consisted of the first volunteer companies to respond to Louisiana's call for troops and was said to be made up of New Orleans' finest gentlemen.[33] In June, 1861, five Louisiana companies stationed at Pensacola, Florida, were mustered into service

29. Casey, "Confederate Units from North Louisiana," SU-A.
30. New Orleans *Daily Crescent,* April 19, 1861.
31. Bartlett, *Military Record of Louisiana,* 46.
32. Compiled Service Records, War Record Group 109, Microcopy 320, Roll 100, NA.
33. DeLeon, *Four Years in Rebel Capitals,* 66.

for twelve months as the 1st Battalion, Louisiana Volunteers, with a sixth company added in July. The battalion's total enrollment during the war was 545, of which 2 were killed and 16 died of disease. The battalion was ordered mustered out of service in April, 1862, but volunteered to remain on duty until after the Battle of Yorktown. After the battalion was disbanded, most of the men reorganized as Fenner's Artillery.

Charles D. Dreux was elected lieutenant-colonel of the battalion and served until he was killed in a skirmish on July 5, 1861. Colonel Dreux was the first Louisianian and the first Confederate field officer killed in the war. He was succeeded by Major N. H. Rightor.

All of the battalion's companies were from New Orleans, except the Shreveport Greys (Shreveport) and the Grivot Guards (Lafourche Parish). The original officers and companies of the battalion were as follows: [34]

Orleans Cadets, Captain Charles D. Dreux commanding. This company was the first Louisiana volunteer company to be mustered into Confederate service (April 11, 1861). Of its 103 members, 37 were under eighteen years old, and it was claimed that Dreux was the only married man in the company. [35]

Shreveport Greys, Captain J. H. Beard commanding. After the disbandment of the battalion, this company was transferred to the 1st Louisiana Volunteers on June 27, 1862. [36]

Grivot Guards, Captain N. H. Rightor commanding. This company was also known as the Terrebonne Rifles.

Crescent City Rifles, Co. A, Captain S. F. Fisk commanding.

Louisiana Guards, Co. A, Captain S. M. Todd commanding.

Louisiana Guards, Co. C. This was the sixth company added to the battalion. [37]

1st Battalion, Louisiana Zouaves

The 1st Battalion, Louisiana Zouaves' muster rolls do not appear in the Bound Volumes at Tulane University. Therefore, some infor-

34. *OR,* Series IV, Vol. I, 747.
35. *Confederate Veteran,* III (1895), 146.
36. *OR,* Vol. LIII, 815–16.
37. William E. Hughes to O. L. Putnam, July 20, 1899, in Flags, LHAC.

mation is lacking. This battalion, commonly known as Coppens' Battalion, was raised under the personal authorization of Jefferson Davis. Davis even promised to increase the battalion to full regimental strength should war come. The battalion's six companies were raised in New Orleans and mustered into service for the duration of the war at Pensacola, Florida, in April, 1861. Despite Davis' promise, however, it was never increased to a full regiment. The battalion was the only complete Louisiana Zouave command sent to Virginia. Its members adopted the French Zouave dress and drill techniques and received all their drill commands in French.[38]

Gaston Coppens was elected lieutenant-colonel of the battalion and served until he was killed on September 17, 1862, at Antietam. His brother, Major Alfred Coppens, then took command. The battalion was eventually mustered into the regular Confederate army as the Confederate States Zouaves. It was detached from the Army of Northern Virginia during the latter half of the war and performed various duties in Virginia. Although the proper names of the battalion's companies are unknown, the Catahoula Guerrillas, Crescent City Blues, and St. Paul's Foot Rifles are known to have transferred to the battalion during the war.[39]

3d Battalion, Louisiana Infantry

The 3d Battalion, Louisiana Infantry, was originally known as the 2d Regiment Polish Brigade and was sometimes referred to as Pendleton's Battalion. It was mustered into service with eight companies for the duration of the war on June 16, 1861. Its total enrollment during the war was 678, but its battalion losses are unknown. See the 15th Louisiana Volunteers for details.

Washington Infantry Battalion

The muster rolls of the Washington Infantry Battalion do not appear in the Bound Volumes at Tulane University. Therefore, some

38. Wallace, "Coppens' Louisiana Zouaves," 269; J. W. Minnich, article on Coppens' Zouaves, in Reminiscences, Executive and Army of Northern Virginia, LHAC; Lonn, *Foreigners in the Confederacy*, 102.
39. Army of Northern Virginia Papers, Part I, LHAC.

information is lacking. This battalion was commonly known as St. Paul's Foot Rifles but was also referred to as the 7th or 19th Louisiana Infantry Battalion. On April 19, 1861, the Confederate secretary of war accepted Belgian-born Henry St. Paul de Lechard's 1st Company of Foot Rifles (Chasseurs a Pied) directly into Confederate service. By October 1, 1861, two more companies had been added to St. Paul's company, and the three were designated the Washington Infantry Battalion, with St. Paul as its major. The battalion's total enrollment during the war was 316, but its losses are unknown. Official records state that the battalion was disbanded in August, 1862, with its companies being distributed among other Louisiana commands. But one veteran claimed the battalion, or at least one of its companies, was detached from the Army of Northern Virginia after the Battle of Fredericksburg and was captured at Fort Gaines on August 5, 1864.[40]

Two of the battalion's companies were from New Orleans, and the third was from Catahoula Parish. They were as follows:

St. Paul's Foot Rifles, Captain Henry St. Paul commanding. Apparently this company transferred to Coppens' Battalion when St. Paul's Battalion was disbanded. This company also appears to have served with the 1st Louisiana Volunteers.[41]

Catahoula Guerrillas, Captain J. W. Buhoup commanding. This company was transferred from Wheat's Battalion to St. Paul's Battalion and eventually became part of the 15th Louisiana Volunteers.[42]

Crescent City Blues, Captain Frank Barlett commanding. This company was composed of members of the Pelican Hook and Ladder Fire Company of New Orleans. It went to Virginia unattached and fought at First Manassas with two other independent companies. In

40. W. S. Michie, article on the 15th Louisiana Volunteers, in Reminiscences, Executive and Army of Northern Virginia, LHAC; List of Companies and Officers, St. Paul's Foot Rifles, Army of Northern Virginia Papers, Part I, LHAC; *Confederate Veteran*, XIII (1905), 277.

41. W. S. Michie, article on 15th Louisiana Volunteers, in Reminiscences, Executive and Army of Northern Virginia, LHAC; List of Companies and Officers, St. Paul's Foot Rifles, Army of Northern Virginia Papers, Part I, LHAC.

42. W. S. Michie, article on 15th Louisiana Volunteers, in Reminiscences, Executive and Army of Northern Virginia, LHAC; List of Companies and Officers, St. Paul's Foot Rifles, Army of Northern Virginia Papers, LHAC.

September, 1861, it was attached for one month to the 49th Virginia Infantry. In October, 1861, it was transferred to St. Paul's Foot Rifles and in May, 1862, was attached to Coppens' Battalion. In August, 1862, it was transferred to the 3d Louisiana Battalion and appears to have later served with the 1st Louisiana Volunteers. Of its members, 38 percent were foreign-born, and it suffered a 24 percent desertion rate.[43]

43. New Orleans *Daily Picayune*, April 18, 1861.

BIBLIOGRAPHY

Primary Sources

MANUSCRIPT COLLECTIONS

Centenary College, Shreveport, Louisiana.
    North Louisiana Historical Association Archives.
Duke University, Durham, North Carolina.
    Beauregard, Pierre Gustave Toutant. Papers.
    Browning, Amos G. Papers.
    Confederate States of America. Archives.
    Confederate Veteran. Papers.
    Dawson, Francis Warrington. Letters.
    Hemphill Family. Papers.
    Hubert, Ben. Papers.
    Morgan, Thomas Gibbes, Sr., and Jr. Papers.
    Solomons, M. J. Scrapbook.
    Stuart, James Ewell Brown. Papers.
    Walkup, Samuel Huey. Journal.
East Carolina University, Greenville, North Carolina.
    East Carolina Manuscript Collection.
Fredericksburg and Spotsylvania National Military Park, Fredericksburg,
    Virginia.
    Patterson, E. A. Collection.
    Slaughter Papers.
Hewitt, Lawrence L. Private Collection. Independence, Louisiana.
Historic New Orleans Collection, New Orleans, Louisiana.
    Walton-Glenny Family. Papers.
Huntington Library, San Marino, California.
    Janin Family. Papers.
Library of Congress, Washington, D.C.
    Ewell, Richard S. Papers.
    Miscellaneous Manuscripts Collection.

Louisiana State Archives, Baton Rouge, Louisiana.
    Hollier, Charles S. Pension File.
Louisiana State University, Baton Rouge, Louisiana.
    Batchelor, Albert A. Papers.
    Boyd, David F. Civil War Papers.
    Boyd, David F. Papers.
    Boyd, David F. Selected Papers.
    Egan, J. S. Family Papers.
    Evans, H. Letter.
    Fitzpatrick, John. Letterbook.
    Flournoy, Alfred. Papers.
    Jastremski, Leon. Family Papers.
    LaVillebeuvre, Jean Ursin. Family Papers.
    Liddell, Moses and St. John R. Family Papers.
    Mandeville, Henry D. Family Papers.
    Newell, Robert A. Papers.
    Nicholls, Francis R. T. Letter.
    Saucier, Gertrude B. Papers.
    Shilg, Merritt M. Memorial Collection.
    Smith, Benjamin. Letter.
    Stephens, John F. Correspondence.
    Stubbs, Jefferson W. Family Papers.
    Taylor, Miles. Family Papers.
    Washburne and Hesler Ledger.
    Wise, James Calvert. Papers.
Louisiana State University at Shreveport, Shreveport, Louisiana.
    Beard, James H. Papers.
    Flournoy, Alfred, Jr. Papers.
Mansfield State Commemorative Area, Mansfield, Louisiana.
    Devine, John. Letters.
    Harris, Robert, Jr. Letter.
    Wharton, William H. Scrapbook.
    Williams, Boling. Diary.
Museum of the Confederacy, Richmond, Virginia.
    MC–3/MSS. 3.
National Archives, Washington, D.C.
    Clothing Account. 7th Regiment of Louisiana Volunteers, 1862. War
        Record Group 109. Chapter V. Volume 205.
    Compiled Service Records of Confederate General and Staff Officers,
        and Nonregimental Enlisted Men. War Record Group 109. Micro-
        copy 331.
    Compiled Service Records of Confederate Soldiers Who Served in Or-

ganizations from the State of Louisiana. War Record Group 109. Microcopy 320.

Early, General Jubal A. Papers, 1861–65. War Record Group 109. Entry 118.

Record Book of the Hospital of the 7th Regiment of Louisiana Volunteers. 1861. War Record Group 109. Chapter VI. Volume 486.

Register of Arrests, 1862–64. War Record Group 109. Chapter IX. Volume 244.

7th Louisiana Volunteers Quartermaster Document, March, 1864. War Record Group 109. Chapter V. Volume 205.

New York Public Library, Rare Books and Manuscripts Division, New York, New York.

Louisiana Troops. 7th Regiment Orderly Book, 1862–64.

Northwestern State University, Natchitoches, Louisiana.

Carver Collection.

Mansfield Museum MSS.

Sandlin, Murphy. Collection.

Melrose Scrapbooks.

Stephens, Judge Paul. Collection.

Tooke, T. A. Letter.

Tulane University, New Orleans, Louisiana.

Behan Family Papers.

Civil War Manuscript Series.

Civil War Scrapbooks.

Herron Family Correspondence.

New Orleans Civil War Scrapbook.

Ogden Family Papers.

Tulane University, Louisiana Historical Association Collection, New Orleans, Louisiana.

Army of Northern Virginia Papers.

Association of the Army of Northern Virginia.

Bibliographic Material. Louisiana Troops.

Confederate Personnel.

Flags.

Moore, Charles, Jr. Diary, 1861–65.

Newsclippings and Miscellaneous Unidentified Material.

Pamphlets.

Reminiscences, Executive and Army of Northern Virginia.

University of Michigan, Ann Arbor, Michigan.

Seymour, Isaac G. Papers. Schoff Civil War Collection.

University of North Carolina at Chapel Hill, Southern Historical Collection, Chapel Hill, North Carolina.

Alexander, Edward Porter. Collection.
Brown, Campbell. Collection.
Coles, Elizabeth P. Collection.
Colston, Raleigh E. Collection.
Hairston, Peter W. Collection.
Janin, Eugene. Collection.
King, Grace. Collection.
McLaws, Lafayette. Collection.
Polk, Ewell, Brown Collection.
Wheat, John T. Collection.
White, Wellford, Taliaferro, and Marshall Collection.
Williams, Marguerite E. Collection.
University of Texas, Austin, Texas.
Moore, William E. Papers.
Virginia Historical Society Library, Virginia Historical Society Collection, Richmond, Virginia.
Carrington Family Papers.
George Family Papers.
Virginia State Library, Richmond, Virginia.
Owen, Henry T. Papers.

STATE AND FEDERAL GOVERNMENT PUBLICATIONS

Adjutant General's Report, State of Louisiana. New Orleans, 1890.
Biennial Report of the Secretary of State of the State of Louisiana to His Excellancy Samuel D. McEnery, Governor of Louisiana, 1886–1887. Baton Rouge, 1888.
The War of the Rebellion: A Compilation of the Official Records of the Union and Confederate Armies. 130 vols. Washington, D.C., 1880–1901.

MEMOIRS AND REMINISCENCES

Alexander, Edward Porter. *Military Memoirs of a Confederate.* New York, 1907.
Baquet, Camille. *History of the First Brigade, New Jersey Volunteers from 1861 to 1865.* Trenton, 1910.
Beers, Fannie A. *Memories: A Record of Personal Experience and Adventure During Four Years of War.* Philadelphia, 1889.
Blackford, Susan Leigh, comp., Charles M. Blackford and C. M. Blackford, eds. *Letters from Lee's Army or Memoirs of Life in and out of the Army of Virginia During the War Between the States.* New York, 1947.
Buckley, Cornelius M., trans. and ed. *A Frenchman, a Chaplain, a Rebel: The War Letters of Pere Louis-Hippolyte Gache, S.J.* Chicago, 1981.

Casler, John Overton. *Four Years in the Stonewall Brigade.* 1906; rpr. Marietta, Ga., 1951.

Cavanagh, Michael. *Memoirs of Gen. Thomas Francis Meagher . . . Including Personal Reminiscences.* Worcester, Mass., 1892.

Chamberlayne, C. G., ed. *Ham Chamberlayne—Virginian: Letters and Papers of an Artillery Officer in the War for Southern Independence, 1861–1865.* Richmond, 1932.

Dawes, Rufus R. *Service with the Sixth Wisconsin Volunteers.* Edited by Alan T. Nolan. 1890; rpr. Madison, 1962.

DeLeon, Thomas Cooper. *Four Years in Rebel Capitals: An Inside View of Life in the Southern Confederacy, from Birth to Death.* Mobile, 1890.

Douglas, Henry Kyd. *I Rode with Stonewall.* Chapel Hill, 1940.

Dunlop, W. S. *Lee's Sharpshooters; or, the Forefront of Battle.* Little Rock, 1899.

Durkin, Rev. Joseph, ed. *Confederate Chaplain: A War Journal of Rev. James B. Sheeran, c.s.s.r., 14th Louisiana, C.S.A.* Milwaukee, 1960.

Early, Jubal Anderson. *A Memoir of the Last Year of the War for Independence . . . in the Year 1864 and 1865.* Lynchburg, 1867.

———. *War Memoirs: Autobiographical Sketch and Narrative of the War Between the States.* Edited by Frank E. Vandiver. 1912; rpr. Bloomington, 1960.

An English Combatant [pseud.]. *Battlefields of the South, from Bull Run to Fredericksburg, with Sketches of Confederate Commanders, and Gossip of the Camps.* New York, 1864.

Goldsborough, W. W. *The Maryland Line in the Confederate Army, 1861–1865.* Baltimore, 1900.

Gordon, John B. *Reminiscences of the Civil War.* New York, 1903.

Handerson, Henry E. *Yankee in Gray: The Civil War Memoirs of Henry E. Handerson with a Selection of His Wartime Letters.* Cleveland, 1962.

Hood, John Bell. *Advance and Retreat: Personal Experiences in the United States and Confederate States Armies.* Edited by Richard N. Current. 1880; rpr. Bloomington, 1959.

Hotchkiss, Jedediah. *Make Me a Map of the Valley: The Civil War Journal of Stonewall Jackson's Topographer.* Edited by Archie P. McDonald. Dallas, 1973.

Howard, McHenry. *Recollections of a Maryland Confederate Soldier and Staff Officer Under Johnston, Jackson and Lee.* 1914; rpr. Dayton, Ohio, 1975.

Howard, Oliver Otis. *Autobiography of Oliver Otis Howard, Major General, United States Army.* New York, 1907.

Huffman, James. *Ups and Downs of a Confederate Soldier.* New York, 1940.

Johnson, R. V., and C. C. Buel, eds. *Battles and Leaders of the Civil War.* 4 vols. New York, 1884–88.

Jones, Rev. John William. *Christ in the Camp or Religion in Lee's Army.* Richmond, 1887.

Lane, Mills, ed. *"Dear Mother: Don't Grieve About Me, If I Get Killed, I'll Only Be Dead." Letters from Georgia Soldiers in the Civil War.* Savannah, 1977.

Myers, Frank M. *The Comanches: A History of White's Battalion, Virginia Cavalry, Laurel Brig., Hampton Div., A.N.V., C.S.A.* 1871; rpr. Marietta, Ga., 1956.

Nisbet, James Cooper. *Four Years on the Firing Line.* Edited by Bell Irvin Wiley. 1914; rpr. Jackson, Tenn., 1963.

Oates, William C. *The War Between the Union and Confederacy and Its Lost Opportunities with a History of the 15th Alabama Regiment and the Forty-eight Battles in Which It Was Engaged.* New York, 1905.

Paver, John M. *What I Saw from 1861 to 1864.* 1906; rpr. Ann Arbor, 1974.

Pryor, Mrs. Roger A. *Reminiscences of Peace and War.* New York, 1905.

Putnam, Sallie A. *Richmond During the War: Four Years of Personal Observation.* New York, 1867.

Quaife, Milo M., ed. *From the Cannon's Mouth: The Civil War Letters of General Alpheus S. Williams.* Detroit, 1959.

Reed, Thomas Benton. *A Private in Gray.* Camden, Ark., 1905.

Reid, Jesse Walton. *History of the Fourth S.C. Volunteers, from the Commencement of the War Until Lee's Surrender.* 1892; rpr. Dayton, Ohio, 1975.

Russell, Sir William Howard. *My Diary North and South.* Edited by Fletcher Pratt. 1863; rpr. New York, 1954.

———. *Pictures of Southern Life, Social, Political and Military.* New York, 1861.

Schurz, Carl. *The Reminiscences of Carl Schurz.* 3 vols. New York, 1907, 1908.

SeCheverell, J. Hamp. *Journal History of the Twenty-Ninth Ohio Veteran Volunteers, 1861–1865, Its Victories and Its Reverses.* Cleveland, 1883.

Stearns, Austin C. *Three Years with Company K.* Edited by Arthur A. Kent. London, 1976.

Stevens, C. A. *Berdan's United States Sharpshooters in the Army of the Potomac, 1861–1865.* St. Paul, 1892.

Stiles, Robert. *Four Years Under Marse Robert.* 4th ed. New York, 1910.

Taylor, Richard. *Destruction and Reconstruction: Personal Experiences of the Late War.* Edited by Charles P. Roland. 1879; rpr. Xerox Corporation, Waltham, Mass., 1968.

Wood, George L. *The Seventh Regiment: A Record.* New York, 1865.

Woodbury, Augustus. *The Second Rhode Island Regiment: A Narrative of Military Operations from the Beginning to the End of the War for the Union.* Providence, 1875.

Worsham, John H. *One of Jackson's Foot Cavalry.* Edited by James I. Robertson, Jr. 1912; rpr. Jackson, Tenn., 1964.

JOURNALS AND ARTICLES

Confederate Veteran.

Conner, Forrest P., ed. "Letters of Lieutenant Robert H. Miller to His Family, 1861–1862." *Virginia Magazine of History and Biography,* LXX (1962), 62–91.

Davis, Edwin A., ed. "A Louisiana Volunteer: Letters of William J. Walter, 1861–1862." *Southwest Review,* XIX (1933), 78–87.

Forman, William Harper, Jr. "William P. Harper in War and Reconstruction." *Louisiana History,* XIII (1972), 47–70.

Lathrop, Barnes F., ed. "An Autobiography of Francis T. Nicholls, 1834–1881." *Louisiana Historical Quarterly,* XVII (1934), 246–67.

Laurence, Debra Nance. "Letters from a North Louisiana Tiger." *North Louisiana Historical Association's Journal,* X (Fall, 1979), 130–47.

Southern Historical Society Papers.

Turner, Charles W., ed. "Major Charles A. Davidson: Letters of a Virginia Soldier." *Civil War History,* XXII (1976), 16–40.

Vandiver, Frank E., ed. "A Collection of Louisiana Confederate Letters." *Louisiana Historical Quarterly,* XXVI (1943), 937–74.

NEWSPAPERS

New Orleans. *Daily Crescent,* April 19, 1861.
———. *Daily Delta,* May 2, 6, 24, 1861.
———. *Daily Picayune,* April 18, 19, 29, September 30, 1861.
———. *Times Picayune,* May 16, 1926.
Richmond. *Enquirer,* July 11, 26, 1861, May 10, 1864.

Secondary Sources

BOOKS

Austin, Aurelia. *Georgia Boys with "Stonewall" Jackson: James Thomas Thompson and the Walton Infantry.* Athens, 1967.

Bartlett, Napier. *Military Record of Louisiana.* Baton Rouge, 1964.

Bean, W. G. *The Liberty Hall Volunteers: Stonewall's College Boys.* Charlottesville, 1964.

Benedict, G. G. *Vermont in the Civil War: A History of the Part Taken by the Vermont Soldiers and Sailors in the War for the Union, 1861–5.* 2 vols. Burlington, 1886.

Bill, Alfred Hoyt. *The Beleaguered City: Richmond, 1861–1865.* New York, 1946.

Booth, Andrew B., comp. *Records of Louisiana Confederate Soldiers and Louisiana Confederate Commands.* 3 vols. New Orleans, 1920.

Brock, R. A. *The Appomattox Roster.* 1887; rpr. New York, n.d.

Dabney, Robert L. *Life and Campaigns of Lieut.-Gen. Thomas J. Jackson.* New York, 1866.

Davis, Burke. *Gray Fox: Robert E. Lee and the Civil War.* New York, 1956.
————. *They Called Him Stonewall: A Life of Lt. General T. J. Jackson, C.S.A.* New York, 1954.
Dimitry, John. *Louisiana.* Vol. X in Clement Evans, ed., *Confederate Military History.* Atlanta, 1899.
Dowdey, Clifford. *The Land They Fought For: The Story of the South as the Confederacy, 1832–1865.* Garden City, 1955.
————. *Lee's Last Campaign: The Story of Lee and His Men Against Grant—1864.* Boston, 1960.
————. *The Seven Days: The Emergence of Lee.* Boston, 1964.
Dufour, Charles L. *Gentle Tiger: The Gallant Life of Roberdeau Wheat.* Baton Rouge, 1957.
Foster, John Y. *New Jersey and the Rebellion: A History of the Services of the Troops and People of New Jersey in Aid of the Union Cause.* Newark, 1868.
Frassanito, William A. *Antietam: The Photographic Legacy of America's Bloodiest Day.* New York, 1978.
Freeman, Douglas Southall. *Lee's Lieutenants: A Study in Command.* 3 vols. New York, 1942, 1944.
————. *R. E. Lee: A Biography.* 4 vols. New York, 1935.
Hamlin, Percy Gatling. *"Old Bald Head" (General R. S. Ewell): The Portrait of a Soldier.* Strasburg, Va., 1940.
LaBree, Ben, ed. *Camp Fires of the Confederacy.* Louisville, 1899.
Lonn, Ella. *Foreigners in the Confederacy.* Chapel Hill, 1940.
Miers, Earl Schenck, and Richard A. Brown, eds. *Gettysburg.* New Brunswick, N.J., 1948.
Moore, Alison. *The Louisiana Tigers, or the Two Louisiana Brigades in the Army of Northern Virginia, 1861–1865.* Baton Rouge, 1961.
Murfin, James V. *The Gleam of Bayonets: The Battle of Antietam and the Maryland Campaign of 1862.* New York, 1965.
Nye, Wilbur S. *Here Come the Rebels!* Baton Rouge, 1965.
Phisterer, Frederick, comp. *New York in the War of the Rebellion, 1861 to 1865.* Albany, 1890.
Pinkowski, Edward. *Pills, Pen and Politics: The Story of General Leon Jastremski, 1843–1907.* Wilmington, Del., 1974.
Robertson, James I., Jr. *The Stonewall Brigade.* 1963; rpr. Baton Rouge, 1977.
Slaughter, Rev. Philip. *A Sketch of the Life of Randolph Fairfax . . . Including a Brief Account of Jackson's Celebrated Valley Campaign.* Baltimore, 1878.
Stafford, Dr. G. M. G. *General Leroy Augustus Stafford, His Forebears and Descendants.* New Orleans, 1943.
Steere, Edward. *The Wilderness Campaign.* New York, 1960.
Tankersley, Allen P. *John B. Gordon: A Study in Gallantry.* Atlanta, 1955.

Tucker, Glenn. *High Tide at Gettysburg: The Campaign in Pennsylvania*. Indianapolis, 1958.
Vandiver, Frank E. *Jubal's Raid: General Early's Famous Attack on Washington in 1864*. New York, 1960.
Warner, Ezra J. *Generals in Gray: Lives of the Confederate Commanders*. Baton Rouge, 1959.
Wellman, Manly Wade. *Rebel Boast: First at Bethel—Last at Appomattox*. New York, 1956.
Wheeler, Richard. *Voices in the Civil War*. New York, 1976.
Wiley, Bell Irvin. *The Life of Johnny Reb: The Common Soldier of the Confederacy*. New York, 1962.
Winters, John D. *The Civil War in Louisiana*. Baton Rouge, 1963.

JOURNAL ARTICLES

Casey, Powell A. "Confederate Units from North Louisiana." *North Louisiana Historical Association's Journal*, VI (Spring, 1975), 105–15.
Forman, William Harper, Jr. "William P. Harper in War and Reconstruction," *Louisiana History*, XIII (1972), 45–70.
Kajencki, Francis C. "The Louisiana Tiger." *Louisiana History*, XV (1974), 49–59.
Nichols, C. Howard. "Some Notes on the Military Career of Francis T. Nicholls." *Louisiana History*, III (1962), 297–315.
Romero, Sidney J. "Louisiana Clergy and the Confederate Army." *Louisiana History*, II (1961), 277–97.
Thomas, Michael R. "Confederate Firing Squad at Centreville." *Northern Virginia Heritage*, June, 1980, pp. 3–6.
———. "Unearthing Two Tigers' Graves." *Northern Virginia Heritage*, June, 1980, pp. 7, 8.
Uminski, Sigmund H. "Poles and the Confederacy." *Polish American Studies*, XXII (1965), 99–106.
———. "Two Polish Confederates." *Polish American Studies*, XXIII (1966), 65–81.
Wallace, Lee A., Jr. "Coppens' Louisiana Zouaves." *Civil War History*, VIII (1962), 269–82.

THESES

Leland, Edwin Albert. "Organization and Administration of the Louisiana Army During the Civil War." M.A. thesis, Louisiana State University, 1938.
Urquhart, Kenneth Trist. "General Richard Taylor and the War in Virginia, 1861–1862." M.A. thesis, Tulane University, 1958.

INDEX